CHRISTIAN BELIEVER

KNOWING GOD WITH HEART AND MIND

Readings

ABINGDON PRESS
Nashville

CHRISTIAN BELIEVER: KNOWING GOD WITH HEART AND MIND
Readings

Copyright © 1999 by Abingdon Press

Acknowledgments for readings are on pages 267– 272,
which constitute an extension of this copyright page.

Stained-glass art by Nell Fisher
Cover and interior design by Ed Wynne

Manufactured in Hong Kong

99 00 01 02 03 04 05 06 07 08 — 10 9 8 7 6 5 4 3 2 1

Contents

As You Begin Your Study

Y ou may have come to this study with little knowledge of the people, events, and documents that contributed to the formulation of the doctrines or beliefs central to the Christian faith. With you in mind we have selected key statements from leading theologians and crucial church councils that express the classical teachings of the Christian faith, what the church has said is essential and has continuously taught as essential.

The readings reflect the richness of thought and discussion within Christianity over two thousand years. Through these readings you have opportunity to hear from and join faithful Christians from across the centuries in seeking understanding of the Christian faith.

This book of readings takes seriously the Great Commandment to "Love the Lord your God with all your heart and with all your soul and with all your mind and with all your strength" (Mark 12:30, NIV)—that is, it calls for committed effort. Grasping the ideas in the readings will take time, thought, and discipline. Writers express themselves in the language of their day. So, some of the language is outdated and the concepts unfamiliar.

Because a high percentage of the readings in this book come from other centuries, masculine language is prevalent. While at the beginning of the twenty-first century we are sensitive to the need for more inclusive language, we also respect people and their ideas set in their own time. We have made no attempt to change masculine language, believing that the power in the ideas can transcend the time-related differences in language.

Readings are grouped by topic and each week's readings relate to the topic of the lesson in the study manual. The approximately ten readings per week are intended to acquaint you with a particular doctrine and the key ideas in that doctrine. Readings are mostly arranged in chronological order, from the earliest to the most recent. All readings are numbered sequentially through the book.

The format for the readings follows a common pattern: a general introduction to the week's readings, an introduction to each individual reading, the reading itself, and the name and date of the author or the document. Sources of all readings are found in the acknowledgments on pages 267–272. Sometimes ellipses appear within a reading to indicate that some material, unnecessary to the purpose of the reading, has been left out.

Steps to Understanding What You Read

The study manual includes daily assignments for reading and taking notes on Scripture and readings in this book. Space for notes is provided in the study manual. You will read the commentary in the study manual after you have completed all of the week's assigned Scripture and readings.

Follow these steps as you read. Understanding will come more easily, and you will be prepared for the discussion in the weekly group meeting.

1. Read sentence by sentence, watching for key terms or phrases.
2. Identify and list the main ideas in the reading.
3. Indicate the points at which you have questions or difficulty with ideas.
4. When you come to a sentence that is hard to understand, keep reading. Often the next few sentences will clarify what the difficult sentence is saying.
5. When you are having difficulty understanding a reading, keep in mind that other members of the group are also reading and making notes and that in the group meeting you will have time together to discuss, clarify, question, and draw conclusions from the various readings.
6. After completing each reading, recall the main ideas and summarize in a sentence or two what the reading is saying.
7. At the end of the week, look back over your notes and list the key ideas for the doctrine being studied. Write a statement of the doctrine.

Christian symbols proclaim the Christian faith in visual language. The eight pages of art in this book depict time-honored Christian symbols for the classical doctrines of the Christian faith. Explanations of the symbols emphasize the message behind each symbol.

*With deep gratitude we acknowledge
the work of
Ted A. Campbell, Young Ho Chun, Will Coleman,
Catherine G. González, Justo L. González,
Scott J. Jones, W. Ellison Jones, John H. Leith,
Rebekah L. Miles, Donald K. McKim, Amy Oden,
and William C. Placher
in selecting the readings in this book.*

*J. Ellsworth Kalas
wrote the introductions for the readings.*

The Message
Behind the Symbols

S tep into the sandals of a first-century Christian believer walking along the road in Galilee. You stop to exchange greetings with a stranger. As you talk, you casually scratch the shape of a fish in the dust with your walking stick. The stranger notices, smiles, clasps your hand—you've met another believer.

Christian symbols point beyond themselves to something else. The first letters of the Greek words for *Jesus Christ, Son of God, Savior* spell the Greek word for *fish*. The fish is an early symbol for Jesus Christ and also for the believer. The sun in full glory symbolizes the self-revealing God. And the tree represents the revelation of God in the created world, a message available to the experience and understanding of all humankind.

An open book represents Scripture, the Word of God revealing the God at work in the call and history of Israel and in the Person of Jesus Christ, God in the flesh. The lamp, another symbol for Scripture, suggests divine inspiration of the Word and calls to mind the words of the psalm, "Your word is a lamp to my feet and a light to my path" (Psalm 119:105).

Believing

The readings for this week are intended to explore the nature of believing, and its significance to our human personality. Are beliefs and the act of believing important enough to justify identifying ourselves as believers? In these readings we will sample what theologians over the centuries have said about the role of believing.

1 Any creed we recite is only a shorthand version of what we believe. Cyril, Bishop of Jerusalem, made that point more than sixteen centuries ago, as he tried to explain to new converts the far-reaching significance of their creedal statements of faith. Our study this year will help us understand what is behind these relatively succinct statements.

But in learning the Faith and in professing it, acquire and keep that only, which is now delivered to thee by the Church, and which has been built up strongly out of all the Scriptures. . . . So for the present listen while I simply say the Creed, and commit it to memory; but at the proper season expect the confirmation out of Holy Scripture of each part of the contents. For the articles of the Faith were not composed as seemed good to men; but the most important points collected out of all the Scripture make up one complete teaching of the Faith. And just as the mustard seed in one small grain contains many branches, so also this Faith has embraced in few words all the knowledge of godliness in the Old and New Testaments.

—Cyril of Jerusalem, 315–387

2 The Nicene Creed was adopted by the Council of Nicaea in 325. This contemporary version of the creed reflects the modifications made in the creed at the Council of Constantinople in 381.

We believe in one God,
    the Father, the Almighty,
    maker of heaven and earth,
    of all that is, seen and unseen.

We believe in one Lord, Jesus Christ,
    the only Son of God,
    eternally begotten of the Father,
    God from God, Light from Light,
    true God from true God,
    begotten, not made,
    of one Being with the Father;
    through him all things were made.
    For us and for our salvation
        he came down from heaven,
        was incarnate of the Holy Spirit and the Virgin Mary
        and became truly human.
        For our sake he was crucified under Pontius Pilate;
        he suffered death and was buried.
        On the third day he rose again
        in accordance with the Scriptures;
        he ascended into heaven
        and is seated at the right hand of the Father.
        He will come again in glory
        to judge the living and the dead,
        and his kingdom will have no end.

We believe in the Holy Spirit, the Lord, the giver of life,
    who proceeds from the Father and the Son,
    who with the Father and the Son
        is worshiped and glorified,
    who has spoken through the prophets.
    We believe in the one holy catholic and apostolic church.
    We acknowledge one baptism
        for the forgiveness of sins.
    We look for the resurrection of the dead,
        and the life of the world to come. Amen.

—The Nicene Creed, 325/381

3 We humans are by nature believers; it is not a question of whether we will believe, but of what and whom we will believe. Saint Augustine, Bishop of Hippo, goes a step further, insisting that our believing will never find satisfaction until it is centered in God. Not only are we believing creatures; something in our nature craves a particular object of belief.

Great art Thou, O Lord, and greatly to be praised; great is Thy power, and of Thy wisdom there is no end. And man, who being a part of Thy creation, desires to praise Thee,—man, who bears about with him his mortality, the witness of his sin, even the witness that Thou "resistest the proud,"—yet man, this part of Thy creation, desires to praise Thee; for Thou hast formed us for Thyself, and our hearts are restless until they find rest in Thee.

—Augustine, 354–430

4 We humans insist on believing something. Saint Augustine reminds us that even the act of doubting is in its own way a declaration of belief—that is, of belief in the power to doubt. He challenges us to employ reasoning rather than to be controlled by it.

Everyone who knows that he has doubts knows with certainty something that is true, namely, that he doubts. He is certain, therefore, about *a* truth. Therefore everyone who doubts whether there be such a thing as *the* truth has at least *a* truth to set a limit to his doubt; and nothing can be true except truth be in it. Accordingly, no one ought to have doubts about the existence of *the* truth, even if doubts arise for him from every possible quarter. Wherever this is seen, there is light that transcends space and time and all phantasms that spring from spatial and temporal things. Could this be in the least destroyed even if every reasoner should perish or grow old among inferior carnal things? Reasoning does not create truth but discovers it. Before it is discovered it abides in itself; and when it is discovered it renews us.

—Augustine, 354–430

5 The Apostles' Creed is no doubt the most familiar of our belief statements; literally tens of millions of us repeat it each week. Tradition says that its twelve summarizing statements came individually from the twelve apostles, but in truth it reached its present form some time in the eighth century, as a declaration of faith for those who wanted to be baptized.

I believe in God the Father Almighty,
   maker of heaven and earth;

And in Jesus Christ his only Son our Lord:
   who was conceived by the Holy Spirit,
      born of the Virgin Mary,
      suffered under Pontius Pilate,
      was crucified, dead, and buried;
   the third day he rose from the dead;
   he ascended into heaven,
      and sitteth at the right hand of God the Father Almighty;
   from thence he shall come to judge the quick and the dead.

I believe in the Holy Spirit,
   the holy catholic church,
   the communion of saints,
   the forgiveness of sins,
   the resurrection of the body,
   and the life everlasting. Amen.

—The Apostles' Creed, title first cited in 390

6 Saint Anselm, Archbishop of Canterbury, is usually ranked among the major philosophical thinkers of history. It is therefore all the more remarkable that he makes believing more basic than understanding. Where some philosophers would consider understanding as the highest expression of the human creature, Anselm elevates the act of believing.

Lord, my heart is made bitter by its desolation; sweeten thou it, I beseech thee, with thy consolation. Lord, in hunger I began to seek thee; I beseech thee that I may not cease to hunger for thee. In hunger I have come to thee; let me not go unfed. . . .
   Be it mine to look up to thy light, even from afar, even from the depths. Teach me to seek thee, and reveal thyself to me, when I seek thee, for I cannot seek thee, except thou teach me, nor find thee, except thou reveal thyself. Let me seek thee in longing, let me long for thee in seeking; let me find thee in love, and love thee in finding. Lord, I acknowledge and I thank thee that thou hast created me in this thine image, in order that I may be mindful of thee, may conceive of thee, and love thee; but that image has been so consumed and wasted away by vices, and obscured by the smoke

of wrong-doing, that it cannot achieve that for which it was made, except thou renew it, and create it anew. I do not endeavor, O Lord, to penetrate thy sublimity, for in no wise do I compare my understanding with that; but I long to understand in some degree thy truth, which my heart believes and loves. For I do not seek to understand that I may believe, but I believe in order to understand. For this also I believe,—that unless I believed, I should not understand.

—Anselm, 1033–1109

7 The process of believing is complex because you and I are complex. Thomas Aquinas, philosopher and theologian, helps us by drawing a distinction between the intellect and the will, reminding us that the two are not necessarily in agreement. Then, to make the point still more emphatic, he introduces the eternal issue.

When we are faced with a contradiction, in which there are two opposing views, our understanding can respond in different ways. Sometimes it does not incline one way or another, either because of lack of evidence, or because of the apparent equality of evidence for both sides. Thus the understanding wavers between two views, and is in a state of doubt. Sometimes the understanding is inclined more to one side than the other; yet the evidence is not of sufficient weight to demand complete assent. Thus the understanding is in a state of opinion. . . .

Sometimes the understanding is immediately convinced that one view is right, because it conforms to fundamental axioms; thus it is in a state of knowledge. Sometimes the understanding does not incline one way or the other, because neither view is obviously in conformity with fundamental axioms. But the will chooses to assent to one view, definitely and positively, through some influence which can move the will, but not the intellect. This influence is such that the will regards it as good and right to assent to one view.

This is the state of belief. We believe in the words of someone, because to believe seems proper and advantageous. In particular we are moved to believe in certain sayings when it seems that eternal life depends on belief.

—Thomas Aquinas, 1225–1274

8 But beliefs are not independent entities, suspended in some philosophical framework; they demonstrate themselves in the fabric of human experience. John Wesley saw this experience of believing as a crucial proof of the integrity of the doctrine. In simple terms, Wesley is saying, "It works!"

What Christianity (considered as a doctrine) promised is accomplished in my soul. And Christianity, considered as an inward principle, is the completion of all those promises. It is holiness and happiness, the image of God impressed on a created spirit, a fountain of peace and love springing up into everlasting life.

And this I conceive to be the strongest evidence of the truth of Christianity. I do not undervalue traditional evidence. Let it have its place and its due honour. It is highly serviceable in its kind and in its degree. And yet I cannot set it on a level with this.

It is generally supposed that traditional evidence is weakened by length of time, as it must necessarily pass through so many hands in a continued succession of ages. But no length of time can possibly affect the strength of this internal evidence. It is equally strong, equally new, through the course of seventeen hundred years. It passes now, even as it has done from the beginning, directly from God into the believing soul. Do you suppose time will ever dry up this stream? Oh no! It shall never be cut off.

—John Wesley, 1703–1791

9 Ask the average person to define a Christian, and she or he is more than likely to answer, "Someone who believes in God." Their emphasis on believing is correct, but the definition is too broad. Christians believe in God in a specific way, as God has been revealed in Jesus Christ. Albert Schweitzer, a twentieth-century theologian-philosopher, insisted that we must go beyond knowing the historical Jesus, until in the process of discipleship we come to know Jesus Christ and the truth he embodied.

Jesus as a concrete historical personality remains a stranger to our time, but His spirit, which lies hidden in His words, is known in simplicity, and its influence is direct. . . .

. . . Jesus, as He is depicted in the Gospels, influenced individuals by the individual word. They understood Him so far as it was necessary for them to understand, without forming any conception of His life as a whole, since this in its ultimate aims remained a mystery even for the disciples.

...The names in which men expressed their recognition of Him as such, Messiah, Son of Man, Son of God, have become for us historical parables. We can find no designation which expresses what He is for us.

He comes to us as One unknown, without a name, as of old, by the lake-side, He came to those men who knew Him not. He speaks to us the same word: "Follow thou me!" and sets us to the tasks which He has to fulfil for our time. He commands. And to those who obey Him, whether they be wise or simple, He will reveal Himself in the toils, the conflicts, the sufferings which they shall pass through in His fellowship, and, as an ineffable mystery, they shall learn in their own experience Who He is.

—*Albert Schweitzer, 1875–1965*

10 Our study suggests that believing is native to the human creature. Roman Catholic theologian, Edward Schillebeeckx, contends that the experience of believing begins in an act of God, the love in which God chooses to make divinity known.

Religion, faith in God, is never the first datum for us to consider in this connection, for religion and faith are a reply, the second word: the first is spoken by God himself. Revelation, upon which the whole of our concrete faith is founded, is the completely personal gesture of God by which he, as it were, steps outside himself to encounter us with the offer of his love; that is to say, with an offer of "communion with him," of a love that only reaches fulfillment in our reciprocal love. It is through this personal relationship to God, a relationship of child to Father, of a child that grows in Christ to the full measure of humanity, that we stand in the grace which sanctifies us. In a somewhat careless way we say that we *have* sanctifying grace. In reality there is more to it than this: we are personally taken up into communion of life with God; we live, we are and we move to the rhythm of the divine life. We abide in God as in our own home. This is a matter of quite special, personal relations between God and us.

—*Edward Schillebeeckx, 1914–*

11 Although Christian thought is discussed and refined century by century by church theologians, Jaroslav Pelikan—himself a theologian and historian—insists that the doctrines of the Christian faith must be seen as the continuing voice of the church, and not confused with the theories of the various teachers.

Christian doctrine is the business of the church. The history of doctrine is not to be equated with the history of theology or the history of Christian thought. If it is, the historian runs the danger of exaggerating the significance of the idiosyncratic thought of individual theologians at the expense of the common faith of the church. The private beliefs of theologians do belong to the history of doctrine, but not simply on their own terms. . . . It is usually difficult, and sometimes impossible, to draw the line of demarcation between the teachings of the church and the theories of its teachers; what the teachers thought often reflected an earlier stage in the development or anticipated a later one. . . .

Doctrine is what is believed, taught, and confessed.

—Jaroslav Pelikan, 1923–

12 Donald Bloesch, a contemporary theologian, offers an insight that can be seen as balancing the statement we have quoted from Wesley. As important as is our personal religious experience, there are also the apostolic testimony and the teachings of the Scriptures.

It is well to bear in mind that faith is deeper and wider than a spiritual experience: it is an acknowledgment of the claims of Jesus Christ and an obedience to his commands. It consists primarily in personal devotion to a living Savior, but it also entails a confidence in the apostolic testimony concerning who he is and what he has done. Our faith is directed not simply to the mystical presence of Christ or to the unconditional, but to Jesus Christ crucified and risen according to the Scriptures. The act of believing *(fides qua creditur),* though supremely important, must never prevail over the content of faith *(fides quae creditur).*

—Donald G. Bloesch, 1928–

Revelation

From the earliest days of the Christian faith, believers have tried to grasp and explain the source of their teachings. But perhaps it is not surprising that some of the most effective statements have emerged in the twentieth century. Our contemporary emphasis on scientific methodology has compelled theologians to think more incisively about the nature of divine revelation. Most of our readings for this chapter come to us from relatively recent church councils or major twentieth-century theologians.

13 In the latter third of the second century, when Irenaeus, Bishop of Lyons, wrote, the Christian faith was spreading more and more into unknown territories. Irenaeus rejoiced that the truths of the gospel remained the same, regardless of ethnic cultures and even of cultural and intellectual differences.

The truths of the gospel are gradually spreading across the world. Yet despite the great distances between groups of believers, it seems as if they all occupy one house. Their common faith draws them together in heart and soul. They speak the same words, and they proclaim the same message. There are many different languages in the world; but one Christian doctrine is conveyed in all of them. Thus the church in Germany believes and proclaims exactly the same message as do the Spanish and Celtic churches; and it is the same message as that preached by Christians in Jerusalem, which is the center of the world. Just as the sun, which was created by God, is the same throughout the world, so the same truth now shines in every nation, and enlightens all those who respond to it in a spirit of faith. Those who are eloquent speakers cannot add to the truth; and those who are stumbling speakers cannot diminish the truth. Since truth is one and the same, regardless of who expresses it, no one can improve on it or undermine it.

—Irenaeus, c. 130–c. 200

14 Martin Luther, father of the Reformation, declares unequivocally that the most important revelation of God has come to us in Jesus Christ. It was daring to do so, since the basic ecclesiastical structures of his day placed all authority in the church. Luther insisted on a prior, higher ground.

Christ is the offspring promised to Abraham; on him God founded all his promises. Therefore Christ alone is the means, the life, and the mirror through which we see God and know his will.

Through Christ God announces his favor and mercy to us. In Christ we see that God is not a wrathful taskmaster and judge but a gracious and kind father, who blesses us, that is, who delivers us from the law, sin, death, and every evil, and endows us with righteousness and eternal life through Christ. This is a sure knowledge of God and a true divine conviction, which does not deceive us but portrays God himself in a specific form, apart from which there is no God.

—Martin Luther, 1483–1546

15 We are always in danger of discrediting the learning of other generations. In truth, most of the basic systems of philosophy and inquiry are hundreds and even thousands of years old. Martin Luther, writing from half a millennium ago, was well-schooled in such a philosophical heritage, holding a doctorate in philosophy. Nevertheless, he vigorously insisted that our search for God would be futile if it were not for God's own willingness to reveal.

When it comes to the knowledge of how one may stand before God and attain to eternal life, that is truly not to be achieved by our work or power, nor to originate in our brain. In other things, those pertaining to this temporal life, you may glory in what you know, you may advance the teachings of reason, you may invent ideas of your own. . . . But in spiritual matters, human reasoning certainly is not in order; other intelligence, other skill and power, are requisite here—something to be granted by God himself and revealed through his Word.

What mortal has ever discovered or fathomed the truth that the three persons in the eternal divine essence are one God; that the second person, the Son of God, was obliged to become man, born of a virgin; and that no way of life could be opened for us, save through his crucifixion? Such truth never would have been heard nor preached, would never in all eternity have been published, learned and believed, had not God himself revealed it.

—*Martin Luther, 1483–1546*

16 So many elements of revelation, such as nature and history, are evidences of grace; or as American theologian Reinhold Niebuhr puts it, "general" revelation. But he reminds us that there is also the point at which divine reality touches us at a personal, specific level.

The revelation of God to man is always a twofold one, a personal-individual revelation, and a revelation in the context of social-historical experience. Without the public and historical revelation the private experience of God would remain poorly defined and subject to caprice. Without the private revelation of God, the public and historical revelation would not gain credence. Since all men have, in some fashion, the experience of a reality beyond themselves, they are able to entertain the more precise revelations of the character and purpose of God as they come to them in the most significant experiences of prophetic history. Private revelation is, in a sense, synonymous with "general" revelation, without the presuppositions of which there could be no "special" revelation. It is no less universal for being private. Private revelation is the testimony in the consciousness of every person that his life touches a reality beyond himself, a reality deeper and higher than the system of nature in which he stands.

—*Reinhold Niebuhr, 1892–1971*

17 H. Richard Niebuhr, theologian and younger brother of Reinhold, developed a book-length study of revelation. Where our study has concentrated on the act and forms of revelation, Richard Niebuhr deals also with the effect of revelation on the receiver, in making events "intelligible."

Revelation means for us that part of our inner history which illuminates the rest of it and which is itself intelligible. Sometimes when we read a difficult book, seeking to follow a complicated argument, we come across a luminous sentence from which we can go forward and backward and so attain some understanding of the whole. Revelation is like that. In his *Religion in the Making* Professor Whitehead has written such illuminating sentences and one of them is this: "Rational religion appeals to the direct intuition of special occasions, and to the elucidatory power of its concepts for all occasions." The special occasion to which we appeal in the Christian church is called Jesus Christ, in whom we see the righteousness of God, his power and wisdom. But from that special occasion we also derive the concepts which make possible the elucidation of all the events in our history. Revelation means this intelligible event which makes all other events intelligible.

—H. Richard Niebuhr, 1894–1962

18 Our study urges caution about visions, dreams, and other dramatic experiences that tend to be very subjective. Swiss theologian Emil Brunner goes still farther, reminding us that the point of revelation is God—not our pleasure or peculiar benefit.

Revelation always means that something hidden is made known, that a mystery is unveiled. But the Biblical revelation is the absolute manifestation of something that had been absolutely concealed. . . . The absolutely Mysterious is not only partially hidden from the natural knowledge of man; it is wholly inaccessible to man's natural faculties for research and discovery. . . .

In the Bible, however, we are not confronted by an impersonal supernatural Absolute, but by One who transcends this earthly life; God, the Creator and Lord, is the absolute Mystery. In the Bible God and revelation are so intimately connected that there is no other revelation than that which comes to us from God, and there is no other knowledge of God than that which is given to us through revelation.

. . . The real content of revelation in the Bible is not "something," but *God* Himself. Revelation is the self-manifestation of God. The real revelation, that is, the revelation with which the whole Bible is concerned, is God's self-manifestation.

—Emil Brunner, 1889–1966

19 Emil Brunner, who had considerable influence on American theology, directs our attention to those who receive the revelation—that is, to us—noting that revelation is incomplete until faith activates it.

[R]evelation is certainly not a "Something", a "thing"; but it is a process, an event, and indeed an event which happens to us and in us. Neither the prophetic Word of the Old Testament, nor Jesus

Christ, nor the witness of the Apostles, nor of the preachers of the Church who proclaim Him, "is" the revelation; the reality of the revelation culminates in the "subject" who receives it. Indeed, it is quite possible that none of these forms of revelation may become revelation to *us*. If there is no faith, then the revelation has not been consummated: it has not actually happened, so to speak, but it is only at the first stage. All objective forms of revelation need the "subject" in whom they become revelation. The Bible itself calls this inward process "revelation". It was a new particular intervention of God which opened the eyes of Peter to the Mystery of the Messiah, so that he could then confess Him as the Son of the Living God. Again, it was the same intervention of God which happened to Paul when "it pleased God to reveal His Son" in him. And the same process of revelation takes place wherever Christ manifests Himself to a human being as the living Lord and is received in faith.

— Emil Brunner, 1889–1966

20 Georgia Harkness, who led the way for women theologians in the twentieth century, makes a basic case for revelation in simple, straightforward language. She reminds us that the very principle of revelation rests on the conviction that there has been a divine disclosure.

There is no simple, clear, universally agreed-upon definition of revelation. In fact, the "hot spot" of the problem as to the relations of revelation to reason lies in what revelation is understood to mean. . . .

The common denominator amongst various views of revelation is the assumption that God has disclosed something. Everybody except the extreme skeptic agrees that there is something in the way of knowledge for man to *discover*. (And even the most thoroughgoing skeptic believes he has discovered skepticism to be true!) However, when the emphasis is not on man's discovery but on the *disclosure* by deity of what is to be accepted by the human mind, this is revelation.

—Georgia Harkness, 1891–1974

21 It is generally agreed that Swiss theologian Karl Barth was one of the most influential theological spokespersons of the twentieth century. While our study approaches the subject of revelation somewhat cautiously, recognizing that it is a difficult concept, Barth speaks sharply and unhesitatingly, insisting that there is no possibility for humans to perceive God except by God's revelation.

Revelation is God's self-offering and self-manifestation. Revelation encounters man on the presupposition and in confirmation of the fact that man's attempts to know God from his own standpoint are wholly and entirely futile; not because of any necessity in principle, but because of a practical necessity of fact. In revelation God tells man that He is God, and that as such He is his Lord. In telling him this, revelation tells him something utterly new, something which apart from revelation he does not know and cannot tell either himself or others. It is true that he could do this, for revelation simply states the truth. If it is true that God is God and that as such He is the Lord of man, then it is also true that man is so placed towards Him, that he could know Him. But this is the very truth which is not available to man, before it is told him in revelation. If he really can know God, this capacity rests upon the fact that he really does know Him, because God has offered and manifested Himself to him. The capacity, then, does not rest upon the fact, which is true enough, that man could know Him. Between "he could" and "he can" there lies the absolutely decisive "he cannot," which can be removed and turned into its opposite only by revelation. The truth that God is God and our Lord, and the further truth that we could know Him as God and Lord, can only come to us through the truth itself. This "coming to us" of the truth is revelation.
—*Karl Barth, 1886–1968*

22 Those who accept the revelation of God may find it a transforming experience. H. Richard Niebuhr uses almost lyrical language to describe this experience. Such a revelation demands a personal response, a "direct confession of the heart."

Revelation means the moment in our history through which we know ourselves to be known from beginning to end, in which we are apprehended by the knower; it means the self-disclosing of that eternal knower. Revelation means the moment in which we are surprised by the knowledge of someone there in the darkness and the void of human life; it means the self-disclosure of light in our darkness. Revelation is the moment in which we find our judging selves to be judged not by ourselves or our neighbors but by one who knows the final secrets of the heart; revelation means the self-disclosure of the judge. Revelation means that we find ourselves to be valued rather than valuing and that all our values are transvaluated by the activity of a universal valuer. When a price is put upon our heads, which is not our price, when the unfairness of all the fair prices we have placed on things is shown up; when the great riches of God reduce our wealth to poverty, that is revelation. When we find out that we are no longer thinking him, but that he first thought us, that is revelation. . . . What this means for us cannot be expressed in the impersonal ways of creeds or other propositions but only in responsive acts of a personal character. We acknowledge revelation by no third-person proposition, such as that there is a God, but only in the direct confession of the heart, "Thou art my God."

—H. Richard Niebuhr, 1894–1962

23 Later our study deals specifically with the Scriptures as a primary means of divine revelation. Karl Barth goes back a step farther to the events to which the Scriptures bear witness, as themselves an element of revelation.

The Bible is the concrete means by which the Church recollects God's past revelation, is called to expectation of His future revelation, and is thus summoned and guided to proclamation and empowered for it. The Bible, then, is not in itself and as such God's past revelation, just as Church proclamation is not in itself and as such the expected future revelation. The Bible, speaking to us and heard by us as God's Word, bears witness to past revelation. Proclamation, speaking to us and heard by us as God's Word, promises future revelation. The Bible is God's Word as it really bears witness to revelation, and proclamation is God's Word as it really promises revelation. . . .

. . . [T]he revelation to which the biblical witnesses direct their gaze as they look and point away from themselves is to be distinguished from the word of the witnesses in exactly the same way as an event itself is to be distinguished from even the best and most faithful account of it. But this distinction is trifling compared with the fact, for which there is no analogy, that in revelation our concern is with the coming Jesus Christ and finally, when the time was fulfilled, the Jesus Christ who has come. Literally, and this time really directly, we are thus concerned with God's own Word spoken by God Himself.

—Karl Barth, 1886–1968

24 In 1963 the World Council of Churches, an ecumenical body including a majority of Protestant and Orthodox communions, issued a statement on Scripture, Tradition, and traditions. While not speaking of revelation as such, this reading refers to several elements of revelation—tradition, the Scriptures, and Christ.

As Christians we all acknowledge with thankfulness that God has revealed himself in the history of the people of God in the Old Testament and in Christ Jesus, his Son, the mediator between God and man. God's mercy and God's glory are the beginning and end of our own history. The testimony of prophets and apostles inaugurated the Tradition of his revelation. The once-for-all disclosure of God in Jesus Christ inspired the apostles and disciples to give witness to the revelation given in the person and work of Christ. No one could, and no one can, "say that Jesus is Lord, save by the Holy Spirit" (I Cor. 12.3). The oral and written tradition of the prophets and apostles under the guidance of the Holy Spirit led to the formation of Scriptures and to the canonization of the Old and New Testaments as the Bible of the Church. The very fact that Tradition precedes the Scriptures points to the significance of tradition, but also to the Bible as the treasure of the Word of God.

... [E]ver since the Reformation "Scripture and Tradition" has been a matter of controversy in the dialogue between Roman Catholic and Protestant theology. On the Roman Catholic side, tradition has generally been understood as divine truth not expressed in Holy Scripture alone, but orally transmitted. The Protestant position has been an appeal to Holy Scripture alone, as the infallible and sufficient authority in all matters pertaining to salvation, to which all human traditions should be subjected. The voice of the Orthodox Church has hardly been heard in these Western discussions until quite recently.

—World Council of Churches, 1963

25 Martin Luther would no doubt be very comfortable with the major modern Catholic statement concerning revelation, as enunciated by Vatican Council II in 1965. This statement refers to both the witness of history and the ultimate revelation in Jesus Christ.

In His goodness and wisdom, God chose to reveal Himself and to make known to us the hidden purpose of His will (cf. Eph. 1:9) by which through Christ, the Word made flesh, man has access to the Father in the Holy Spirit and comes to share in the divine nature (cf. Eph. 2:18; 2 Pet. 1:4). Through this revelation, therefore, the invisible God (cf. Col. 1:15; 1 Tim. 1:17) out of the abundance of His love speaks to men as friends (cf. Ex. 33:11; Jn. 15:14-15) and lives among them (cf. Bar. 3:38), so that He may invite and take them into fellowship with Himself. This plan of revelation is realized by deeds and words having an inner unity: the deeds wrought by God in the history of salvation manifest and confirm the teaching and realities signified by the words, while the words proclaim the deeds and clarify the mystery contained in them. By this revelation then, the deepest truth about God and the salvation of man is made clear to us in Christ, who is the Mediator and at the same time the fullness of all revelation.

—Second Vatican Council, 1962–1965

26 Daniel L. Migliore, American theologian, contributes further to this idea that general revelation must go on to personal experience of revelation. The end of revelation is not simply knowledge of God, but knowledge of God accepted; and it is always at God's initiative.

Yet the meaning of revelation in Christian theology is much more specific. It refers to the self-disclosure of God in the creation, in the history of the people of Israel, and above all in the person of Jesus. Revelation is not the transmission of a body of knowledge but the personal disclosure of one subject to other subjects. God has taken the initiative and has freely made known the divine identity and purpose. In brief, the knowledge given in revelation is not simply knowledge *that,* or knowledge *about,* but knowledge *of.*

—Daniel L. Migliore, 1935–

Scripture

Theologians and Bible students have different views about the nature of divine inspiration, but all will agree that the Bible is the basic document of the Christian faith. Our lesson quotes liberally from the Scriptures, in a kind of internal evidence of inspiration. The following materials trace the teachings of the church and its leaders concerning the place of the Scriptures in the belief system of the church.

27 For a period during the early history of the church, it was very popular to read the Bible allegorically, attaching symbolic significance to each person and element in a story. Origen taught that Scripture must be understood in three senses—the literal, historical; the moral; and the allegorical.

Since, in our investigation of matters of such importance, not satisfied with the common opinions, and with the clear evidence of visible things, we take in addition, for the proof of our statements, testimonies from what are believed by us to be divine writings, ... from that which is called the Old Testament, and that which is styled the New, and endeavor by reason to confirm our faith. ...

And while we thus briefly demonstrate the deity of Christ, and (in so doing) make use of the prophetic declarations regarding Him, we demonstrate at the same time that the writings which prophesied of Him were divinely inspired; and that those documents which announced His coming and His doctrine were given forth with all power and authority, and that on this account they obtained the election from the Gentiles. We must say, also, that the divinity of the prophetic declarations, and the spiritual nature of the law of Moses, shone forth after the advent of Christ. For before the advent of Christ it was not altogether possible to exhibit manifest proofs of the divine inspiration of the ancient Scripture; whereas His coming led those who might suspect the law and the prophets not to be divine, to the clear conviction that they were composed by (the aid of) heavenly grace.

—Origen, 185–254

28 We have noted that the Scriptures were often communicated by unlikely persons, many of them humble and nameless. Jerome, the first great translator of the Bible, though himself a scholar, gladly confesses that both learned and unlearned can benefit from the Scriptures.

I beg you, my dearest brother, to live among these [sacred books], to meditate on them, to know nothing else, to seek nothing else. Does not this seem to you to be a little bit of heaven here on earth ...? Do not take offence on account of the simplicity of Holy Scripture or the unsophistication of its words . . . , for these are either due to translation faults or have some deeper purpose. For Scripture offers itself in such a way that an uneducated congregation can more easily learn from it, some benefit there and both the learned and the unlearned can discover different meanings in the same sentence. I am not so arrogant nor so forward as to claim that I know this, which would be like wanting to pick on earth the fruits of trees whose roots are in heaven. However, I confess that I would like to do so . . . The Lord has said: "ask, and it shall be given; knock, and it shall be opened; seek, and you will find" (Matthew 7:7). So let us study here on earth that knowledge which will continue with us in heaven.

—Jerome, 345–420

29 Thomas á Kempis, ascetic and writer, has blessed generations by the beauty of his devout faith. His counsel on reading the Scriptures is marked by the same sense of humble piety; he reminds us that to understand the Bible best, we must come under its discipline and authority.

Truth, not eloquence, is to be sought for in Holy Scripture.

Each part of the Scripture is to be read with the same Spirit wherewith it was written.

We should rather search after profit in the Scriptures, than after subtle arguments.

We ought to read plain and devout books as willingly as those high and profound.

Let not the authority of the writer be a stumbling-block, whether he be of great or small learning; but let the love of pure truth draw thee to read. Enquire not who spoke this or that, but mark what is spoken.

Men pass away, but the truth of the Lord remaineth for ever. God speaks unto us in sundry ways without respect of persons.

Our own curiosity often hindereth us in reading of the Scriptures, when we will examine and discuss that which we should rather pass over without more ado.

If thou desire to profit, read with humility, simplicity, and faithfulness; nor ever desire the repute of learning.

Enquire willingly, and hear with silence the words of holy men. Let not the parables of the Elders displease thee, for they are not given without cause.

—Thomas á Kempis, c. 1380–1471

30 As surely as the Bible has come to us through varieties of human voices over a period of several centuries, it has also been open to varieties of interpretations. Ulrich Zwingli, Swiss reformer, gave twelve rules for reading the Bible profitably, several of which are listed here. Zwingli comes to us from the Calvinist tradition.

I ... thought it might be good at this point to give some instruction in the way to come to a true understanding of the Word of God and to a personal experience of the fact that you are taught of God. For if we are not versed in Scripture, how are we to tell whether the priest who teaches us is expounding the pure truth unadulterated by his own sinful desires? ...

Fifth, it is the nature and property of the Word to humble the high and mighty and to exalt the lowly. . . .

Sixth, the Word of God always attracts and helps the poor, comforting the comfortless and despairing, but opposing those who trust in themselves, as Christ testifies.

Seventh, it does not seek its own advantage: for that reason Christ commanded his disciples to take neither scrip nor purse.

Eighth, it seeks only that God may be revealed to men, that the obstinate may fear him and the lowly find comfort in God. Those who preach in that manner are undoubtedly right. . . .

Ninth, when you find that the Word of God renews you, and begins to be more precious to you than formerly when you heard the doctrines of men, then you may be sure that this is the work of God within you.

Tenth, when you find that it gives you assurance of the grace of God and eternal salvation, it is of God.

Eleventh, when you find that it crushes and destroys you, but magnifies God himself within you, it is a work of God.

Twelfth, when you find that the fear of God begins to give you joy rather than sorrow, it is a sure working of the Word and Spirit of God.

May God grant us that Spirit. Amen.

—Ulrich Zwingli, 1484–1531

31 Our lesson indicates that the preservation of the Scriptures was itself a kind of miracle. Sometimes even the guardian of the Scriptures, the Church, was a doubtful ally. Martin Luther sought to restore the Bible to its original place in the faith of God's people.

We must make a great difference between God's Word and the word of man. A man's word is a little sound, that flies into the air, and soon vanishes; but the Word of God is greater than heaven and earth, yea, greater than death and hell, for it forms part of the power of God, and endures everlastingly; we should, therefore, diligently study God's Word, and know and assuredly believe that God himself speaks unto us.

—Martin Luther, 1483–1546

32 The Formula of Concord, hardly a generation after Luther's death, sought to ensure that the Bible would be seen as the absolute base of Lutheran theology. Teachers and interpreters of the faith come and go, but the Scriptures remain the ultimate standard.

We believe, teach and confess that there is only one rule and norm according to which all teachings (*dogmata*) and teachers are to be appraised and judged, which is none other than the prophetic and apostolic writings of the Old and New Testaments . . . Other writings, whether of the fathers or more recent theologians, no matter what their names may be, cannot be regarded as possessing equal status to Holy Scripture, but must all be considered to be subordinate to it, and to witness to the way in which the teaching of the prophets and apostles was preserved in post-apostolic times and in different parts of the world . . . Holy Scripture remains the only judge, rule and norm according to which all doctrines are to be understood and judged, as to which are good or evil, and which are true or truly false. Certain other creeds (*symbola*) and writings . . . do not themselves possess the authority of judges, as in the case of Holy Scripture, but are witnesses of our religion as to how [the Holy Scriptures] were explained and presented.

—*The Formula of Concord, 1577*

33 At a time when literacy was on the increase, Philip Jacob Spener, founder of German Pietism, urged Christians to make Scripture a priority in their lives. He established what we would now call "Bible study groups" wherever he could, emphasizing that the Word builds faith and provides guidance.

Thought should be given to the more extensive use of the Word of God among us. We know that by nature we have no good in us. If there is to be any good in us, it must be brought about by God. To this end the Word of God is the powerful means, since faith must be enkindled through the gospel, and the law provides the rules for good works and many wonderful impulses to attain them. The more at home the Word of God is among us, the more we shall bring about faith and its fruits.

—*Philip Jacob Spener, 1635–1705*

34 Because of his emphasis on religious experience, John Wesley, Anglican priest and founder of Methodism, is sometimes perceived as less emphatic in his attitude toward the Scriptures. In truth, he held to the Bible with particular passion, as the following reading indicates.

To candid, reasonable men I am not afraid to lay open what have been the inmost thoughts of my heart. I have thought, I am a creature of a day, passing through life as an arrow through the air. I am a spirit come from God and returning to God; just hovering over the great gulf, till a few moments hence I am no more seen—I drop into an unchangeable eternity! I want to know one thing, the way to heaven—how to land safe on that happy shore. God himself has condescended to teach the way: for this very end he came from heaven. He hath written it down in a book. O give me that book! At any price, give me the Book of God! I have it: here is knowledge enough for me. Let me be *homo unius libri* [a man of one book]. Here then I am, far from the busy ways of men. I sit down alone: only God is here. In his presence I open, I read his Book; for this end, to find the way to heaven. Is there a doubt concerning the meaning of what I read? Does anything appear dark or intricate? I lift up my heart to the Father of lights: 'Lord, is it not thy Word, "If any man lack wisdom, let him ask of God"? . . .' I then search after and consider parallel passages of Scripture, 'comparing spiritual things with spiritual.' I meditate thereon, with all the attention and earnestness of which my mind is capable. If any doubt still remains, I consult those who are experienced in the things of God, and then the writings whereby, being dead, they yet speak. And what I thus learn, that I teach.

—John Wesley, 1703–1791

35 Probably every religious body has written into its official declaration its attitude toward the Scriptures. The following statements from the Docrinal Standards of The United Methodist Church also reflect the Anglican statements, from which they were drawn by Methodism's founder, John Wesley.

Article V—Of the Sufficiency of the Holy Scriptures for Salvation

The Holy Scripture containeth all things necessary to salvation; so that whatsoever is not read therein, nor may be proved thereby, is not to be required of any man that it should be believed as an article of faith, or be thought requisite or necessary to salvation. In the name of the Holy Scripture we do understand those canonical books of the Old and New Testament of whose authority was never any doubt in the church. . . .

Article VI—Of the Old Testament

The Old Testament is not contrary to the New; for both in the Old and New Testament everlasting life is offered to mankind by Christ, who is the only Mediator between God and man, being both God and Man. Wherefore they are not to be heard who feign that the old fathers did look only for transitory promises. Although the law given from God by Moses as touching ceremonies and rites doth not bind Christians, nor ought the civil precepts thereof of necessity be received in any commonwealth; yet notwithstanding, no Christian whatsoever is free from the obedience of the commandments which are called moral.

—*The Articles of Religion, 1784*

36 Theologian Alan Richardson reasoned with the continuing doubts of the twentieth-century mind, noting the long history of the Bible's effective witness, and reminding us that part of the issue is the attitude of the reader.

[O]nly the mind which has learnt to read the language of the Bible can understand what God is saying in the events of these stirring days; only the man who has understood the message of the biblical prophets in the great crises of far-away Samaria and Judea will recognize the signs of the times. The inhabitants of the world may learn righteousness when God's judgments are in the earth, but only if they have listened to the thunder in the voices of the prophets of the Old Covenant; they will learn to hope, amidst the chaos of twentieth-century civilization, only if they have caught the authentic Galilean accent of the New Testament, as it speaks of the sure mercies of God's covenanted grace. The Bible, the Old Testament as well as the New, teaches us the vocabulary of the divine language; unless we have learnt to understand this tongue, the words of God spoken through the events of our day will be lost in the babel of conflicting voices, and the meaning of the twentieth-century crisis will remain hidden from us. God speaks to men through contemporary events, if they have learnt from the Bible the idiom of His speech. The Bible interprets for us the events of to-day, if we will question it to discover what God has said in the events of biblical history.

. . . A cloud of witnesses in every Christian century bears unanimous and unbroken testimony to the fact that God speaks to men through the Bible. The only thing required of those who would hear is that they should come to their study of the Bible in an attitude of expectancy, that they should read it in a spirit of prayer. He that seeketh findeth, and to him that knocketh it shall be opened. This is a truth which has been confirmed over and over again in the prayerful and expectant approach of Christians to their Bible; had it not been proved true, Christianity would long ago have perished as an imposture and the biblical promises would have been discredited long before the twentieth century. The trouble with most of us is that we do not come really expecting to hear and to receive: the law of the spiritual world abides, "Be it unto you according to your faith."

—Alan Richardson, 1905–1975

37 The twentieth century, like many centuries before it, has produced numbers of incisively critical statements regarding the Scriptures. But no one has spoken more vigorously regarding the integrity and importance of the Scriptures than Emil Brunner.

From time immemorial the Church has always called the Scriptures of the Old and the New Testament the "Word of God." In so doing, the Church expresses the fundamental truth of the Christian faith, namely, that in these books the historical self-manifestation of God is offered to faith in an incomparable, decisive, and unique manner; this means that no Christian faith can either arise or be preserved which ignores "Holy Scripture." . . .

. . . The Christian Church stands and falls with the written New Testament, and the written Apostolic testimony to Christ is not only the foundation of all the later witness of the Church to Christ; it is also its norm.

—Emil Brunner, 1889–1966

38 During the latter part of the nineteenth century and continuing into the twentieth, scholars came to study the Scriptures in a much more critical way. For some, this seemed to diminish the authority of the Bible. Karl Barth, recognizing the value of such studies, nevertheless declared the unique authority of the Scriptures.

It is the Bible itself, it is the straight inexorable logic of its on-march which drives us out beyond ourselves and invites us, without regard to our worthiness or unworthiness, to reach for the last highest answer, in which all is said that can be said, although we can hardly understand and only stammeringly express it. And that answer is: A new world, the world of God. There is a spirit in the Bible that allows us to stop awhile and play among secondary things as is our wont—but presently it begins to press us on; and however we may object that we are only weak, imperfect, and most average folk, it presses us on to the primary fact, whether we will or no. There is a river in the Bible that carries us away, once we have entrusted our destiny to it—away from ourselves to the sea. The Holy Scriptures will interpret themselves in spite of all our human limitations. We need only dare to follow this drive, this spirit, this river, to grow out beyond ourselves toward the highest answer. This daring is *faith;* and we read the Bible rightly, not when we do so with false modesty, restraint, and attempted sobriety, for these are passive qualities, but when we read it in faith. And the invitation to dare and to reach toward the highest, even though we do not deserve it, is the expression of *grace* in the Bible: the Bible unfolds to us as we are met, guided, drawn on, and made to grow by the grace of God.

—Karl Barth, 1886–1968

39 During the latter half of the twentieth century several theological movements have arisen in the church to emphasize positions of their societal segment that they felt had previously been ignored. One of the most significant is the feminist movement. Bible scholar Letty M. Russell offers a biblical basis for her understanding of feminist theology.

The evidence for a biblical message of liberation for women, as for other marginalized groups, is not found just in particular stories about women or particular female images of God. It is found in God's intention for the mending of all creation. The Bible has authority in my life because it makes sense of my experience and speaks to me about the meaning and purpose of my humanity in Jesus Christ. In spite of its ancient and patriarchal worldviews, in spite of its inconsistencies and mixed messages, the story of God's love affair with the world leads me to a vision of New Creation that impels my life.

. . . .

I am one of those for whom the Bible continues to be a liberating word as I hear it together with others and struggle to live out its story. For me the Bible is "scripture," or sacred writing, because it functions as "script," or prompting for life. Its authority in my life stems from its story of God's invitation to participation in the restoration of wholeness, peace, and justice in the world. Responding to this invitation has made it my own story, or script, through the power of the Spirit at work in communities of struggle and faith.

—Letty M. Russell, 20th century

The Message Behind the Symbols

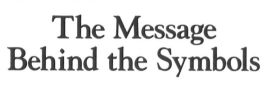

God: Creator ◆ God: Personal
God: Providence ◆ Covenant/Election

God the Creator is depicted in the hand extending from the clouds. The small circle around the hand is a three-rayed nimbus or circle of light, which indicates divinity and a Person of the Trinity. The larger circle enclosing the hand represents the eternal existence of God without beginning or ending, completeness, continuity, perfection.

The six-pointed star is known as the Creator's star. Its two triangles, a double reference to the Trinity, indicate that God the Creator is a triune God—one God in three Persons, a personal God. The six points of the star symbolize the six attributes of God—power, wisdom, majesty, love, mercy, justice—and recall the six days in which God created the heavens and the earth.

The descending dove, with its three-rayed nimbus indicating deity, symbolizes the presence and the power of God the Spirit hovering over the waters at creation.

Our total dependence on the providence of God, the sustaining power and the loving care of God, is eloquently depicted in the mother hen and baby chicks. And shining through the stars of the night is God's endless covenant with Abraham and with all people, "Look toward heaven and count the stars, if you are able to count them" (Genesis 15:5).

God: Creator

Our study of the doctrine of God begins with insights on God as Creator, because it is probably at this level that we are first conscious of God. The readings that follow deal not only with proofs of God as Creator, but also with celebrations of the beauty of creation and the human responsibility to the created trust.

40 We contemporary readers are sometimes surprised by the close and intricate way ancient writers reasoned. Our patterns of thought are often more abbreviated, and at times, more superficial. Read these few lines from Irenaeus with great care, because he is saying so much in a few words.

For creatures must have the origin of their being from some great cause; and the Origin of all is God, since It Itself was not made by anyone, but by It were made all things whatsoever. Therefore, first, one must believe that there is one God, the Father, who made and fashioned everything, and brought being out of nothing, and, while holding all things, is alone beyond grasp. But in "all things" is included this world of ours, with man in it; so this world too was created by God.

—Irenaeus, c. 130–c. 200

41 Although we think of Saint Augustine primarily as theologian and philosopher, he might have identified himself first as a believing worshiper. This is the quality of the following statement from his *Confessions*.

I love you, Lord, with no doubtful mind but with absolute certainty. . . .
But what am I loving when I love you? . . .
I put my question to the earth, and it replied, "I am not he";
I questioned everything it held, and they confessed the same.
I questioned the sea and the great deep,

and the teeming live creatures that crawl,
and they replied,
"We are not God; seek higher."
I questioned the gusty winds,
and every breeze with all its flying creatures told me,
"Anaximenes was wrong: I am not God."
To the sky I put my question, to sun, moon, stars,
but they denied me: "We are not the God you seek."
And to all things which stood around the portals of my flesh
    I said,
"Tell me of my God.
You are not he, but tell me something of him."
Then they lifted up their mighty voices and cried,
"He made us."
My questioning was my attentive spirit,
and their reply, their beauty.

—*Augustine, 354–430*

42 For Saint Augustine the creation not only is the work of God, as described in the Scriptures, but it is also a witness to God. Our faith rests upon both the Scriptures and the wonder of creation.

Of all visible things, the world is the greatest; of all invisible, the greatest is God. But, that the world is, we see; that God is, we believe. That God made the world, we can believe from no one more safely than from God Himself. But where have we heard Him? Nowhere more distinctly than in the Holy Scriptures, where His prophet said, "In the beginning God created the heavens and the earth." Was the prophet present when God made the heavens and the earth? No; but the wisdom of God, by whom all things were made, was there, and wisdom insinuates itself into holy souls, and makes them the friends and prophets of God and His prophets, and noiselessly informs them of His works. They are taught also by the angels of God, who always behold the face of the Father, and announce His will to whom it befits. Of these prophets was he who said and wrote, "In the beginning God created the heavens and the earth." And so fit a witness was he of God, that the same Spirit of God, who revealed these things to him, enabled him also so long before to predict that our faith would be forthcoming.

—*Augustine, 354–430*

43 The Scriptures speak more as poets than as scientists. Francis of Assisi writes both as poet and as lover as he thanks God for the wonders of creation, even while embracing the elements of creation as his kin.

Most high, all-powerful and good Lord!
To you are due the praises, the glory, the honor and every blessing,
To you only, O highest one, are they due
and no human being is worthy to speak of you.

Be praised, my Lord, with all your creatures
especially by brother sun
by whom we are lightened every day
for he is fair and radiant with great splendor
and bears your likeness, O highest one.

Be praised, my Lord, for sister moon and the stars
you have set them in heaven, precious, fair and bright.

Be praised, my Lord, by brother wind
and by air and cloud and sky and every weather
through whom you give life to all your creatures.

Be praised, my Lord, by sister water
for she is useful and humble and precious and chaste.

Be praised, my Lord, by brother fire
by him we are lightened at night
and he is fair and cheerful and sturdy and strong.

Be praised, my Lord, by our sister, mother earth
she sustains and governs us
and brings forth many fruits and coloured flowers and plants.

Be praised, my Lord, by those who have been pardoned
    by your love
and who bear infirmity and tribulation;
blessed are those who suffer them in peace
for by you, O highest one, they shall be crowned.

Be praised, my Lord, by our sister, physical death
From whom no one who lives can escape
woe to those who die in mortal sin

but blessed are those who are found in your most holy will
for the second death can do them no harm.

May I bless and praise you, my Lord, and give you thanks and
serve you with great humility.

—Francis of Assisi, 1181–1226

44 Many generations of believers memorized catechisms—training man-
uals for confirmands—in order to establish a sound foundation for their
beliefs. Here the Heidelberg Catechism, a German catechism, gives us a
summary statement regarding the doctrine of creation.

*26. What do you believe when you say: "I believe in God the
Father Almighty, Maker of heaven and earth"?*
A. That the eternal Father of our Lord Jesus Christ, who out of
nothing created heaven and earth with all that is in them, who also
upholds and governs them by his eternal counsel and providence,
is for the sake of Christ his Son, God and my Father. I trust in him
so completely that I have no doubt that he will provide me with all
things necessary for body and soul. Moreover, whatever evil he
sends upon me in this troubled life he will turn to my good, for he
is able to do it, being almighty God, and is determined to do it,
being a faithful Father.

—Heidelberg Catechism, 1562

45 Susanna Wesley worked as a theologian in preparing a manual of
belief for her own children. Her statement about God as Creator draws
from Scripture and is expressed in the language of reverent wonder.

[T]hough we cannot fully comprehend or have any adequate conceptions of what so far surpasseth the reach of human understanding, yet it is plainly demonstrable that he is omnipotent from his
being the Maker of Heaven and Earth—"of all things visible and
invisible." Nor could anything less than almighty power produce
the smallest most inconsiderable thing out of nothing. Not the least
spire of grass or most despicable insect but bears the divine signa-
ture and carries in its existence a clear demonstration of the deity.
For could we admit of such a wild supposition as that anything
could make itself, it must necessarily follow that a thing had being

before it had a being, that it could act before it was, which is a palpable contradiction. From whence among other reasons we conclude that this beauteous world, that celestial arch over our heads, and all those glorious heavenly bodies, sun, moon, and stars, etc. in fine, the whole system of the universe, were in the beginning made or created out of nothing by the eternal power, wisdom, and goodness of the ever blessed God according to "the counsel of his own will" or, as St. Paul better expresses it, Colossians 1:16, "By him were all things created that are in heaven, and that are in earth, visible and invisible, whether they be thrones, or dominions, or principalities, or powers: all things were created by him."

—*Susanna Wesley, 1670–1742*

46 We will observe that our beliefs inevitably affect our whole outlook on life. John Wesley makes this point in comments about God as Creator.

[A Christian] is happy in knowing there is a God, an intelligent Cause and Lord of all, and that he is not the produce either of blind chance or inexorable necessity. He is happy in the full assurance he has that this Creator and End of all things is a Being of boundless wisdom, of infinite power to execute all the designs of His wisdom, and of no less infinite goodness to direct all His power to the advantage of all His creatures. Nay, even the consideration of His immutable justice, rendering to all their due, of His unspotted holiness, of His all-sufficiency in Himself, and of that immense ocean of all perfections which centre in God from eternity to eternity, is a continual addition to the happiness of a Christian.

—*John Wesley, 1703–1791*

47 The Scriptures teach that the creation, as it came from God's hand, was perfect, but that it has since gone wrong. C.S. Lewis, defender of the Christian faith, reasons that it is the believer's task to help get it right again. He too underlines the distinction between the Creator and creation.

Pantheists usually believe that . . . the universe almost *is* God, so that if it did not exist He would not exist either, and anything you find in the universe is a part of God. . . . But, of course, if you think some things really bad, and God really good, then you cannot talk like that. You must believe that God is separate from the world and that some of the things we see in it are contrary to His will. Confronted with a cancer or a slum the Pantheist can say, "If you could only see it from the divine point of view, you would realise that this also is God." The Christian replies, "Don't talk damned nonsense."* For Christianity is a fighting religion. It thinks God made the world—that space and time, heat and cold, and all the colours and tastes, and all the animals and vegetables, are things that God "made up out of his head" as a man makes up a story. But it also thinks that a great many things have gone wrong with the world that God made and that God insists, and insists very loudly, on our putting them right again.

*One listener complained of the word *damned* as frivolous swearing. But I mean exactly what I say—nonsense that is *damned* is under God's curse, and will (apart from God's grace) lead those who believe it to eternal death.

—*C.S. Lewis, 1898–1963*

48 Christianity draws a sharp distinction between the Creator and creation. Karl Barth emphasizes this distinction in his doctrine of creation.

The proposition that God created heaven and earth and man asserts that this whole sphere is from God, willed and established by Him as a reality which is distinct from His own. In this respect, too, it contains within itself a negative and a positive. The negative is that the world is not alone—much less so than God. God could be alone; the world cannot. The world would not exist at all if God did not exist, and if it were not from Him. It is because it does not exist at all of itself, but only because God willed and created it, that it has no power over its existence and form; that it does not belong to itself; and that it cannot control itself. And the positive is that God is before the world; that He is an absolutely distinct and individual being in relation to it; that unlike the world He belongs to Himself and controls Himself; that He is completely self-sufficient because established and determined by Himself. And God is before the world in the strictest sense that He is its absolute origin, its purpose, the power which rules it, its Lord. For He created it. Through Him it came into being and through Him it is.

—*Karl Barth, 1886–1968*

49 Langdon Gilkey, professor of theology, notes that the creation reveals not only who the Creator is, but the character of the Creator.

Among the many activities of God, His creative activity is surely the one most essential for our existence. It is through this activity that we are brought into being, and it is this activity, therefore, that establishes our deepest, because our most essential, relation to God: He is our Creator and thus our Lord. Correspondingly, the doctrine of God as Creator is, perhaps, the most fundamental conception we can have of God. That is, creation is that activity of God by means of which we define what we mean by the word "God." It is quite natural, of course, that Christian devotion and Christian thought should concern themselves most with God's redeeming activity in Jesus Christ, for upon this our knowledge of God as Loving Father, and so of our hope for salvation, most directly depends. Nevertheless, the centrality of God's redeeming activity to our life and thought should not blind Christians to the divine work of creation, which, if not so close to our hearts, is just as significant for our existence and just as important if we are to think rightly about God. Through God's redeeming works we know that He is supremely righteous and supremely loving. But when we ask *who* is supremely righteous and loving, the answer comes in terms of God's original activity, creation: the Creator of heaven and earth, the Lord, is He who judges and redeems us.

—Langdon Gilkey, 1919–

50 Science and faith approach creation from different vantage points, and each needs—and ought to respect—the other. Georgia Harkness underlines this fact, then goes on to observe the quality of goodness in creation that is conveyed in the Genesis account.

There is, first, the affirmation that *God is the Creator of all that is.* . . .

The truth is that we know nothing at all about the manner of God's initial creative act. We were not there when it happened, and the scientists cannot tell us. What we do know is that God created, and controls, and continues to create an infinitely complex world. About the various natural and biological processes in which His creativity is discerned, science can tell us much. What can be learned about God's ways of working through the regularities of nature, we ought gratefully to receive. What we must not do is to confuse ultimate causation with chemical, physical, or biological processes and try to make the latter a substitute for God.

A second truth to be appropriated from the first chapter of Genesis is *the goodness of creation.* This is expressed in the refrain that is repeated at the end of nearly every stanza of this great hymn, "And God saw that it was good." (Gen. 1:10, 12, 18, 21, 25, 31.) James Weldon Johnson in his sermon (in reality a poem) on "Creation" in *God's Trombones* expresses this feeling in moving words second only to the biblical account itself. For example he thus describes the creation of the sun, moon, and stars:

Then God reached out and took the light in his hands,
And God rolled the light around in his hands
Until he made the sun;
And he set the sun a-blazing in the heavens.
And the light that was left from making the sun
God gathered it up in a shining ball
And flung it against the darkness,
Spangling the night with moon and stars.
Then down between
The darkness and the light
He hurled the world;
And God said: That's good!

—*Georgia Harkness, 1891–1974*

51 God sustains as well as creates. The creation is not the end of God's involvement in our universe. Theologian Sallie McFague relates this concept to our responsibility in an ecological, nuclear world.

Let us now look more carefully at some features of the sustaining work of God in an ecological, nuclear world. The issues with which we will deal are summarized in two questions: Who is the sustaining God? And what sort of community is formed by the work of God the sustainer? In attempting to answer the first question, we recall that what solidarity friendship says, most fundamentally, is that we are not our own and we are not on our own. As a model for God's relationship with the world, it is a model of hope, defying despair. It says that God is with us, Emmanuel, our companion, who steadfastly accompanies us in both joy and suffering. We are not left alone to struggle against the forces of sin and evil, the forces in ourselves and our world that pit being against being, build walls of discrimination, deny nourishment to many, oppress some in order to privilege others. And this is also what the church and the tradition have said both in the appearance stories of Jesus . . . and in the arrival of the Holy Spirit at Pentecost (Acts 2).

—Sallie McFague, 20th century

52 The Korean Creed is a relatively recent addition to the creeds of Christendom, but a significant one as an expression of the church in what was once a mission field, but which is now one of the most rapidly growing Christian populations in all of the world.

We believe in the one God,
    creator and sustainer of all things, Father of all nations,
    the source of all goodness and beauty, all truth and love.
We believe in Jesus Christ,
    God manifest in the flesh,
    our teacher, example, and Redeemer, the Savior of the world.
We believe in the Holy Spirit,
    God present with us for guidance, for comfort, and for strength.
We believe in the forgiveness of sins,
    in the life of love and prayer,
    and in grace equal to every need.
We believe in the Word of God
    contained in the Old and New Testaments
    as the sufficient rule both of faith and of practice.
We believe in the church,
    those who are united in the living Lord
    for the purpose of worship and service.
We believe in the reign of God
    as the divine will realized in human society,
    and in the family of God,
    where we are all brothers and sisters.
We believe in the final triumph of righteousness
    and in the life everlasting. Amen.

—A Statement of Faith of the Korean Methodist Church, 1989

God: Personal

At the point of our understanding and experiencing God, no element in the doctrine of God is more important than the names and the character by which we know God. While there has always been some latitude of description, one is impressed that these expressions have not often slipped over into what the church would judge to be heresy.

53 We have noted in our reading that we humans haven't the capacity to comprehend the fullness of God; no wonder, then, that we come up with partial descriptions and figures of speech. Cyril, Bishop of Jerusalem, suggests that our best knowledge is "confessing that we have none." But this is an expression of worship, not of despair.

Now the mind thinks with great rapidity, but the tongue needs expressions and a long outpouring of words before it reaches a conclusion. For, in one instant, the eye takes in a vast multitude of stars, but if anyone should want to discourse on any particular stars, as, for instance, to pick out the morning star or the evening star, or any single star, he will need to say a good deal. Again in like manner the mind comprehends earth and sea and all the bounds of the world in a flash, but it takes it many words to express what it understands in a twinkling. The example, then, that I have adduced is a very strong one, and yet it is weak and inadequate for the purpose in hand. For what we say about God is not what should be said (for that is known only to him) but only what human nature takes in, and only what our infirmity can bear. For what we expound is not what God is, but (and we frankly acknowledge it) the fact that we have no sure knowledge about him; and that is to say that our chief theological knowledge is confessing that we have none. Therefore, "magnify the Lord with me, and let us exalt his name together," since one alone is unequal to the task. Rather I should say, if all of us unite for it, it will still be beyond us; and in saying that I do not mean just us who are here, but that if all the children of the Church throughout the world, both to this day and for all time to come, united to the task, we still should not be able worthily to hymn our Shepherd.

—*Cyril of Jerusalem, 314–386*

54 We have noted that our names for God and the qualities we find in God are likely to intersect. Julian of Norwich demonstrates as much, in the language of a devout mystic. She worships even as she seeks to explain.

And then I saw that God rejoiceth that he is our Father: and God rejoiceth that he is our Mother: and God rejoiceth that he is our true Spouse, and our soul his beloved wife. And Christ rejoiceth that he is our Brother: and Jesus rejoiceth that he is our Savior.

...God is kind in his Being. That is to say: the Goodness which is Kind, is God. He is the Ground: he is the Substance: he is the very thing called Kindness. And he is the very Father and the very Mother of kinds. And all kinds that he hath made to flow out of him to work his will, they must be restored and brought again into him, by the salvation of man, through the working of grace. For of all the kinds that he hath set in various creatures separately, only in man is all the whole—in fullness and in power, in beauty and in goodness, in royalty and nobility: in all manner of eminence, of preciousness and honour.

Here may we see that we are all indebted to God for kind, and we are indebted to God for grace.

—*Julian of Norwich, 1342–after 1416*

55 We have seen that the biblical writers used a variety of images to express their experience of God. One of the most vivid images from the world of theologians comes from Martin Luther, in his picture of God as his fortress in the struggles of life. Although the word *fortress* is used only once, the full imagery of the poem is one of strength in the midst of conflict.

A mighty fortress is our God,
a bulwark never failing;
our helper he amid the flood
of mortal ills prevailing.
For still our ancient foe
doth seek to work us woe;

his craft and power are great,
and armed with cruel hate,
on earth is not his equal.

Did we in our own strength confide,
our striving would be losing,
were not the right man on our side,
the man of God's own choosing.
Dost ask who that may be?
Christ Jesus, it is he;
Lord Sabaoth, his name,
from age to age the same,
and he must win the battle.

And though this world, with devils filled,
should threaten to undo us,
we will not fear, for God hath willed
his truth to triumph through us.
The Prince of Darkness grim,
we tremble not for him;
his rage we can endure,
for lo, his doom is sure;
one little word shall fell him.

That word above all earthly powers,
no thanks to them, abideth;
the Spirit and the gifts are ours,
thru him who with us sideth.
Let goods and kindred go,
this mortal life also; the body
they may kill; God's truth abideth still;
his kingdom is forever.

—Martin Luther, 1483–1546

56 Any study of the nature of God must be pursued with great humility. We confess readily that not only can we not contain the subject; we cannot really approach it, except as the Subject draws us and reveals to us. John Wesley wrestles with the relationship between understanding and revelation in our pursuit of God.

'There are three that bear record in heaven. . . : and these three are one.' I believe this *fact* also (if I may use the expression)—that God is Three and One. But the *manner*, *how*, I do not comprehend; and I do not believe it. Now in this, in the *manner*, lies the mystery. And so it may; I have no concern with it. It is no object of my faith; I believe just so much as God has revealed and no more. But this, the *manner*, he has not revealed; therefore I believe nothing about it. But would it not be absurd in me to deny the fact because I do not understand the manner? That is, to reject *what God has revealed* because I do not comprehend *what he has not revealed?*

This is a point much to be observed. There are many things which 'eye hath not seen, nor ear heard, neither hath it entered into the heart of man to conceive'. Part of these God hath 'revealed to us by his Spirit'—*revealed*, that is, unveiled, uncovered. That part he requires us to believe. Part of them he has not revealed. That we need not, and indeed cannot, believe; it is far above, out of our sight.

—John Wesley, 1703–1791

57 Although our understanding of God should never be limited to our personal experience, the fact remains that these experiences either support or weaken whatever divine character we perceive. Georgia Harkness helps us to understand the relationship of logic and experience.

Only a personal God can know or care what happens to persons. A deity conceived to be an impersonal force or process, or an abstract principle, or the totality of all that exists, or the sum total of human ideals cannot be personally concerned with individuals or their destiny. Such a God may be worshiped in the sense of being held in reverence; to such a deity some form of human adjustment can be made. But such a God cannot be prayed to or trusted to give providential guidance to any person's life. . . .

A personal God is one of supreme intelligence, supreme goodness, and supreme creative and controlling power. One who grants the presence of an infinitely complex, yet ordered, structure in the universe and the predominance of value over evil in human existence may be ready to affirm the existence of a personal God upon these grounds. Yet this is not foundation enough for a doctrine of providence. The Christian's faith in providence requires a further and to many minds a more difficult affirmation, for it roots in the conviction that the God who guides the stars and atoms in their courses also guides and cares *for you and me.*

—Georgia Harkness, 1891–1974

58 If anything is basic to our Christian understanding of God, it is the belief that God is personal. Georgia Harkness tells us that this understanding is basic not only to our understanding of God, but to our whole structure of belief.

Though the Bible does not use the philosophical term "personal God," its assumption throughout is that God is personal. The God who not only creates but loves, rebukes, judges, redeems, delivers, guides, guards, and sustains His people; the God who sorrows for their sins and in mercy offers salvation; the God who is the basis of the Christian's faith and hope and love is meaningless unless conceived in personal terms. The Bible does not argue this position; it assumes it, for the Bible is not written as speculative philosophy but as the record of living religion. On this assumption the entire structure of the great drama of creation, judgment, and redemption rests.

—Georgia Harkness, 1891–1974

59 We learned in an earlier lesson that what we know of God begins with the divine revelation. Emil Brunner draws us back to that revelation, warning us that without it our perception of God will quickly slip over into a form of idolatry.

Truth and grace can be spoken with the same breath: truth like grace is encounter between God and man; grace and truth came into being in Jesus Christ.

...God, apart from his revelation in the form of a human being, is mystery. What we speculate about God is idolatrous interpretation of the divine mystery, of which we are all aware. The personal God can be known only in his personal revelation, and his personal revelation is the incarnation of the Word. The incarnation of the eternal Son of God is the unveiling of his quality of being person and hence at the same time his will to fellowship. For this is the Biblical conception of God's quality of being Person: love, self-communication—that love which through all eternity the Father has for the Son, and the Son for the Father. God's quality of being Person, revealed in Jesus Christ, is itself of such a nature that it establishes fellowship. . . . Such is the Biblical concept of the personality of God. The revelation of himself as Person is therefore at the same time revelation of himself as Love; consequently truth and grace are the same.

—Emil Brunner, 1889–1966

60 While the qualities of God are unchanging, our human perceptions and prejudices shift notably from one generation to the next. The love of God is more appealing to the late twentieth century than the justice of God. But Martin Luther King, Jr., makes a case for God's justice, as well.

At times we need to know that the Lord is a God of justice. When slumbering giants of injustice emerge in the earth, we need to know that there is a God of power who can cut them down like the grass and leave them withering like the green herb. When our most tireless efforts fail to stop the surging sweep of oppression, we need to know that in this universe is a God whose matchless strength is a fit contrast to the sordid weakness of man. But there are also times when we need to know that God possesses love and mercy. When we are staggered by the chilly winds of adversity and battered by the raging storms of disappointment and when through our folly and sin we stray into some destructive far country and are frustrated because of a strange feeling of homesickness, we need to know that there is Someone who loves us, cares for us, understands us, and will give us another chance. When days grow dark and nights grow dreary, we can be thankful that our God combines in his nature a creative synthesis of love and justice which will lead us through life's dark valleys and into sunlit pathways of hope and fulfillment.

—Martin Luther King, Jr., 1929–1968

61 The idea that God is personal can be reached by way of logic and reasoning. But in most cases it also includes some elements of experience. Such is the witness of Martin Luther King, Jr., civil rights leader, as he traces a journey from a "metaphysical category" to a "living reality."

In recent months I have also become more and more convinced of the reality of a personal God. True, I have always believed in the personality of God. But in past years the idea of a personal God was little more than a metaphysical category which I found theologically and philosophically satisfying. Now it is a living reality that has been validated in the experiences of everyday life. Perhaps the suffering, frustration and agonizing moments which I have had to undergo occasionally as a result of my involvement in a difficult struggle have drawn me closer to God. Whatever the cause, God has been profoundly real to me in recent months. In the midst of outer dangers I have felt an inner calm and known resources of strength that only God could give. In many instances I have felt the power of God transforming the fatigue of despair into the buoyancy of hope. I am convinced that the universe is under the control of a loving purpose and that in the struggle for righteousness man has cosmic companionship. Behind the harsh appearances of the world there is a benign power. To say God is personal is not to make him an object among other objects or attribute to him the finiteness and limitations of human personality; it is to take what is finest and noblest in our consciousness and affirm its perfect existence in him. It is certainly true that human personality is limited, but personality as such involves no necessary limitations. It simply means self-consciousness and self-direction. So in the truest sense of the word, God is a living God. In him there is feeling and will, responsive to the deepest yearnings of the human heart: this God both evokes and answers prayers.

—Martin Luther King, Jr., 1929–1968

62 The Bible, and the theology that springs from it, does a daring thing, by portraying God in the concepts of our everyday human relationships. Theologian Thomas Oden gives us several biblical examples, while explaining the significance of such everyday concepts for our understanding of the nature of God.

A personal relationship involves and requires an interactive speaking and listening relationship of free beings. Even though God's way of being a person far transcends human ways of being persons, nonetheless the divine-human encounter is portrayed by Scripture as a personal relationship of meeting, speaking, listening, getting acquainted, becoming mutually committed and involved, experiencing frustrations and failures, splitting up, and becoming reconciled (Exod. 28:43; Num. 11:33; 1 Sam. 10:1-5; Pss. 4:1; 17:1; 74:1; Hos. 14:1 . . .).

Scripture speaks constantly of God by means of these personal and interpersonal analogies: God is viewed as a self-determining, conscious, feeling, and willing Self who has relationships with other personal beings (Matt. 7:21; 26:39 . . .). God is known and celebrated in the life of prayer as personal, and understood by means of metaphors of human personal responsiveness (Matt. 6:10; John 6:38-40).

Persons by definition have feelings. Each one has an identifiable self, intellect, and capacity for response. God is represented in Scripture as having much of the psychological makeup of what we know as personhood. God has intellect and emotion; God speaks (Gen. 1:3), sees (Gen. 11:5), and hears (Ps. 94:9). Metaphorically it is said that God repents (Gen. 6:6) and can be angry (Deut. 1:37), jealous (Exod. 20:5), and compassionate (Ps. 111:4). Only personal beings can feel such emotions. . . . No stone or abstract idea or amoeba can speak words, listen, care for others, get angry, respond to hurts—only persons do these things.

—Thomas C. Oden, 1931–

63 Our study concentrates especially on the holiness and the love of God, since these are the divine qualities that touch our lives so intimately, and since they seem in many ways to subsume other divine qualities. Paul K. Jewett, theologian, speaks of the relationship of love and holiness.

The God who is the Holy One is the God who is in our midst as Love. We must now probe the meaning of the apostle John's remarkable statement God *is* Love (1 Jn. 4:8). The paradox in our doctrine of the divine nature becomes evident at once. Holiness speaks of God's transcendence, his otherness, his remoteness from us; love, of his immanence, his giving of himself to us. The one affirmation is distance-making, the other distance-breaking. Yet the authors of Scripture never think of God's holiness and love as mutually exclusive; they rather view them as mutually inclusive. Not that God's holiness and love are ultimately synonymous; to say that God is the Holy One and that he is Love is not to speak in tautologies. But his holiness and love encompass each other, contain and comprise each other in a mysterious embrace. Hence for the prophet Isaiah, the divine purpose in Israel's judgment is salvation! It is as the Holy One who judges Israel that God becomes Israel's Redeemer and Savior (Is. 41:14; 43:3; 47:4).

—Paul K. Jewett, 20th century

64 What we believe about God always affects (even if sometimes subtly) what we believe about ourselves as human beings. Sallie McFague puts this issue in enchanting fashion, urging us to a new appreciation of ourselves as physical beings.

When Moses in an audacious moment asks of God, "Show me your glory," God replies that "no one can see me and live," but he does allow Moses a glimpse of the divine body—not the face, but the back (Exodus 33:20-23). The passage is a wonderful mix of the outrageous (God has a *backside*?!) and the awesome (the display of divine glory too dazzling for human eyes). The passage unites guts and glory, flesh and spirit, the human and the divine, and all those other apparent dualisms with a reckless flamboyance that points to something at the heart of the Hebrew and Christian traditions: God is not afraid of the flesh. We intend to take this incarnationalism seriously and see what it does, could, mean in terms of the picture of reality from postmodern science. Were we to imagine "the Word made flesh" as not limited to Jesus of Nazareth but as the body of the universe, all bodies, might we not have a homey but awesome metaphor for both divine nearness *and* divine glory? Like Moses, when we ask, "Show me your glory," we might see the humble bodies of our own planet as visible signs of the invisible grandeur. Not the face, not the depths of divine radiance, but enough, more than enough. We might begin to see (for the first time, perhaps) the marvels at our feet and at our fingertips: the intricate splendor of an Alpine forget-me-not or a child's hand. We might begin to realize the extraordinariness of the ordinary. We would begin to delight in creation, not as the work of an external deity, but as a sacrament of the living God. We would see creation as bodies alive with the breath of God. We might realize what this tradition has told us, although often shied away from embracing unreservedly: we live and move and have our being *in* God. We might see ourselves and everything else as the living body of God.

—Sallie McFague, 20th century

God: Providence

To recognize the activity of God as demonstrations of providence calls for more faith than to recognize God as Creator. Especially, it asks us to see God as personal, and as interested and involved in this planet and its inhabitants; indeed, as participating in the unfolding of daily life on this planet. Faith may testify to this theme with gladness; centuries of theologians have responded with both cautious reasoning and personal trust.

65 We have been reminded that "providence" contains the word and concept of "provide." This mood is accentuated in John Calvin's explanation of God's continuing involvement in our world. Calvin, Protestant reformer, contends that God is not truly Creator if he is only Creator.

It were cold and lifeless to represent God as a momentary Creator, who completed his work once for all, and then left it. Here, especially, we must dissent from the profane, and maintain that the presence of the divine power is conspicuous, not less in the perpetual condition of the world than in its first creation. For, although even wicked men are forced, by the mere view of the earth and sky, to rise to the Creator, yet faith has a method of its own in assigning the whole praise of creation to God. To this effect is the passage of the Apostle already quoted, that by faith we understand that the worlds were framed by the Word of God (Heb. xi.3); because, without proceeding to his Providence, we cannot understand the full force of what is meant by God being the Creator, how much soever we may seem to comprehend it with our mind, and confess it with our tongue. ... But faith must penetrate deeper. After learning that there is a Creator, it must forthwith infer that he is also a Governor and Preserver, and that, not by producing a kind of general motion in the machine of the globe as well as in each of its parts, but by a special Providence sustaining, cherishing, superintending, all the things which he has made, to the very minutest, even to a sparrow.

—*John Calvin, 1509–1564*

66 Most of us would define providence as the activity of God in our world. Jacobus Arminius, a Dutch Reformed theologian, (whose name is preserved for us in the theological system known as Arminianism) defines providence by its two aspects, and by the four ways in which he perceives it to operate.

Divine providence is the process by which God ensures good relations with all creatures, in order that their natures might be fulfilled. The actions of God in his providence demonstrate his wisdom. In his wisdom he is sometimes severe, and sometimes merciful; but always he is just.

We may distinguish two aspects of providence. The first is preservation, by which God sustains all creatures. The second is government, by which God guides their feelings and actions.

We may also distinguish four ways in which providence operates. The first is motion, by which God prompts creatures to feel and act in a particular fashion. The second is assistance, by which God strengthens the good inclinations of creatures. The third is concurrence, by which God supports and opposes the feelings and actions of creatures. And the fourth is permission, by which God allows his creatures to feel and act in a particular fashion.

—*Jacobus Arminius, 1560–1609*

67 As we have seen, the character of God is particularly an issue in the matter of God's continuing involvement in our world. John Wesley meets this issue head-on.

And is the Creator and Preserver of the world unconcerned for what he sees therein? Does he look upon these things either with a malignant or heedless eye? Is he an Epicurean god? Does he sit at ease in the heaven, without regarding the poor inhabitants of earth? It cannot be. He hath made us, not we ourselves; and he cannot despise the work of his own hands. We are his children. . . . Consequently he is concerned every moment for what befalls every creature upon earth; and more especially for everything that befalls any of the children of men. It is hard indeed to comprehend this; nay, it is hard to believe it, considering the complicated wickedness and the complicated misery which we see on every side. But believe it we must unless we will make God a liar, although it is sure no man can comprehend it. . . .

He is infinite in wisdom as well as in power; and all his wisdom is continually employed in managing all the affairs of his creation for the good of all his creatures. For his wisdom and goodness go hand in hand; they are inseparably united, and continually act in concert with almighty power. . . . And to him all things are possible. He doth whatsoever pleaseth him. And we cannot doubt of his exerting all his power, as in sustaining, so in governing all that he has made.

—*John Wesley, 1703–1791*

68 As we have indicated before, providence has to be grasped with some measure of faith. No wonder, then, that some of the most moving insights on providence come in the unpretentious language of believers—and never more eloquently than in a hymn by Civilla D. Martin.

Why should I feel discouraged,
Why should the shadows come,
Why should my heart be lonely
And long for heaven and home,
When Jesus is my portion?
My constant friend is He:
His eye is on the sparrow,
And I know He watches me;
His eye is on the sparrow,
And I know He watches me.

"Let not your heart be troubled,"
His tender word I hear,
And resting on His goodness,
I lose my doubts and fears;
Though by the path He leadeth,
But one step I may see:
His eye is on the sparrow,
And I know He watches me;
His eye is on the sparrow,
And I know He watches me.

Whenever I am tempted,
Whenever clouds arise,
When songs give place to sighing,
When hope within me dies,
I draw the closer to Him,
From care He sets me free:
His eye is on the sparrow,
And I know He watches me;
His eye is on the sparrow,
And I know He watches me.

I sing because I'm happy,
I sing because I'm free,
For His eye is on the sparrow,
And I know He watches me.
—*Civilla D. Martin, 1869–1948*

69 We can't help wondering how much God is involved in personal and general history, and why that involvement, from our point of view, seems selective. William Temple, Archbishop of Canterbury, deals with such issues, giving theological substance to a common word, *accident*.

What men call an "accident" is an event in which some causal sequence in nature comes into intimate relationship with the purposive action of a mind that had not taken that sequence into account. All purposive action of men rests upon and presupposes the constant operation of natural forces. I plan for tomorrow and for next year on the supposition that the revolution of the earth upon its own axis and about the sun will continue. If in following up my plan I walk along a street at the precise moment when a chimney is blown down so that it nearly or quite kills me, that is an "accident"; the fall of rocks from a mountain into an empty valley is not called an accident unless there is a person, or a building representing the purpose of a person, near where the rocks fall. It appears then that while the constancy of natural processes is the necessary prerequisite for intelligent, purposive and moral action, that same constancy may sometimes cut across the sequence of purposive actions and hinder the fulfillment of purpose. It is at such times that religious people are driven to ask why God permits the occurrence of events that involve apparently useless waste and sorrow. . . . First, the whole possibility of that moral life, from the implications of which the difficulty arises, depends upon the general constancy of natural processes, which leads to the particular regretted accident. If that constancy is to be modified every time it would lead to what is in itself regrettable for somebody, it would become a totally insecure foundation for the purposiveness of the moral life. Secondly, it is good for a man to know that the course of nature is not devised for his convenience; for his benefit indeed it is devised—for it is to his benefit that his individual convenience should not be considered. Consequently there is an immense *a priori* probability that it is good for the normal process to take its course, even though it make havoc of many human purposes and even of human affections. But the religious man's difficulty is not imaginary; it springs from a principle more fundamental than that of nature's constancy; it springs from recognition of what is implied by belief in Divine Personality.

—*William Temple, 1881–1944*

70 German theologian Paul Tillich's experiences in Hitler's Germany gave him a powerful sense of what he called "the daemonic." His doctrine of providence affirms vigorously the final victory of God over even the most destructive forces that seem to operate in our world and in history.

But the content of the faith in Providence is this: when death rains from heaven as it does now, when cruelty wields power over nations and individuals as it does now, when hunger and persecution drive millions from place to place as they do now, and when prisons and slums all over the world distort the humanity of the bodies and souls of men as they do now—we can boast in that time, and just in that time, that even all of this cannot separate us from the love of God. In this sense, and in this sense alone, all things work together for good, for the *ultimate* good, the eternal love, and the Kingdom of God. Faith in divine Providence is the faith that nothing can prevent us from fulfilling the ultimate meaning of our existence. Providence does not mean a divine planning by which everything is predetermined, as is an efficient machine. Rather, Providence means that there is a creative and saving possibility implied in every situation, which cannot be destroyed by any event. Providence means that the daemonic and destructive forces within ourselves and our world can never have an unbreakable grasp upon us, and that the bond which connects us with the fulfilling love can never be disrupted.

—Paul Tillich, 1886–1965

71 Although we use the words *providence* and *providential* often enough, we might be hard put to offer a definition. Georgia Harkness gives not only a good definition, but also explains the difference between general and special providence.

The providence of God means the goodness of God and His guiding, sustaining care. Belief in providence in the most general sense implies the goodness as well as the power of God in the creation, ordering, and maintaining of His world, embracing the entire world of physical nature, biological life, and human persons. . . .

. . . [A] distinction needs to be drawn between what is often called the "general providence" of God and "special providences." General providence means the goodness of God as seen in the overall, inclusive structure of creation. . . . What is basic to a Christian doctrine of general providence is expressed with great beauty and dignity in the refrain of the Genesis story of creation, "And God saw that it was good." This is echoed in the familiar words of Jesus about the heavenly Father who feeds the birds of the air and clothes the grass of the field. . . .

The term "special providences" is much more ambiguous. It may mean events thought to happen outside the regular course of nature by the supernatural power of God, that is, miracles. It may mean that God does for one person what He ordinarily does not do for others in the form of special favors or some special protection, and it is then usually linked with specific answers to prayer.

—Georgia Harkness, 1891–1974

72 Like many less well-known believers, Martin Luther King, Jr., found his theology of providence in life's crucible as well as in his study.

At the center of the Christian faith is the conviction that in the universe there is a God of power who is able to do exceedingly abundant things in nature and in history. This conviction is stressed over and over in the Old and the New Testaments. Theologically, this affirmation is expressed in the doctrine of the omnipotence of God. The God whom we worship is not a weak and incompetent

God. He is able to beat back gigantic waves of opposition and to bring low prodigious mountains of evil. The ringing testimony of the Christian faith is that God is able. . . .

Let us notice, first, that God is able to sustain the vast scope of the physical universe. . . .

Let us notice also that God is able to subdue all the powers of evil. . . .

Let us notice, finally, that God is able to give us interior resources to confront the trials and difficulties of life. Each of us faces circumstances in life which compel us to carry heavy burdens of sorrow. Adversity assails us with hurricane force. Glowing sunrises are transformed into darkest nights. Our highest hopes are blasted and our noblest dreams are shattered. . . .

Only God is able. It is faith in him that we must rediscover. With this faith we can transform bleak and desolate valleys into sunlit paths of joy and bring new light into the dark caverns of pessimism. Is someone here moving toward the twilight of life and fearful of that which we call death? Why be afraid? God is able. Is someone here on the brink of despair because of the death of a loved one, the breaking of a marriage, or the waywardness of a child? Why despair? God is able to give you the power to endure that which cannot be changed. Is someone here anxious because of bad health? Why be anxious? Come what may, God is able.

Let this affirmation be our ringing cry. It will give us courage to face the uncertainties of the future. It will give our tired feet new strength as we continue our forward stride toward the city of freedom. When our days become dreary with low-hovering clouds and our nights become darker than a thousand midnights, let us remember that there is a great benign Power in the universe whose name is God, and he is able to make a way out of no way, and transform dark yesterdays into bright tomorrows.

—*Martin Luther King, Jr, 1929–1968*

73 What we believe plays a key part in what we are. This is part of the mood of theologian Albert Outler, as he describes the spirit in which the believer faces life, and the unselfishness with which he or she lives it.

The really "stylish" Christian takes it for granted that existence is tenuous and untoward—the nice guys do often finish last, if they aren't finished off first. But, oddly enough, he is seldom bitter and outraged that it should be so; he is not smothered with self-pity, nor driven to strike out blindly against his tormentors. . . . The stylish Christian finds life *good—this* life in *this* world. And so he takes the bitter and the sweet with tears and laughter because he is so sure that this life and this world are all as fully and really in God's care and keeping as the affairs of the angels and saints in heaven. He sees his joys and sorrows in the perspective of life as a training ground for growing persons—all of it provided and cared for by grace. He is not "patient" with any misery that human wit and effort can prevent or allay—his own or others—but his courage and devotion do not fluctuate with the odds against his "success." He is, as Luther said, "the most free lord of all and subject to no one"—in this sense undominated by society and "the world"—and yet also he is "most bound by love and subject to every one." He is a man for others precisely because he is not a man on his own. . . .

But the life of grace that lives fully in the present is also life open to the future and to death. For all that life means now must really await judgment as to what it will have meant when it can all be seen in just perspective. For the Christian, this turns on his faith in God's providence for the human future as well as the past. Such a faith knows as well as any skeptic that our proximate futures are inscrutable and that our final future is, literally, inconceivable. But it does believe that God's providence for our freedom, identity and power to love will continue to "the end" as it has from "the beginning."

—*Albert C. Outler, 1909–1989*

74 While the Old Testament prophets see God at work in the unfolding of history, we may not expect a professional historian to do so. But Herbert Butterfield, a premier twentieth-century British historian, insists that history inevitably includes providence.

For let us make sure of one thing—in the long run there are only two alternative views about life or about history. Here is a fact which was realized thousands of years ago and it is still as true as ever. Either you trace everything back in the long run to sheer blind Chance, or you trace everything to God. Some of you might say that there is a third alternative—namely that everything just happens through the operation of the laws of nature. But that is not an explanation at all and the mind cannot rest there, for such a thesis does not tell us where the laws themselves can have come from. Either we must say that there is a mind behind the laws of nature—there is a God who ordered things in that particular way—or we must say that in the infinity of time all possible combinations of events are exhausted by the blind work of Chance, which produces amongst all the planets of the sky at any rate one where vegetation is possible and where animal life develops, and where in human beings matter itself acquires the quality of mind.

—Herbert Butterfield, 1900–

75 As our lesson notes, people who do not accept the idea of providence sometimes refer to God as an "absentee landlord." Daniel L. Migliore explains the idea of providence while drawing upon the classical language of the Heidelberg Catechism.

Christians confess the lordship and providential care of God over the world. God the creator does not abandon the creation, leaving it to run on its own, as deism teaches. The true God is no absentee landlord but remains ever faithful, upholding, blessing, and guiding the creation to its appointed goal. God's continuing care for all creatures is attested in many passages of Scripture (e.g., Ps. 104:27-30), perhaps the most familiar being the teaching of Jesus that God sends rain on both the just and the unjust (Matt. 5:45), feeds the birds of the air, clothes the lilies of the field (Matt. 6:26-30), and knows every hair on our head (Matt. 10:30).

A brief but pointed definition of providence is offered by the Heidelberg Catechism of 1563: providence is "the almighty and ever-present power of God whereby he still upholds, as it were by his own hand, heaven and earth together with all creatures, and rules in such a way that leaves and grass, rain and drought, fruitful and unfruitful years, food and drink, health and sickness, riches and poverty, and everything else, come to us not by chance but by his fatherly hand."

—Daniel L. Migliore, 1935–

Covenant/Election

Most students of doctrine have had a strong sense of covenant. Taking a comprehensive view of both Scripture and life, they see evidence of God's pursuing a covenant, and of humanity's alternately pursuing it and fleeing from it.

76 Part of the work of a theologian is to define the language of faith. Our study has provided pieces of a definition through the Scriptures and through the biblical story of covenant. Zacharias Ursinus, a Calvinist theologian who helped to compile the Heidelberg Catechism, summarizes defining material with helpful clarity.

A covenant in general is a mutual contract, or agreement between two parties, in which the one party binds itself to the other to accomplish something upon certain conditions, giving or receiving something, which is accompanied with certain outward signs and symbols, for the purpose of ratifying in the most solemn manner the contract entered into, and for the sake of confirming it, that the engagement may be kept inviolate. From this general definition of a covenant, it is easy to perceive what we are to understand by the Covenant here spoken of, which we may define as a mutual promise and agreement, between God and men, in which God gives assurance to men that he will be merciful to them, remit their sins, grant unto them a new righteousness, the Holy Spirit, and eternal life by and for the sake of his Son, our Mediator. And, on the other side, men bind themselves to God in this covenant that they will exercise repentance and faith, or that they will receive with a true faith this great benefit which God offers, and render such obedience as will be acceptable to him. This mutual engagement between God and man is confirmed by those outward signs which we call sacraments, which are holy signs, declaring and sealing unto us God's good will, and our thankfulness and obedience.

—*Zacharias Ursinus, 1534–1583*

77 To be part of God's covenant people is a gift beyond estimation. No wonder, then, that it is seen as a matter of election. John Calvin rejoices in the certainty of this election. Not only is it wonderful; it is ultimately secure.

Moreover, since the church is the people of God's elect [John 10:28], it cannot happen that those who are truly its members will ultimately perish [John 10:28], or come to a bad end. For their salvation rests on such a sure and solid bed, that, even if the whole fabric of the world were to fall, it itself could not tumble and fall. First, it stands with God's election, nor can it change or fail, unless along with that eternal wisdom. Therefore they can totter and waver, even fall, but not contend against one another for the Lord supports their hand; that is what Paul says, "for the gifts and calling of God are without repentance" [Rom. 11:29]. Then those whom the Lord has chosen, have been turned over to the care and keeping of Christ his Son so that "he may lose none of them but may revive all on the last day." [John 6:39f.]. Under such a good watchman [cf. II Cor. 4:9] they can wander and fall, but surely they cannot be lost.

—John Calvin, 1509–1564

78 One of the key factors of the divine-human covenant is this, that God initiates the action; it would be human presumption, indeed, to conceive of it any other way. The English Reformers put this matter sharply, noting that our covenant is thus a covenant of grace.

The distance between God and the creature is so great that although reasonable creatures do owe obedience unto Him as their Creator, yet they could never have any fruition of Him as their blessedness and reward but by some voluntary condescension on God's part which He hath been pleased to express by way of covenant.

The first covenant made with man was a covenant of works wherein life was promised to Adam, and in him to his posterity, upon condition of perfect and personal obedience.

Man by his fall, having made himself incapable of life by that covenant, the Lord was pleased to make a second, commonly called the covenant of grace, wherein He freely offereth unto sinners life and salvation by Jesus Christ, requiring of them faith in Him that they may be saved, and promising to give unto all those that are ordained unto eternal life His Holy Spirit, to make them willing and able to believe.

This covenant of grace is frequently set forth in Scripture by the name of a testament, in reference to the death of Jesus Christ the Testator and to the everlasting inheritance, with all things belonging to it, therein bequeathed.

—*Westminster Confession, 1646*

79 The doctrine of election is a point of issue between several major theological bodies within Christendom. John Calvin emphasized one point of view; here John Wesley tries to explain the issues from another vantage point.

"But do not the Scriptures speak of election? They say, St. Paul was 'an elected or chosen vessel;' nay, and speak of great numbers of men as 'elect according to the foreknowledge of God.' You cannot, therefore, deny there is such a thing as election. And, if there is, what do you mean by it?"

I will tell you, in all plainness and simplicity. I believe it commonly means one of these two things: First, a divine appointment of some particular men, to do some particular work in the world. And this election I believe to be not only personal, but absolute and unconditional. Thus Cyrus was elected to rebuild the temple, and St. Paul, with the twelve, to preach the gospel. But I do not find this to have any necessary connexion with eternal happiness. . . .

I believe election means, Secondly, a divine appointment of some men to eternal happiness. But I believe this election to be conditional, as well as the reprobation opposite thereto. I believe the eternal decree concerning both is expressed in those words: "He that believeth shall be saved; he that believeth not shall be damned." And this decree, without doubt, God will not change, and man cannot resist. According to this, all true believers are in Scripture termed elect, as all who continue in unbelief are so long properly reprobates, that is, unapproved of God, and without discernment touching the things of the Spirit.

—*John Wesley, 1703–1791*

80 Because covenant involves election, it also involves our understanding of human freedom. The issues are complicated, and often involve close and intense reasoning. William Temple helps us find our way through some of these complicated insights.

And to that very freedom the divine appeal must be addressed. If God exercised compulsion by forcing obedience or by remaking the character of a self against its will, He would have abandoned omnipotence in the act which should assert it, for the will that was overridden would remain outside His control. The only obedience congruous with the nature of either God or man is an obedience willingly, and therefore freely, offered—a response which is given because the self finds it good to offer it. Our question therefore is this: How can the self find it good to submit willingly to removal from its self-centredness and welcome reconstitution about God as centre? There is in fact one power known to men, and only one, which can effect this, not only for one or another function of the self (as beauty and truth can do) but for the self as a whole in its entirety and integrity. When a man acts to please one whom he loves, doing or bearing what apart from that love he would not choose to do or bear, his action is wholly determined by the other's pleasure, yet in no action is he so utterly free—that is, so utterly determined by his apparent good. And when love is not yet present, there is one power and only one that can evoke it; that is the power of love expressed in sacrifice, of love (that is to say) doing and bearing what apart from love would not be willingly borne or done. *The one hope, then, of bringing human selves into right relationship to God is that God should declare His love in an act, or acts, of sheer self-sacrifice, thereby winning the freely offered love of the finite selves which He has created.*

—*William Temple, 1881–1944*

81 As we already know, the covenant account begins with Israel, the people of God. Emil Brunner notes the singular quality of this relationship, and in doing so uses a term with which we became acquainted earlier, *election.*

Israel experienced its election as an historical event: "For thou art an holy People unto the Lord thy God, and the Lord hath chosen thee to be a peculiar people unto Himself, above all peoples that are upon the face of the earth." Through Moses and the Prophets this people became aware that Yahweh was speaking to it in the events of history, as God's incomprehensible, free, unfathomable act, an act which is also a Word. Its election is the same as the peculiar course of History by which God leads this People—and this people alone, among all nations. The Election of Israel, indeed, consists in this historical encounter in which the Holy and Merciful God manifests Himself to it as "the Lord *thy* God", and thus makes Israel His own People, and in so doing singles it out from all other nations upon earth. The fact that this election is based solely upon the free election of God, upon the unfathomable love of Yahweh, and not upon any quality inherent in Israel itself, is brought home to it in the fact that Yahweh can, and may, reject and cast out His chosen People. The basis of election never lies in the one who is chosen, but exclusively in the One who chooses. Election means precisely this: that Israel knows itself to be wholly dependent upon the grace of the One who has chosen her, and that she ought to live in this attitude of continual dependence. The historical character of the fact of election, and the freedom of God in election, are one and the same thing. "The Lord hath taken you, and brought you forth out of the iron furnace, out of Egypt, to be unto Him a people of inheritance. . . . For this historical fact of election is truth which cannot be deduced by arguments: it is God in action, Unique and Unfathomable.

—*Emil Brunner, 1889–1966*

82 This covenant process begun with Israel, in the Hebrew Scriptures, moves on to include the church in the New Testament. Jesus Christ (as our study has indicated) is the key figure in the instituting of the church as God's covenant people. Theologian James H. Cone traces this Israel-Church progression.

The history of Israel is a history of God's election of a special, oppressed people to share in his creative involvement in the world on behalf of man. The call of this people at Sinai into a covenant relationship for a special task may be said to be the beginning of the Church. In the Old Testament, Israel often refers to herself as the *qahal*, the assembly or people of God. Israel is called into being as a people of the covenant in which Yahweh promises to be their God and they his people. Israel's task is to be a partner in

God's revolutionary activity and thus to be an example to the whole world of what God intends for all men. . . .

With him [Jesus] also comes a new people which the New Testament calls the *ekklesia* (church). Like the people of Old Israel, they are called into being by God himself—to be his agent in this world until Christ's second coming. Like Old Israel, they are an oppressed people, created to cooperate in God's liberation of all men. Unlike Old Israel, their membership is not limited by ethnic or political boundaries, but includes all who respond in faith to the redemptive act of God in Christ with a willingness to share in God's creative activity in the world.

—James H. Cone, 1938–

83 The issue of covenant is one of mutual responsibilities. Scripture makes clear that God is always faithful to the divine side of the covenant, but we humans find it more difficult to uphold our part. Marjorie Hewitt Suchocki, theology professor, defines some of the human responsibility, and reminds us that God is always prodding us on to its fulfillment.

How does God create that people [Israel], save through a covenant that reveals the divine nature? Whether the covenant is considered through the dim recesses of the past, recorded as a relationship with Adam, Noah, and Abraham, or through the giving of the law through Moses, or through the call and response represented by the prophets, always the covenant is at once revealing and creating. Through the covenant, God's will toward justice in relationships is revealed; through the people's participation in the covenant, justice in relationships is enacted in society. Faithfully, God lures the people into being a people who will reflect the divine character. Insofar as the people become a society of justice, the image of God is created in human society; insofar as they fall away, the image is distorted. Always the constancy of God is like a goad, pricking the people into relationships which exhibit justice, and therefore fulfill the covenant.

—Marjorie Hewitt Suchocki, 20th century

84 We have seen already that *election* is a difficult word, open to much debate and misunderstanding. Because it is such an important element in the concept of covenant, educator Mary Potter Engel helps us by her explanation of the term, and by facing the problems it raises.

Election is that act of grace by which God chooses a companion with whom to live in an intimate relationship of love and responsibility. This companion is identified in the scriptures variously as humankind, Abraham, the people Israel, David, Jesus Christ, and the community called church. Election has been and remains one of the more disputed doctrines in Christian theology. In the classical and Reformation periods the debate centered on the question, How is God's electing grace related to free will? Augustine, Luther, and Calvin devised a pastoral view of election that emphasized God's grace as free (devoid of consideration of merit) and prevenient (preceding human acts). This was hardened and narrowed by some theologians into a deterministic, metaphysical view of predestination that denied all human freedom. Others (e.g., Aquinas) attempted to reconcile God's electing grace with human freedom. Still others attacked the doctrine as incompatible with human responsibility.

In the modern period two different questions concerning election came to the fore, particularly among Reformed theologians: What is the unit of divine care? and, Does God choose to save all persons or only some? Friedrich Schleiermacher answered the first question by rejecting the classical assumption that God singles out individuals for this special relationship and argued that communities or the totality of the world were the focus of divine care. Karl Barth answered the second question by criticizing the traditional, dualistic view that God chooses some and rejects others and by affirming the election of all persons in Jesus Christ.

—Mary Potter Engel, 20th century

The Message Behind the Symbols

Humankind: Made in God's Image
Human Condition: Sin
Grace ◆ Salvation

Symbols are signs. Before human beings read words, they read signs and symbols. The Christian faith uses symbols as sign language for communicating essential teachings and ideas. Think of symbols as transparent. They fulfill their function when we look right through them to the message of truth behind them.

Symbols arising out of the early stories in Genesis depict a relationship between God and humankind. Humankind, made in God's image but marred by sin, is depicted by a spade, representing the fact that humans must earn their bread by hard work. Thistles are symbolic reminders of the fall of humankind and of the sorrow that accompanies the curse put upon the earth as a result of sin.

A visual representation of a serpent sends several messages: sin, Satan, tempter. And the snake, coiled around the world, dramatically and powerfully symbolizes the sinful nature of humankind and the spread of sin everywhere.

God's ever-present grace and offer of salvation are depicted in the ark, a saving refuge in a time when earth was overwhelmed by flood. Later the ark came to symbolize the church proclaiming the word of grace and salvation.

Humankind: Made in God's Image

We often speak of "the human story." This term is especially appropriate when we look at the biblical account, because so much of what the Bible says about us humans is by way of stories. It is left to theologians to bring structure to that story, and to present in a kind of philosophical diagnosis what the Bible gives us in saga, poem, and exhortation.

85 The first chapter of Genesis declares that we humans are made in God's own image. Such a statement may seem to us to be more poetry than true description. Athanasius, Bishop of Alexandria, expounds on this theme, and links it with the story of human redemption in Christ.

[I]n fact, the good God has given them [human beings] a share in His own Image, that is, in our Lord Jesus Christ, and has made even themselves after the same Image and Likeness. Why? Simply in order that through this gift of God-likeness in themselves they may be able to perceive the Image Absolute, that is the Word Himself, and through Him to apprehend the Father; which knowledge of their Maker is for men the only really happy and blessed life.

But, as we have already seen, men, foolish as they are, thought little of the grace they had received, and turned away from God. . . .

What, then, was God to do? What else could He possibly do, being God, but renew His Image in mankind, so that through it men might once more come to know Him? And how could this be done save by the coming of the very Image Himself, our Saviour Jesus Christ? Men could not have done it, for they are only made after the Image; nor could angels have done it, for they are not the images of God. The Word of God came in His own Person, because it was He alone, the Image of the Father, Who could recreate man made after the Image.

—Athanasius, 296–373

86 The concept of humans being made in God's image has intrigued and challenged theologians in every generation. Ulrich Zwingli examines the possibilities, then draws implications from the conclusions he has reached.

When in the beginning of creation Almighty God purposed to create the wonderful creature man he deliberated with himself as follows: "Let us make man in our image and likeness; let him have dominion over the fish of the sea, the fowl of the air, the cattle and all the earth, and everything that creepeth upon the earth! And God created man in his own image, in the image of God created he him" (Gen. 1). . . . At this point we must enquire with what part of our nature we are made in the divine image, with the body or the soul. Now if we are made in the divine image in respect of the body, then that means that God has a body composed of different members and that our body is a copy of his. But if we grant that, then it follows that God is a being which has been constituted and may finally be dissolved. But this is a negation of the constancy of the divine essence, and it is therefore non-Christian, heretical and blasphemous. . . .

It remains then that it is in respect of the mind or soul that we are made in the image of God. The exact form of that likeness it is not for us to know except that the soul is the substance upon which that likeness is particularly stamped. The opinion of Augustine . . . and the early doctors is that the three faculties of intellect, will and memory, which are distinct and yet constitute the one soul, are a similitude of the one God in respect of the existence and the trinity of the Persons. This I do not dispute, so long as we are not led astray by the three faculties and imagine that in God as in us there is a conflict of will. . . .

. . . I do not reject the opinion of Augustine, but I think that there are many things which give us an awareness of the divine likeness apart from those which Augustine singled out as the chief. There is in particular that looking to God and to the words of God which is a sure sign of the divine relationship, image and similitude within us. . . .

We are taught then that the desire for salvation is present within us by nature, not the nature of the flesh and its lusts, but the likeness which God the masterworkman has impressed upon us.

—Ulrich Zwingli, 1484–1531

87 What exactly do we mean by the phrase, "in God's image"? Except for a New Testament reference (Ephesians 4:24), we are left to imagine what might be included in this term. Martin Luther uses his imagination reverently but freely as he explains what the biblical writer had in mind.

Wherefore that image of God in which Adam was created was a workmanship the most beautiful, the most excellent, and the most noble, while as yet no leprosy of sin adhered either to his reason or to his will. Then all his senses, both internal and external, were the most perfect and the most pure. His intellect was most clear, his memory most complete, and his will the most sincere, and accompanied with the most charming security, without any fear of death and without any care or anxiety whatsoever. To these internal perfections of Adam was added a power of body, and of all his limbs, so beautiful and so excellent, that therein he surpassed all other animate natural creatures. For I fully believe that, before his sin, the eyes of Adam were so clear and their sight so acute, that his powers of vision exceeded those of the lynx. Adam, I believe, being stronger than they, handled lions and bears, whose strength is so great, as we handle the young of any animal. I believe also that to Adam the sweetness and the virtue of the fruits which he ate were far beyond our enjoyment of them now.

—Martin Luther, 1483–1546

88 What does being in God's image have to do with our moral nature, or our ability to govern the earth? And what is the relationship of this image to the Genesis statement that God was pleased with the creation? John Wesley gives further insights on these questions.

The foundation of it lies near as deep as the creation of the world, in the scriptural account whereof we read, 'And God,' the three-one God, 'said, Let us make man in our image, after our likeness. So God created man in his own image, in the image of God created he him.' [Gen. 1:26-27] Not barely in his *natural image*, a picture of his own immortality, a spiritual being endued with understanding, freedom of will, and various affections; nor merely in his *political image*, the governor of this lower world, having 'dominion over the fishes of the sea, and over the fowl of the air, and over the cattle, and over all the earth'; but chiefly in his *moral image*, which, according to the Apostle, is 'righteousness and true holiness'. [Eph. 4:24] In this image of God was man made. 'God is love:' accordingly man at his creation was full of love, which was the sole principle of all his tempers, thoughts, words, and actions. God is full of justice, mercy, and truth: so was man as he came from the hands of his Creator. God is spotless purity: and so man was in the beginning pure from every sinful blot. Otherwise God could not have pronounced *him* as well as all the other works of his hands, 'very good'. [Gen. 1:31] This he could not have been had he not been pure from sin, and filled with righteousness and true holiness. For there is no medium. If we suppose an intelligent creature not to love God, not to be righteous and holy, we necessarily suppose him not to be good at all; much less to be 'very good'.

—John Wesley, 1703–1791

89 The Creation account in Genesis 1 says that God made the human race "male and female." The language of the following document—probably by Sarah Fell—maintains the emphasis upon both men and women being part of the original creation. Fell, a Quaker, dates from the latter part of the seventeenth century.

So here is the blessed Image of the living God, restored againe, in which he made them male and female in the beginning: and in this his own Image God blessed them both, and said unto them increase and multiply, and replenish the earth, and subdue it, and have dominion over the fish of the sea, and have dominion over the fowles of the heavens, and have dominion over the beasts, and over the cattel, and over the earth, and over every creeping thing on the face of the earth. And in this dominion and power, the Lord God is establishing his own seed, in the male and female, over the head of the serpent, and over his seed, and power. And he makes no difference in the seed, between the male and the female, as Christ saith, that he which made them in the beginning made them male and female, &c. they were both in the work of God in the beginning, and so in the restoration, but if the work of the old serpent, put them out of the work of god, and as he did the beginning tempt them to sinne and transgression, and disobedience, so he would still keep them there, and make a difference, and keep a superiority one over another, that Christ the head should not rule in male and female: and so keep them in bondage, and slavery, and in difference and dissention one with another, and then they are fit for his temptations.

—Quaker woman, 17th century

90 Emil Brunner observes that the New Testament has little extra to say about the Genesis definition of our being made in the divine image. But this *imago dei* calls for a quality of response from the human creature.

The New Testament simply presupposes this fact that man—in his very nature—has been "made in the image of God"; it does not develop this any further. To the Apostles what matters most is the "material" realization of this God-given quality; that is, that man should really give *the* answer which the Creator intends, the response in which God is honoured, and in which He fully imparts Himself, the response of reverent, grateful love, given not only in words, but in his whole life. The New Testament, in *its* doctrine of the *Imago Dei*, tells us that this right answer has not been given; that a quite different one has been given instead, in which the glory is not given to God, but to men and to creatures, in which man does not live in the love of God, but seeks himself. Secondly, the New Testament is the proclamation of what God has done in order that He may turn this false answer into the true one.

. . . The restoration of the *Imago Dei*, the new creation of the original image of God in man, is identical with the gift of God in Jesus Christ received by faith.

—Emil Brunner, 1889–1966

91 Part of the uniqueness of humans is suggested in the idea of our being created in the divine image. No other created being has this distinction. Karl Barth investigates something of this significance.

"He created them male and female." This is the interpretation immediately given to the sentence "God created man." As in this sense man is the first and only one to be created in genuine confrontation with God and as a genuine counterpart to his fellows, it is he first and alone who is created "in the image" and "after the likeness" of God. ... It [God-likeness] is not a quality of man. Hence there is no point in asking in which of man's peculiar attributes and attitudes it consists. It does not consist in anything that man is or does. It consists as man himself consists as the creature of God. He would not be man if he were not the image of God. ... But the divine form of life, repeated in the man created by Him, consists in that which is the obvious aim of the "Let us." In God's own being and sphere there is a counterpart: a genuine but harmonious self-encounter and self-discovery; a free co-existence and co-operation; an open confrontation and reciprocity. Man is the repetition of this divine form of life; its copy and reflection. He is this first in the fact that he is the counterpart of God, the encounter and discovery in God Himself being copied and imitated in God's relation to man. But he is it also in the fact that he is himself the counterpart of his fellows and has in them a counterpart, the co-existence and co-operation in God Himself being repeated in the relation of man to man.

—*Karl Barth, 1886–1968*

92 Our quality, in being made in the divine image, includes a great variety of possibilities. It is clear that the biblical writer meant other than a physical resemblance; indeed, such an idea would have been repugnant to the Genesis writer. Georgia Harkness explores some of the potential that is suggested in this great phrase.

Made in God's own spiritual image, made male and female, man is God's supreme creation. There is a telling answer to every social system that impugns the dignity of man or that belittles the importance of women in the words, "So God created man in his own image, in the image of God he created him; male and female he created them." (Gen. 1:27).

The *imago dei* means that man is created with qualities of mind and spirit that make him truly a person, not a biological organism only or subhuman animal. As God is personal, so is man a person in terms of his capacity for making moral choices, his rational intelligence, his concern for love and goodness, truth and beauty, though always with the limitation that man's personality is derivative and incomplete while only God's is infinite and perfect. The most distinctive attribute of man is his free spirit, whereby he may either sin or seek after God in obedient love, and in this he reflects the image of the eternal.

Creation in the image of God means that *all* men, and not some fortunate few or some unusually righteous few, are precious to God. It is the final answer to race prejudice, class distinctions, national cleavages, and every other form of man-made separation.

—*Georgia Harkness, 1891–1974*

93 The significance of the *imago dei* idea extends naturally into issues of human rights and innate human dignity. Martin Luther King, Jr., notes the specific relationship to the issue of race.

There must be a recognition of the sacredness of human personality. Deeply rooted in our political and religious heritage is the conviction that every man is an heir to a legacy of dignity and worth. Our Hebraic-Christian tradition refers to this inherent dignity of man in the Biblical term *the image of God*. This innate worth referred to in the phrase the image of God is universally shared in equal portions by all men. There is no graded scale of essential worth; there is no divine right of one race which differs from the divine right of another. Every human being has etched in his personality the indelible stamp of the Creator.

—*Martin Luther King, Jr, 1929–1968*

94 Those who are made in God's image must then ponder the divine expectations for creatures such as they. This is the point of theologian Anthony A. Hoekema's exploration.

The image of God . . . describes not just something that man *has*, but something man *is*. It means that human beings both mirror and represent God. Thus, there is a sense in which the image includes the physical body. The image of God, we found further, includes both a structural and a functional aspect (sometimes called the broader and narrower image), though we must remember that in the biblical view structure is secondary, while function is primary. The image must be seen in man's threefold relationship: toward God, toward others, and toward nature. When originally created, humans imaged God sinlessly in all three relationships. After the Fall the image of God was not annihilated but perverted, so that human beings now function wrongly in each of the three relationships. In the process of redemption, however, the image is being renewed, so that man is now enabled to be properly directed toward God, others, and nature. The renewal of the image of God is seen in its richest form in the church. The image is therefore not static but dynamic—a constant challenge to God-glorifying living. In the life to come the image of God will be perfected; glorified human beings will then live perfectly in all three relationships. After the resurrection, redeemed man will be in a higher state than man before the Fall, since he will then no longer be able either to sin or to die.

—*Anthony A. Hoekema, 1913–*

95 There is always a danger that grand ideas such as the *imago dei* (Genesis 1) and being God-breathed (Genesis 2) will leave us with little practical understanding of ourselves as very earthly creatures. Christopher Morse, professor of theology, prods us with this issue, especially as our humanness involves relationships.

When we ask how humankind is to be understood in Christian faith, we are not asking about something other than ourselves, but about our own proper identification and true destiny. . . . The underlying question behind all the church's teachings regarding our human being is, "How are we most truly revealed as being who we really are?"

We know from a psychological standpoint that there is a profound sense in which who we are is only revealed in our relationships with others. When we enter into a relationship with someone we become who we could not be otherwise and learn things about ourselves that we did not know before. Not uncommonly we are surprised to realize how we tend to interact with others. In being children, and having children, in being loved, and loving another, in being rejected and misunderstood, as well as in being accepted and welcomed, we develop self-awareness and self-understanding, and the promise of our own life becomes a story.

—*Christopher Morse, 1935–*

Human Condition: Sin

Someone has said that if it were not for sin, the news-papers and newscasts would go out of business. Certainly a good deal of what makes up each day's headlines is either the act of sin or its results. But sin is far too complicated a subject to leave to headline writers or to news analysts. In these readings, we see how theologians over the centuries have tried to get beyond a superficial understanding of this profound human issue.

96 To what degree has our whole human race been affected by the act of sin described in Genesis 3? Saint Augustine examined this subject at length, and concluded that the connection was fatal. Needless to say, centuries of theologians have seen this issue from a variety of positions.

Through Adam's sin his whole posterity were corrupted, and were born under the penalty of death, which he had incurred.

Thence, after his sin, he was driven into exile, and by his sin the whole race of which he was the root was corrupted in him, and thereby subjected to the penalty of death. And so it happens that all descended from him, and from the woman who had led him into sin, and was condemned at the same time with him,—being the offspring of carnal lust on which the same punishment of disobedience was visited,—were tainted with the original sin, and were by it drawn through divers errors and sufferings into that last and endless punishment which they suffer in common with the fallen angels, their corrupters and masters, and the partakers of their doom. And thus "by one man sin entered into the world, and death by sin; and so death passed upon all men, for that all have sinned."

By "the world" the apostle, of course, means in this place the whole human race.

—Augustine, 354–430

97 As our study manual says, part of the subtle power of sin lies in the fact that it springs from legitimate desires that are then drawn beyond legitimate bonds. One of our defenses against sin, says Julian of Norwich, is our love of God.

Then we hope that God has forgiven us our sins. And so he has! It is then that our Lord in his courtesy shows himself to the soul, gaily and with cheerful countenance, giving it a friendly welcome as though it had been suffering in prison. 'My beloved,' he says, 'I am glad that you have come to me. In all your trouble I have been with you. Now you can see how I love you. We are made one in blessedness.' So sins are forgiven through merciful grace, and our soul is honourably and joyfully received (just as it will be when it gets to heaven!) whenever it experiences the gracious work of the Holy Spirit, and the virtue of Christ's passion. . . .

But if, because of all this spiritual comfort we have been talking of, one were foolish enough to say, 'If this is true, it is a good thing to sin because the reward will be greater', or to hold sin to be less sinful, then beware! Should such a thought come it would be untrue, and would stem from the enemy of the very love that tells of all this comfort. The same blessed love teaches us that we should hate sin for Love's sake alone. I am quite clear about this: the more a soul sees this in the courtesy and love of our Lord God, the more he hates to sin, and the greater is his sense of shame. For if there could be set before us all the pains of hell, purgatory, earth, death, and so on, on the one hand, and sin on the other, we should choose to have all that pain rather than to sin. For sin is so vile and utterly hateful that no pain can compare with it which is not sin. I was shown no harder hell than sin. The soul by its very nature can have no hell but sin.

—Julian of Norwich, 1342–after 1416

98 The language of Scripture makes no exception in its discussions of sin. It sees sin as a malady affecting the whole human race, and with equal deadliness. John Calvin insists on the logic of this scriptural approach but sees therein the need and the possibility of divine mercy.

The Apostle, when he would humble man's pride, uses these words: "There is none righteous, no, not one: there is none that understandeth, there is none that seeketh after God. They are all gone out of the way, they are together become unprofitable; there is none that doeth good, no, not one. Their throat is an open sepulchre; with their tongues they have used deceit; the poison of asps is under their lips: Whose mouth is full of cursing and bitterness: their feet are swift to shed blood: destruction and misery are in their ways: and the way of peace have they not known: there is no fear of God before their eyes" (Rom. iii.10–18). Thus he thunders not against certain individuals, but against the whole posterity of Adam—not against the depraved manners of any single age, but the perpetual corruption of nature. His object in the passage is not merely to upbraid men in order that they may repent, but to teach that all are overwhelmed with inevitable calamity, and can be delivered from it only by the mercy of God. As this could not be proved without previously proving the overthrow and destruction of nature, he produced those passages to show that its ruin is complete.

—John Calvin, 1509–1564

99 Sin, like so many other profound matters, is often understood best if explained in picture language. The Bible does this admirably, in the Genesis story, and in Paul's description in Romans 7 of his struggle with the "dead body" of sin. Saint Teresa of Avila, Carmelite nun and mystic, reflects her own passionate faith as she describes the distastefulness of sin.

I know of a person to whom Our Lord wished to show what a soul was like when it committed mortal sin. That person says that, if people could understand this, she thinks they would find it impossible to sin at all, and, rather than meet occasions of sin, would put themselves to the greatest trouble imaginable. . . . For, just as all the streamlets that flow from a clear spring are as clear as the spring itself, so the works of a soul in grace are pleasing in the eyes both of God and of men, since they proceed from this spring of life, in which the soul is as a tree planted. It would give no shade and yield no fruit if it proceeded not thence, for the spring sustains it and prevents it from drying up and causes it to produce good fruit. When the soul, on the other hand, through its own fault, leaves this spring and becomes rooted in a pool of pitch-black, evil-smelling water, it produces nothing but misery and filth.

It should be noted here that it is not the spring, or the brilliant sun which is in the centre of the soul, that loses its splendour and beauty, for they are always within it and nothing can take away their beauty. If a thick black cloth be placed over a crystal in the sunshine, however, it is clear that, although the sun may be shining upon it, its brightness will have no effect upon the crystal.

—Teresa of Avila, 1515–1582

100 We have seen that the blood sacrifice theme is closely tied to the issue of sin, and that in turn, the Christian celebration of Holy Communion is related to the matter of the blood sacrifice. The ritual of Holy Communion not only recognizes the seriousness of sin but defines our experience of sin in the categories of "thought, word, and deed."

Almighty God, Father of our Lord Jesus Christ,
    maker of all things, judge of all people:
We acknowledge and bewail our manifold sins and wickedness,
    which we from time to time most grievously have committed,
    by thought, word, and deed, against thy divine majesty.
We do earnestly repent,
    and are heartily sorry for these our misdoings;
    the remembrance of them is grievous unto us.
Have mercy upon us, have mercy upon us, most merciful Father.
For thy Son our Lord Jesus Christ's sake,
    forgive us all that is past;
and grant that we may ever hereafter
    serve and please thee in newness of life,
    to the honor and glory of thy name;
through Jesus Christ our Lord. Amen.

—Prayer of Confession, The United Methodist Hymnal

101 Paul's writings remind us that even the most devout must constantly be on guard against sin. John Wesley puts that fact in the most emphatic and the most practical terms.

Is it sin which occasions darkness? What sin? Is it outward sin of any kind? Does your conscience accuse you of committing any sin, whereby you grieve the Holy Spirit of God? Is it on this account that He is departed from you, and that joy and peace are departed with Him? And how can you expect they should return, till you put away the accursed thing? "Let the wicked forsake his way"; "cleanse your hands, ye sinner"; "put away the evil of your doings"; so shall your "light break out of obscurity"; the Lord will return and "abundantly pardon."

If, upon the closest search, you can find no sin of commission which causes the cloud upon your soul, inquire next, if there be not some sin of omission which separates between God and you. . . .

But perhaps you are not conscious of even any sin of omission which impairs your peace and joy in the Holy Ghost. Is there not, then, some inward sin, which, as a root of bitterness, springs up in your heart to trouble you? Is not your dryness, and barrenness of soul occasioned by your heart's "departing from the living God"? . . . It is vain to hope for a recovery of His light, till you pluck out the right eye, and cast it from you. O let there be no longer delay!

—John Wesley, 1703–1791

102 Reinhold Niebuhr leads us still further into the meaning of the human rebellion against God. After all, we humans rarely declare ourselves to be rebellious, or even think ourselves to be. Perhaps this is part of the subtlety of sin that we find in the story in Genesis 3.

Man is insecure and involved in natural contingency; he seeks to overcome his insecurity by a will-to-power which overreaches the limits of human creatureliness. Man is ignorant and involved in the limitations of a finite mind; but he pretends that he is not limited. He assumes that he can gradually transcend finite limitations until his mind becomes identical with universal mind. All of his intellectual and cultural pursuits, therefore, become infected with the sin of pride. Man's pride and will-to-power disturb the harmony of creation. The Bible defines sin in both religious and moral terms. The religious dimension of sin is man's rebellion against God, his effort to usurp the place of God. The moral and social dimension of sin is injustice. The ego which falsely makes itself the centre of existence in its pride and will-to-power inevitably subordinates other life to its will and thus does injustice to other life.

Sometimes man seeks to solve the problem of the contradiction of finiteness and freedom, not by seeking to hide his finiteness and comprehending the world into himself, but by seeking to hide his

freedom and by losing himself in some aspect of the world's vital-
ities. In that case his sin may be defined as sensuality rather than
pride.

—*Reinhold Niebuhr, 1892–1971*

103 Our study examines the subject of sin through a number of biblical
examples. Georgia Harkness defines sin in a more philosophical way, but
noting—as does our study—that God is the issue in sin, specifically in our
response to God.

Sin. There is perhaps no word in our language which is used more
ambiguously, in spite of its apparent simplicity. . . .

Sin to the understanding Christian means rebellion against God
and disobedience to His holy will. Sin ought never to be defined
moralistically, simply as deviation from accepted human standards. . . . Yet it must persistently be made clear that the rejection
of moralism means no repudiation of Christian morality. There is
no true possibility of defining sin in relation to God by disregard
of relations with one's fellow men, for God is intimately concerned with these same fellow men and obedience to Him requires
of us Christian *agape* (self-giving love) toward them. . . .

Sin, then, is a relationship to God focused in self-centeredness,
which shows itself in unloving attitudes and acts toward our fellow men. . . . It is when we seek our own wills instead of God's will
and regulate our lives by such self-seeking that sin corrupts our
nature. This we all do. Thus, all men are sinners. Paul's insight,
verified constantly throughout the Bible and empirically evident,
is a true one, "none is righteous, no, not one." (Rom. 3:9).

Sin is rebellion against God, disobedience to the will of God. . . .

Sin, therefore, is "original" in the sense of a persistent human
tendency, and the Fall of man happened not once but is a perpetual falling away from the life of loving obedience which God
requires of us.

—*Georgia Harkness, 1891–1974*

104 The Genesis story describes the deceptive way sin gains control of
our lives, and Paul describes the intensity of that control in his letter to the
Romans. Paul Tillich, a twentieth-century philosopher and theologian,
puts this experience into sophisticated theological language.

Sin is our act of turning away from participation in the divine Ground from which we come and to which we go. Sin is the turning towards ourselves, and making ourselves the center of our world and of ourselves. Sin is the drive in everyone, even those who exercise the most self-restraint, to draw as much as possible of the world into oneself. But we can be fully aware of this only if we have found a certain level of life above ourselves. Whoever has found himself after he has lost himself knows how deep his loss of self was. If we look at our estrangement from the point of reunion, we are no longer in danger of brooding over our estrangement. We can speak of Sin, because its power over us is broken.

. . . Sin uses the commandments in order to become alive. Prohibition awakens sleeping desire. It arouses the power and consciousness of sin, but cannot break its power. Only if we accept with our whole being the message that it *is* broken, is it also broken in us.

—Paul Tillich, 1886–1965

105 We humans constantly ask about the origins of evil and of sin, and it sometimes seems that the Bible's answer is enigmatic; but in any event, sin is inevitably linked to our freedom; and particularly, to our misuse of freedom. Kallistos Ware, a contemporary Orthodox spiritual writer, enlarges upon the biblical answer.

In man's possession and exercise of free will we find, by no means a complete explanation, but at least the beginnings of an answer to our problem. Why has God allowed the angels and man to sin? Why does God permit evil and suffering? We answer: Because he is a God of love. Love implies sharing, and love also implies freedom. As a Trinity of love, God desired to share his life with created persons made in his image, who would be capable of responding to him freely and willingly in a relationship of love. *Where there is no freedom, there can be no love.* Compulsion excludes love; as Paul Evdokimov used to say, God can do everything except compel us to love him. God, therefore—desiring to share his love—created, not robots who would obey him mechanically, but angels and human beings endowed with free choice. And thereby, to put the matter in an anthropomorphic way, God took a risk: for with this gift of freedom there was given also the possibility of sin. But he who takes no risks does not love.

Without freedom there would be no sin. But without freedom man would not be in God's image; without freedom man would not be capable of entering into communion with God in a relationship of love.

—*Kallistos Ware, 1934–*

106 Our contemporary culture downplays the significance of sin, with responses that range from redefinition to amusement. Daniel Migliore brings us back to the basic issue of sin, namely, that it disrupts our relationship with God. The more seriously we take God, the more clearly we understand sin.

If being human in the image of God means life in free response to God who freely and graciously addresses us, then sin can be described as the denial of our relatedness to God and our need for God's grace. From this vantage point, sin is fundamentally opposition to grace, saying No to the invitation to be human in grateful service to God and in friendship with our fellow creatures. Sin is the great refusal to live thankfully and gladly by the grace of God that makes personal life in community with diverse others possible.

Thus we misunderstand the depth of sin if we see it only as a violation of a moral code; it is, instead, primarily the disruption of our relationship with God. As the Psalmist writes, "against you, you alone, have I sinned" (Ps. 51:4). This disruption of our relationship with God that is the essence of sin appears in vastly different forms. . . . Sin may take the form of rejecting God's grace and absolutizing ourselves. Declaring our freedom to be infinite, we proclaim ourselves God. This is the sin of the prideful, titanic, egocentric self. Often referred to simply as the sin of pride, it is an active and self-centered idolatry. It is the refusal to recognize the limits of the self and the need that the self has of others. Finitude and limitation are not evil in themselves, but they are often the occasion of anxiety and insecurity. Instead of living by a grace whose source is beyond ourselves, in our insecurity we seek to be our own God.

—*Daniel Migliore, 1935–*

Grace

As we read the Scripture selections, we see that grace is often defined in events and experiences rather than simply in orderly explanations. We note the same characteristic in many of our readings from centuries of theologians; and if we know their stories in some detail, the biographical sense is all the more prominent.

107 Not only do we find it difficult to accept the gift of grace; we are inclined at times to explain it away by pointing to our own sense of merit. Few people would be better equipped to deal with this human anomaly than Saint Augustine.

First I shall try to grasp the apostle's purpose which runs through the whole Epistle, and I shall seek guidance from it. It is that no man should glory in meritorious works, in which the Israelites dared to glory, alleging that they had served the law that had been given to them, and that for that reason they had received evangelical grace as due to their merits. So they were unwilling that the same grace should be given to the Gentiles, as if they were unworthy of it unless they undertook to observe the Jewish sacred rites. This problem arose and is settled in the Acts of the Apostles. The Jews did not understand that evangelical grace, just because of its very nature, is not given as a due reward for good works. Otherwise grace is not grace. In many passages the apostle frequently bears witness to this, putting the grace of faith before works; not indeed that he wants to put an end to good works, but to show that works do not precede grace but follow from it. No man is to think that he has received grace because he has done good works. Rather he could not have done good works unless he had received grace through faith. A man begins to receive grace from the moment when he begins to believe in God, being moved to faith by some internal or external admonition.

—Augustine, 354–430

108 While grace is an unmerited gift from God, it is received by us humans, and our level of reception varies greatly—not only from person to person, but from time to time in each person. Generations ago, Pseudo-Macarius, author of spiritual homilies, dealt with this problem in one of his *Homilies.*

Grace, indeed, is unceasingly present and is rooted in us and mingled with our nature from our earliest years. It is as something natural and real which adheres to a person as though it formed one substance. Still, it operates in a person in various ways, depending on one's cooperation as far as this is given.

At times the fire flares out and burns with more vehement flames. At other times it burns more gently and slowly. The light that it gives off flames up at times and shines more brightly. At other times it goes down and barely gives off any light. So it is also with the lamp of grace. It is always burning and giving off light, but when it is especially trimmed, it burns more brilliantly as though intoxicated by the love of God. But again, by a certain dispensation of God, the light is still there but it barely shines.

—Pseudo-Macarius, 4th–5th centuries

109 We can't really understand grace, or apprehend it for ourselves, except as we acknowledge our need—and that acknowledging depends on our recognizing that we are sinners. This is the emphasis Martin Luther gives in the following reading.

Now the true meaning of Christianity is this: that a man first acknowledge, through the Law, that he is a sinner, for whom it is impossible to perform any good work. For the Law says: "You are an evil tree. Therefore everything you think, speak, or do is opposed to God. Hence you cannot deserve grace by your works. But if you try to do so, you make the bad even worse; for since you are an evil tree, you cannot produce anything except evil fruits, that is, sins. 'For whatever does not proceed from faith is sin' (Rom. 14:23)." Trying to merit grace by preceding works, therefore, is trying to placate God with sins, which is nothing but heaping sins upon sins, making fun of God, and provoking His wrath. When a man is taught this way by the Law, he is frightened and humbled. Then he really sees the greatness of his sin and finds in himself not one spark of the love of God; thus he justifies God in His Word and confesses that he deserves death and eternal damnation. Thus the first step in Christianity is the preaching of repentance and the knowledge of oneself.

The second step is this: If you want to be saved, your salvation does not come by works; but God has sent His only Son into the world that we might live through Him. He was crucified and died for you and bore your sins in His own body (1 Peter 2:24).

—Martin Luther, 1483–1546

110 One of the most important concepts of grace is that manifestation theologians call "prevenient grace"—the grace of God that pursues us so that we are ready to accept grace when at last we see it. John Wesley compares this to what some people call "natural conscience."

Yet this is no excuse for those who continue in sin, and lay the blame upon their Maker by saying: 'It is God only that must quicken us; for we cannot quicken our own souls.' For allowing that all the souls of men are dead in sin by *nature*, this excuses none, seeing there is no man that is in a state of mere nature; there is no man, unless he has quenched the Spirit, that is wholly void of the grace of God. No man living is entirely destitute of what is vulgarly called 'natural conscience'. But this is not natural; it is more properly termed 'preventing grace'. Every man has a greater or less measure of this, which waiteth not for the call of man. Everyone has sooner or later good desires, although the generality of men stifle them before they can strike deep root or produce any considerable fruit. Everyone has some measure of that light, some faint glimmering ray, which sooner or later, more or less, enlightens every man that cometh into the world. And everyone, unless he be one of the small number whose conscience is seared as with a hot iron, feels more or less uneasy when he acts contrary to the light of his own conscience. So that no man sins because he has not grace, but because he does not use the grace which he hath.

Therefore inasmuch as God works in you, you are now able to work out your own salvation. Since he worketh in you of his own good pleasure, without any merit of yours, both to will and to do, it is possible for you to fulfil all righteousness.

—John Wesley, 1703–1791

111 As we have mentioned earlier, references to the doctrine of grace often include some type of personal testimony, because grace is not simply perceived intellectually; it is also experienced. John Wesley records in his own *Journal* some elements of his pilgrimage.

And now first it was that I had that full assurance of my own reconciliation to God through Christ. For many years I had had the forgiveness of my sins, and a measure of the peace of God; but I had not till now that witness of his Spirit, which shuts out all doubt and fear. In all my trials I had always a confidence in Christ, who had done so great things for me. But it was a confidence mixed with fear: I was afraid *I had not done enough.* There was always something dark in my soul till now. But now the clear light shined; and I saw that what I had hitherto so constantly insisted on, the *doing* so much and *feeling* so much, the long repentance and preparation for believing, the bitter sorrow for sin, and that deep contrition of heart which is found in some, were by no means essential to justification. Yea, that wherever the free grace of God is rightly preached, a sinner in the full career of his sins will probably receive it, and be justified by it, before one who insists on such previous preparation.

—John Wesley, 1703–1791

112 In the providence of God, different theologians have emphasized different themes. Sometimes these themes became the impetus for mass renewals of faith. In the eighteenth century, John Wesley shed new light on grace in general, and on prevenient grace in particular.

The grace or love of God, whence cometh our salvation, is FREE IN ALL, and FREE FOR ALL.

It is free IN ALL to whom it is given. It does not depend on any power or merit in man; no, not in any degree, neither in whole, nor in part. It does not in anywise depend either on the good works or righteousness of the receiver; not on anything he has done, or anything he is. It does not depend on his endeavours. It does not depend on his good tempers, or good desires, or good purposes and intentions; for all these flow from the free grace of God; they are the streams only, not the fountain. They are the fruits of free grace, and not the root. They are not the cause, but the effects of it. Whatsoever good is in man, or is done by man, God is the author and doer of it. Thus is his grace free in all; that is, no way depending on any power or merit in man, but on God alone, who freely gave us his own Son, and "with him freely giveth us all things."

—John Wesley, 1703–1791

113 The apostle Paul declared that all have sinned. The eighteenth-century Anglican poet-cleric, Augustus M. Toplady, carefully calculated how many sins a person was likely to commit in a lifetime of eighty years, and came up with a number in excess of two and one-half million. It is out of such a sense of need that his familiar poem declares its confidence in the grace of God.

> Rock of Ages, cleft for me,
> let me hide myself in thee;
> let the water and the blood,
> from thy wounded side which flowed,
> be of sin the double cure;
> save from wrath and make me pure.
>
> Not the labors of my hands
> can fulfill thy law's demands;
> could my zeal no respite know,
> could my tears forever flow,
> all for sin could not atone;
> thou must save, and thou alone.
>
> Nothing in my hand I bring,
> simply to the cross I cling;
> naked, come to thee for dress;
> helpless, look to thee for grace;
> foul, I to the fountain fly;
> wash me, Savior, or I die.

—Augustus M. Toplady, 1740–1778

114 Every doctrine has its hazards as that doctrine is lived out in our daily lives. One of the dangers of grace is that we will take it for granted, or exploit it. Dietrich Bonhoeffer, a German theologian and one of the twentieth century's most notable martyrs, warned of the danger of what he called "cheap grace."

Cheap grace is the preaching of forgiveness without requiring repentance, baptism without church discipline, Communion without confession, absolution without personal confession. Cheap grace is grace without discipleship, grace without the cross, grace without Jesus Christ, living and incarnate.

Costly grace is the treasure hidden in the field; for the sake of it a man will gladly go and sell all that he has. It is the pearl of great price to buy which the merchant will sell all his goods. It is the kingly rule of Christ, for whose sake a man will pluck out the eye which causes him to stumble, it is the call of Jesus Christ at which the disciple leaves his nets and follows him.

Costly grace is the gospel which must be *sought* again and again, the gift which must be *asked* for, the door at which a man must *knock*.

Such grace is *costly* because it calls us to follow, and it is *grace* because it calls us to follow *Jesus Christ*. It is costly because it costs a man his life, and it is grace because it gives a man the only true life.

—*Dietrich Bonhoeffer, 1906–1945*

115 Grace is sometimes forced to deal with our doubts. Paul suggests as much in his letter to the Romans when he describes his sense of wretchedness that he isn't all he knows he should be. A twentieth-century theologian, Paul Tillich, makes the same point, apparently in reflecting upon his own experience.

We cannot transform our lives, unless we allow them to be transformed by that stroke of grace. ... Grace strikes us when we are in great pain and restlessness. It strikes us when we walk through the dark valley of a meaningless and empty life. It strikes us when we feel that our separation is deeper than usual, because we have violated another life, a life which we loved, or from which we were estranged. It strikes us when our disgust for our own being, our indifference, our weakness, our hostility, and our lack of direction and composure have become intolerable to us. It strikes us when, year after year, the longed-for perfection of life does not appear, when the old compulsions reign within us as they have for decades, when despair destroys all joy and courage. Sometimes at that moment a wave of light breaks into our darkness, and it is as though a voice were saying: "You are accepted. *You are accepted, accepted by that which is greater than you, and the name of which you do not know. Do not ask for the name now; perhaps you will find it later. Do not try to do anything now; perhaps later you will do much. Do not seek for anything; do not perform anything; do not intend anything. Simply accept the fact that you are accepted!"* If that happens to us, we experience grace. After such an experience we may not be better than before, and we may not believe more than before. But everything is transformed. In that moment, grace conquers sin, and reconciliation bridges the gulf of estrangement. And nothing is demanded of this experience, no religious or moral or intellectual presupposition, nothing but *acceptance*.

—Paul Tillich, 1886–1965

116 Our biblical readings come from both Testaments. As noted, the word *grace* does not necessarily appear in many of the Old Testament readings, but the concept is clearly there. Emil Brunner takes us faithfully through a series of New Testament references in order to give us a solid foundation for understanding this theme of grace.

Grace, like almost all the important words of the New Testament, is a personal term, more exactly a word denoting a personal relationship. Grace is God's condescending to man (Tit. 2:11), who is not worthy of it but stands in need of it (Rom. 4:25; 2 Cor. 8:9). Grace is the love of God, with the additional meaning that it is immotivated giving and unmerited love (Rom. 3:24, 9:12; Eph. 2:5ff.), love "without any cause", "simply because God wills it so" (Rom. 9:15). Grace therefore stands in the sharpest contrast to "merit" (Rom. 11:6) and to everything achieved and gained by oneself (Gal. 2:21; Eph. 2:8). Grace always denotes that which comes from God. It is thus in Paul's message actually almost identical with Jesus Christ (Rom. 5:2, 15). He is the great gift; indeed, rightly understood, he is the great giving of God (Rom. 5:15ff.). For Jesus Christ is truly a person, yet he is above all God's gift (Eph. 1:5ff.). Jesus Christ is God's bestowing hand, God's acquitting word, God's saving arm; in Jesus Christ God's eye beholds us mercifully and graciously. He is the Grace of God in person.

The thought underlying grace is always that of judicial verdict.

Grace is pardon, acquittal from that punishment which we deserved by right and which would be to our eternal ruin (Rom. 3:24f.). Grace therefore is also exemption from merited condemnation (Rom. 5:16). Yet Paul is careful never to leave it in this merely negative form. Grace is never merely the setting aside of condemnation but the royal bestowal of gifts at the banquet; the granting of the highest good, eternal life (Rom. 5:21). Of course, grace, like faith, leads only to the threshold of this last thing of all, the divine glory (2 Cor. 5:7; 12:9).

—Emil Brunner, 1889–1966

117 As our readings and Scripture lessons have indicated, grace is a much broader and more complex subject than we indicate when we sing of "Amazing Grace." Albert Outler describes some of the breadth of this subject.

Christians from the Methodist tradition ought to know how massively John Wesley's whole theology swung round the axial theme of grace as the reign of Christ here on earth by the power of the Holy Spirit. His view of the *ordo salutis* (the *order* of salvation) is governed, in its entirety, by a complex understanding of the levels and stages of grace. 'Prevenient' or 'preventing grace' is the Holy Spirit's initiative in human consciences and spiritual aspirations. It would take a book (yet to be written) to expound the full range of these stages and types of grace: 'accompanying', 'convincing', 'following', 'cooperating', 'justifying', 'regeneration', 'sanctifying', 'glorifying'. All of these, and each in its own way, signify God's unstinted benevolence, his spontaneous love and mercy. In each case, grace is a *gift of God,* unmerited in the most literal sense. And yet grace as 'given' is also a moral influence in the human heart, enlarging its freedom and making its dispositions grace-full. Thus, Wesley spoke of grace as quietly persuasive ('whispers of grace') and of grace as a stable quality ('the state of grace'). Grace is a healing power that reinvigorates the human will, deadened and contorted by sin; it rehabilitates the *iustitia originalis* (original righteousness) with which we were created. Grace is the fruit of the Spirit's influence in the believer's heart, maturing it toward its original design: 'inward holiness' (the love of God above all else) and 'outward holiness' (love of neighbour in his need). Life 'in grace' and 'under grace' is free, persuaded, communal, sustained by the authority that comes from true greatness, viz. [namely] pre-eminence in service.

—Albert C. Outler, 1908–1989

118 We should never assume that theology is the exclusive domain of professional theologians. Some of the clearest expressions of theology have come to us through poets and novelists. Here Denise Levertov, twentieth-century poet, puts the doctrine of grace in an unforgettable picture.

The Avowal

As swimmers dare
to lie face to the sky
and water bears them,
as hawks rest upon air
and air sustains them,
so would I learn to attain
freefall, and float
into Creator Spirit's deep embrace,
knowing no effort earns
that all-surrounding grace.

—Denise Levertov, 1923–1997

Salvation

The concept of salvation dominates the entire Bible; as scholars have sometimes said, the Bible is nothing other than salvation history. But the forms in which biblical salvation appears are very broad, ranging from military deliverance for individuals or a nation to spiritual salvation. Theologians have concentrated more often on the spiritual salvation, but our writers will introduce us to a variety of views.

119 By its innate definition, salvation comes from outside ourselves; it is not our accomplishment. But who is capable of saving us? Hildegard of Bingen, Abbess of a convent in Germany, who wrote of her visions, points to Jesus Christ, and the love that God has extended to us.

Why so? Because in this way GOD loved us; another salvation has sprung up, than that which we had in the creation, when we were heirs of innocence and of sanctity, because the Father above showed His love, when we in our peril were placed in punishment, sending His Word, Who alone among the sons of men was perfect in holiness, into the darkness of this world, where that same Word, doing all good works, led them back to life through His meekness, who were cast out by the malice of transgression, nor were they able to return to that holiness which they had lost.

Why so? Because through that fountain of life came the paternal love of the embrace of God, which educated us to life, and in our dangers was our help, and is the most deep and beautiful light teaching us repentance.

In what way? God mercifully remembered His great work and His most precious pearl, man, I say, whom He formed from the dust of the earth, and into whom He breathed the breath of life. In what manner? He taught (us) how to live in repentance whose efficacy will never perish. . . .

Thence this salvation of love did not spring from us, because we did not know, neither were we able to love God unto salvation, but because He the Creator and Lord of all so loved the world, that He sent His Son for its salvation, the Prince and Saviour of the faithful, Who washed and dried our wounds, and from Him also came that most sweet medicine, from which all the good things of salvation flow.

—Hildegard of Bingen, 1098–1179

120 As our study continues, we will see the relationship between God's gift of salvation and our response. The ancient Heidelberg Catechism links these two factors, the divine and the human, in its series of questions.

Q. 60.   How are you righteous before God?

A. Only by true faith in Jesus Christ. In spite of the fact that my conscience accuses me that I have grievously sinned against all the commandments of God, and have not kept any one of them, and that I am still ever prone to all that is evil, nevertheless, God, without any merit of my own, out of pure grace, grants me the benefits of the perfect expiation of Christ, imputing to me his righteousness and holiness as if I had never committed a single sin or had ever been sinful, having fulfilled myself all the obedience which Christ has carried out for me, if only I accept such favor with a trusting heart.

Q. 61.   Why do you say that you are righteous by faith alone?

A. Not because I please God by virtue of the worthiness of my faith, but because the satisfaction, righteousness, and holiness of Christ alone are my righteousness before God, and because I can accept it and make it mine in no other way than by faith alone.

—Heidelberg Catechism, 1562

121 The human experience of salvation has produced hundreds of poems and hymns. English religious poet George Herbert put the issue in especially graphic form, drawing upon the Old Testament insight of the kinsman redeemer, tying it to the act of Christ at Calvary.

REDEMPTION

Having been tenant long to a rich Lord,
   Not thriving, I resolved to be bold,
   And make a suit unto him, to afford
A new small-rented lease, and cancel th' old.

In heaven at his manor I him sought:
   They told me there, that he was lately gone
   About some land, which he had dearly bought
Long since on earth, to take possession.

I straight return'd, and knowing his great birth,
   Sought him accordingly in great resorts;
   In cities, theaters, gardens, parks, and courts:
At length I heard a ragged noise and mirth

   Of thieves and murderers: there I him espied,
   Who straight, *Your suit is granted,* said, and died.
           —*George Herbert, 1593–1633*

122 The average person often perceives salvation as primarily a deliverance from eternal punishment. Not so; it is also an experience that changes life on this earth. John Wesley makes this point clear in one of his sermons.

What is *salvation*? The salvation which is here spoken of is not what is frequently understood by that word, the going to heaven, eternal happiness. It is not the soul's going to paradise, termed by our Lord, 'Abraham's bosom'. It is not a blessing which lies on the other side death, or (as we usually speak) in the other world. The very words of the text itself put this beyond all question: 'Ye *are* saved.' It is not something at a distance: it is a present thing, a blessing which, through the free mercy of God, ye are now in possession of. . . .

. . . And this consists of two general parts, justification and sanctification.

Justification is another word for pardon. It is the forgiveness of all our sins, and (what is necessarily implied therein) our acceptance with God. . . .

And at the same time that we are justified, yea, in that very moment, *sanctification* begins. In that instant we are 'born again', 'born from above', 'born of the Spirit'. There is a *real* as well as a *relative* change. We are inwardly renewed by the power of God. We feel the 'love of God shed abroad in our heart, by the Holy Ghost which is given unto us', producing love to all mankind, and more especially to the children of God; expelling the love of the world, the love of pleasure, of ease, of honour, of money; together with pride, anger, self-will, and every other evil temper—in a word, changing the 'earthly, sensual, devilish' mind into 'the mind which was in Christ Jesus'.

—John Wesley, 1703–1791

123 The salvation that we receive on earth is complex enough that we use a variety of terms to describe it. John Wesley identifies those terms in relationship to our various experiences.

Whatsoever else it [salvation by faith] imply, it is a present salvation. It is something attainable, yea, actually attained on earth, by those who are partakers of this faith. For thus saith the Apostle to the believers at Ephesus, and in them to the believers of all ages, not, 'Ye *shall be*' (though that also is true), but 'Ye *are* saved through faith.'

Ye are saved (to comprise all in one word) from sin.... Through faith that is in him they are saved both from the guilt and from the power of it.

First, from the guilt of all past sin....

And being saved from guilt, they are saved from fear....

This then is the salvation which is through faith, even in the present world: a salvation from sin, and the consequences of sin, both often expressed in the word 'justification', which, taken in the largest sense, implies a deliverance from guilt and punishment, by the atonement of Christ actually applied to the soul of the sinner now believing on him, and a deliverance from the power of sin, through Christ 'formed in his heart'. So that he who is thus justified or saved by faith is indeed 'born again'. He is 'born again of the Spirit' unto new 'life which is hid with Christ in God'. ['He is a new creature: old things are passed away; all things in him are become new.'] And as a 'newborn babe he gladly receives the ... sincere milk of the word, and grows thereby'; 'going on in the might of the Lord his God', 'from faith to faith', 'from grace to grace', 'until at length he comes unto a perfect man, unto the measure of the stature of the fullness of Christ'.

—John Wesley, 1703–1791

124 A later lesson deals specifically with our human response to God's act of salvation, but one cannot completely isolate the two subjects. Here we have a statement from Rudolf Bultmann, theologian and New Testament scholar, explaining the essential quality of our human response by faith.

[T]he apostolic preaching which originated in the event of Easter Day is itself a part of the eschatological event of redemption. The death of Christ, which is both the judgment and the salvation of the world, inaugurates the "ministry of reconciliation" or "word of reconciliation" (2 Cor. 5:18 f.) This word supplements the cross and makes its saving efficacy intelligible by demanding faith and confronting men with the question whether they are willing to understand themselves as men who are crucified and risen with Christ. Through the word of preaching the cross and the resurrection are made present: the eschatological "now" is here, and the promise of Isa. 49:8 is fulfilled: "Behold, now is the acceptable time; behold, now is the day of salvation" (2 Cor. 6:2). That is why the apostolic preaching brings judgment. For some the apostle is "a saviour from death unto death" and for others a "saviour from life unto life" (2 Cor. 2:16). St. Paul is the agent through whom the resurrection life becomes effective in the faithful (2 Cor. 4:12). The promise of Jesus in the fourth gospel is eminently applicable to the preaching in which he is proclaimed: "Verily I say unto you, he that heareth my words and believeth on him that sent me, hath eternal life, and cometh not unto judgment, but hath passed out of death into life. . . . The hour cometh and now is, when the dead shall hear the voice of the Son of God; and they that hear shall live" (John 5:24 f.). In the word of preaching and there alone we meet the risen Lord. "So belief cometh of hearing, and hearing by the word of Christ" (Rom. 10:17).

—Rudolf Bultmann, 1884–1976

125 Karl Barth preached regularly to persons in prison. His theme of salvation takes on particular significance in light of the congregation he is addressing. But he makes clear that the need of deliverance is as great for persons who are outside as for those who are incarcerated.

'By grace *you* have been saved!' How strange to have this message addressed to us! Who are we, anyway? Let me tell you quite frankly: we are all together great sinners. . . . We spend our life in the midst of a whole world of sin and captivity and suffering.

But now listen. Into the depth of our predicament the word is spoken from on high: *By grace you have been saved!* To be saved does not just mean to be a little encouraged, a little comforted, a little relieved. It means to be pulled out like a log from a burning fire. You have been saved! We are not told: you may be saved sometimes, or a little bit. No, you *have been* saved, totally and for all times. You? Yes, we! Not just any other people, more pious and better than we are, no, we, each one of us.

This is so because Jesus Christ is our brother and, through his life and death, has become our Saviour who has wrought our salvation. He is the word of God for us. And this word is: *By grace you have been saved!*

—Karl Barth, 1886–1968

126 The biblical understanding of salvation is so profound that the Scriptures use several words and figures of speech in referring to it. Georgia Harkness considers not only the several terms, but also the nature of change that happens when salvation is experienced.

There is no one word that expresses the full meaning of salvation. Yet all the great traditional words of our faith indicate a genuine change of life, goals, and motive power. As regeneration in its derivation means to be "born again," and as conversion means to "turn around," so redemption means to be "bought back" and brought back to our Father's home and fellowship through the love and the self-giving of Christ. Atonement means "at-one-ment" and refers to the new unity of the soul with God which one who has been alienated and estranged by his sin and self-will finds in the grace, mercy, and peace that God in Christ stands ready to impart. Reconciliation does not mean that God must be reconciled to us, but that "God was in Christ reconciling the world to himself, not counting their trespasses against them, and entrusting to us the message of reconciliation" (2 Corinthians 5:19). . . .

If the regeneration is deep-going, a person's choices and decisions are different from the time when it happens. Feelings, words, and acts take on a different tenor....

Sometimes the change is so radical that it seems miraculous. Sometimes there is a gradual, ... almost imperceptible, change in values, motives, feelings, and modes of responding to situations. If there is no difference at all, regeneration has not occurred.

—*Georgia Harkness, 1891–1974*

127 As we have observed, the Old Testament pictures of salvation often include salvation in battle, and the psalmists sometimes cry for salvation from shame or poverty. Latin American theologian Gustavo Gutiérrez applies the concept of salvation to personal, social, and historical elements in our present life.

Salvation is not something otherworldly, in regard to which the present life is merely a test. Salvation—the communion of human beings with God and among themselves—is something which embraces all human reality, transforms it, and leads it to its fullness in Christ: "Thus the center of God's salvific design is Jesus Christ, who by his death and resurrection transforms the universe and makes it possible for the person to reach fulfillment as a human being. This fulfillment embraces every aspect of humanity: body and spirit, individual and society, person and cosmos, time and eternity. Christ, the image of the Father and the perfect God-Man, takes on all the dimensions of human existence."

Therefore, sin is not only an impediment to salvation in the afterlife. Insofar as it constitutes a break with God, sin is a historical reality, it is a breach of the communion of persons with each other, it is a turning in of individuals on themselves which manifests itself in a multifaceted withdrawal from others. And because sin is a personal and social intrahistorical reality, a part of the daily events of human life, it is also, and above all, an obstacle to life's reaching the fullness we call salvation.

... One looks then to this world, and now sees in the world beyond not the "true life," but rather the transformation and fulfillment of the present life. The absolute value of salvation—far from devaluing this world—gives it its authentic meaning and its own autonomy because salvation is already latently there.

—*Gustavo Gutiérrez, 1928–*

The Message Behind the Symbols

Jesus Christ: Human/Divine
Jesus Christ: Savior ◆ Atonement
Jesus Christ: Lord ◆ Faith

The olive and the balsam together symbolize the human and divine nature of Jesus Christ. Olive oil, used to sooth pain and restore the body, represents Jesus, who ministered to the sick, the tired, the needy. Balsam, valued for its healing power, points to the Christ who by his life and death heals the broken relationship between us and God. The humble violet expresses the humility of the Son of God in becoming a human being. Another symbol of the Incarnation is the swallow. Look for it in paintings depicting the birth of Jesus.

The fish with the letters ICHTHUS symbolizes the Second Person of the Trinity, Jesus Christ, Son of God, Savior. And the most familiar symbol of Christianity is the Latin cross, the form of the cross on which Jesus our Savior gave his life for our redemption.

John the Baptist called Jesus "the Lamb of God who takes away the sin of the world" (John 1:29). The figure of the lamb as a symbol of Christ the sacrifice for atonement echoes the sacrifice of the Passover lamb in the Old Testament. The lamb, with its three-rayed nimbus indicating divinity, carries a staff shaped like a cross and bearing a banner of victory over sin and death—Jesus is Lord, the object of our faith.

According to legend, the pelican, in a time of famine, tears open its breast to feed its young with its lifeblood, a depiction of our salvation through the blood of Christ.

Jesus Christ: Human/Divine

The glory of Christianity is Jesus Christ. He is also its primary issue. While the Scriptures provided the basis for the church's understanding of Jesus Christ as both human and divine, it took a series of church councils to define the matter in a fashion that would prevent various heresies and that would provide a foundation of doctrinal belief for the succeeding centuries of church history.

128 Our Scripture readings are taken from both the Old Testament and the New, because the early church, before there was a New Testament, saw its Lord in the Old. Tertullian, father of Latin theology, does the same.

[T]he truth is, we find that He is expressly set forth as both God and man. . . . Thus does the apostle . . . teach respecting His two substances, saying, "who was made of the seed of David;" in which words He will be Man and Son of Man. "Who was declared to be the Son of God, according to the Spirit;" in which words He will be God, and the Word—the Son of God. We see plainly the twofold state, which is not confounded, but conjoined in One Person— Jesus, God and Man. Concerning Christ, . . . the property of each nature is so wholly preserved, that the Spirit on the one hand did all things in Jesus suitable to Itself, such as miracles, and mighty deeds, and wonders; and the Flesh, on the other hand, exhibited the affections which belong to it. It was hungry under the devil's temptation, thirsty with the Samaritan woman, wept over Lazarus, was troubled even unto death, and at last actually died.

—Tertullian, 160–225

129 Biblical references to Jesus Christ offer no systematic study of the humanity and divinity of our Lord. Apparently readers must determine how they will find their way through these materials. In Athanasius we have one good example.

Being God, he became a human being: and then as God he raised the dead, healed all by a word, and also changed water into wine. These were not the acts of a human being. But as a human being, he felt thirst and tiredness, and he suffered pain. These experiences are not appropriate to deity. As God he said, "I in the father, the Father in me"; as a human being, he criticized the Jews, thus: "Why do you seek to kill me, when I am a man who has told you the truth, which I heard from my Father?" And yet these are not events occurring without any connection, distinguished according to their quality, so that one class may be ascribed to the body, apart from the divinity, and the other to the divinity, apart from the body. They all occurred in such a way that they were joined together; and the Lord, who marvellously performed those acts by his grace, was one. He spat in human fashion; but his spittle had divine power, for by it he restored sight to the eyes of the man blind from birth. When he willed to make himself known as God, he used his human tongue to signify this, when he said, "I and the Father are one." He cured by his mere will. Yet it was by extending his human hand that he raised Peter's mother-in-law when she had a fever, and raised from the dead the daughter of the ruler of the synagogue, when she had already died.

—Anthanasius, 296–373

130 How complete was God's involvement in our human race in the coming of Jesus Christ? Augustine explains that God became totally involved with our humanness in the act of incarnation—a concept that gives new dignity to the human race. What greater thing can be said for our race than that God chose to take on our form of body?

Christ did not assume for only a brief time the human form in which he appeared to men, with that form later passing away. Rather, he took the visible form of the man to the unity of his person, while the invisible form of God remained. Not only was he born from a human mother in the visible form of a man, but he also grew up in it, and ate and drank and slept in it. He was killed in it, rose in it and ascended into heaven and is seated at the right hand of the Father in it. He will come in it to judge the living and the dead, and in his kingdom he will be subject in it to him who has subjected all things to him.

—Augustine, 354–430

131 Many biblical scholars think that Philippians 2:6-11 may have been a hymn or a response that was popularly sung in the early Christian church. Augustine analyzes the doctrine that resides in this ancient poem.

Wherefore Christ Jesus, the Son of God, is both God and man; God before all worlds; man in our world: God, because the Word of God (for "the Word was God"); and man, because in His one person the Word was joined with a body and a rational soul. Wherefore, so far as He is God, He and the Father are one; so far as He is man, the Father is greater than He. For when He was the only Son of God, not by grace, but by nature, that He might be also full of grace, He became the Son of man; and He Himself unites both natures in His own identity, and both natures constitute one Christ; because, "being in the form of God, He thought it not robbery to be," what He was by nature, "equal with God." But He made Himself of no reputation, and took upon Himself the form of a servant, not losing or lessening the form of God. And, accordingly, He was both made less and remained equal, being both in one, as has been said: but He was one of these as Word, and the other as man. As Word, He is equal with the Father; as man, less than the Father. One Son of God, and at the same time Son of man; one Son of man, and at the same time Son of God; not two Sons of God, God and man, but one Son of God: God without beginning; man with a beginning, our Lord Jesus Christ.

—Augustine, 354–430

132 A series of church councils struggled to perfect statements that would clarify beyond debate the nature of Jesus Christ. The Council of Chalcedon (A.D. 451) declared what became orthodox Christian teaching.

Therefore, following the holy Fathers, we all with one accord teach men to acknowledge one and the same Son, our Lord Jesus

Christ, at once complete in Godhead and complete in manhood, truly God and truly man, consisting also of a reasonable soul and body; of one substance ... with the Father as regards his Godhead, and at the same time of one substance with us as regards his manhood; like us in all respects, apart from sin; as regards his Godhead, begotten of the Father before the ages, but yet as regards his manhood begotten, in the last days, for us men and for our salvation, of Mary the Virgin, the God-bearer ...; one and the same Christ, Son, Lord, Only-begotten, recognized IN TWO NATURES, WITHOUT CONFUSION, WITHOUT CHANGE, WITHOUT DIVISION, WITHOUT SEPARATION; the distinction of natures being in no way annulled by the union, but rather the characteristics of each nature being preserved and coming together to form one person and subsistence ..., not as parted or separated into two persons, but one and the same Son and Only-begotten God the Word, Lord Jesus Christ; even as the prophets from earliest times spoke of him, and our Lord Jesus Christ himself taught us, and the creed of the Fathers has handed down to us.

—The Definition of Chalcedon, 451

133 When the New Testament writers speak of the human elements in the life of Jesus, they do so without any explanation. Leo the Great, who became pope in 440, seeks to show the relationship between the humanness in Jesus and in ourselves.

Thus there was born true God in the entire and perfect nature of true man, complete in his own properties, complete in ours. By 'ours' I mean those which the Creator formed in us at the beginning, which he assumed in order to restore; for in the Saviour there was no trace of the properties which the deceiver brought in, and which man, being deceived, allowed to enter. He did not become partaker of our sins because he entered into fellowship with human infirmities. He assumed the form of a servant without the stain of sin, making the human properties greater, but not detracting from the divine. For that 'emptying of himself', whereby the invisible rendered himself visible, and the Creator and Lord of all willed to be a mortal, was a condescension of compassion, not a failure of power. Accordingly, he who made man, while he remained in the form of God, was himself made man in the form of a servant. Each nature preserves its own characteristics without diminution, so that the form of a servant does not detract from the form of God.

—Leo the Great, 400?–461

134 Since the Bible so rarely declares doctrine in systematic fashion, the generations of theologians naturally brought organization of their own. Here Leo the Great seeks in admirable detail to offer clarity for believers.

[We must] believe that at no moment of time was the power of the Word wanting to the flesh and soul which she [the blessed Virgin] conceived. . . . but through Himself and in Himself was the beginning given to the New Man, so that in the one Son of GOD and Man there might be Godhead without a mother, and Manhood without a Father. . . .

. . . [Nestorius] dared to maintain that the blessed Virgin Mary was the mother of Christ's manhood only. . . . This can in no wise be tolerated by catholic ears, which are so imbued with the gospel of Truth that they know of a surety there is no hope of salvation for mankind unless He were Himself the Son of the Virgin who was His mother's Creator. . . .

. . . The man, therefore, assumed into the Son of GOD, was in such wise received into the unity of Christ's Person from His very commencement in the body, that without the Godhead He was not brought forth, without the Godhead he was not nursed. It was the same Person in the wondrous acts, and in the endurance of insults; through His human weakness crucified, dead and buried: through His Divine power, being raised the third day, He ascended to the heavens, sat down at the right hand of the Father, and in His nature as man received from the Father that which in His nature as GOD He Himself also gave.

—Leo the Great, 400?–461

135 Like other theologians over the centuries, Leo the Great wrestled with the question, if Jesus Christ was human, did he also partake of our human weaknesses? Leo's explanation is systematic, but also devotional.

Therefore, when the time came, dearly beloved, which had been fore-ordained for men's redemption, there enters these lower parts of the world, the Son of GOD, descending from His heavenly throne and yet not quitting His Father's glory, begotten in a new order, by a new nativity. In a new order, because being invisible in His own nature He became visible in ours, and He whom nothing could contain, was content to be contained: abiding before all time He began to be in time: the LORD of all things, He obscured His immeasurable majesty and took on Him the form of a servant: being GOD, that cannot suffer, He did not disdain to be man that can, and immortal as He is, to subject Himself to the laws of death.

—Leo the Great, 400?–461

136 Humans are complex, and God is quite beyond our full comprehension. How then do we describe the Incarnation, when God becomes human in Jesus Christ? It is no simple matter, so it is no wonder theologians have been struggling with definitions for centuries. Here is a fifth-century word from Cyril of Alexandria.

For we do not affirm that the nature of the Word underwent a change and became flesh, or that it was transformed into a whole or perfect man consisting of soul and body; but we say that the Word, having in an ineffable and inconceivable manner personally united to Himself flesh instinct with a living soul, became man and was called the Son of Man, yet not of mere will or favor, nor again by the simple taking to Himself of a person (i.e. of a human person to His divine person), and that while the natures which were brought together into this true unity were divrse, there was of both one Christ and one Son: not as though the diverseness of the natures were done away by this union, but rather the Godhead and Manhood completed for us the one Lord and Christ and Son by their inutterable and unspeakable concurrence and unity. And thus, although He subsisted and was begotten of the Father before the worlds, He is spoken of as having been born also after the flesh of a woman. . . . For He was not first born an ordinary man of the holy Virgin, and then the Word descended upon Him, but having been made one with the flesh from the very womb itself, He is said to have submitted to a birth according to the flesh, as appropriating and making His own the birth of His own flesh.

—Cyril of Alexandria, died 444

137 Such New Testament books as the Gospel of John and the epistles to Ephesus and Colossae speak of the pre-existence of Christ. Greek theologian John of Damascus tries to explain such mysteries in more structured, philosophical language.

And therefore we hold that there has been a union of two perfect natures, one divine and one human; not with disorder or confusion, or intermixture . . . but by synthesis, that is, in subsistence, without change or confusion or alteration or difference or separation, and we confess that in two perfect natures there is but one subsistence of the Son of God incarnate, holding that there is one and the same subsistence belonging to His divinity and His humanity, and granting that the two natures are preserved in Him after the union, but we do not hold that each is separate and by itself, but that they are united to each other in one compound subsistence. For we look upon the union as essential, that is, as true and not imaginary. We say that it is essential, moreover, not in the sense of two natures resulting in one compound nature, but in the sense of a true union of them in one compound subsistence of the Son of God, and we hold that their essential difference is preserved. For the created remaineth created, and the uncreated, uncreated: the mortal remaineth mortal; the immortal, immortal: the circumscribed, circumscribed: the uncircumscribed, uncircumscribed: the visible, visible: the invisible, invisible. "The one part is all glorious with wonders: while the other is the victim of insults."

—John of Damascus, 655–750

138 The New Testament church insisted that persons can be saved only through the name of Jesus Christ. Dorothy L. Sayers, popular English novelist and playwright, but a theologian as well, put the issue clearly in her summary of doctrine.

That you cannot have Christian principles without Christ is becoming increasingly clear, because their validity as principles depends on Christ's authority. . . . If "the average man" is required to "believe in Christ" and accept His authority for "Christian principles," it is surely relevant to inquire who or what Christ is, and why His authority should be accepted. But the question, "What think ye of Christ?" lands the average man at once in the very knottiest kind of dogmatic riddle. . . .

It is not true at all that dogma is "hopelessly irrelevant" to the life and thought of the average man. What is true is that ministers of the Christian religion often assert that it is, present it for consideration as though it were, and, in fact, by their faulty exposition of it make it so. The central dogma of the Incarnation is that by which relevance stands or falls. If Christ was only man, then He is entirely irrelevant to any thought about God; if He is only God, then He is entirely irrelevant to any experience of human life. It is, in the strictest sense, *necessary* to the salvation of relevance that a man should believe *rightly* the Incarnation of Our Lord Jesus Christ.

—*Dorothy L. Sayers, 1893–1957*

139 The New Testament writers generally presented doctrinal statements more in the language of devotion than of debate. Monika K. Hellwig, professor of theology, summarizes the logic of doctrinal development.

If Jesus is personally and literally divine, is he really a human being like the rest of us, or is he really a divine being appearing to us as a man so that we might see him and relate to him? Or is he perhaps a divine being somehow expressing himself in a human body but not really subject to our limitations? For instance, did Jesus really suffer? Were there things he did not know? Did he have to consider situations, think about them, pray about them, and struggle to come to a decision? Or did the divine fullness of being, omnipotence, and omniscience preclude all this? That certainly is a very important set of questions because these issues relate immediately to what we understand by redemption and how we see our own role in accepting and responding to the divine initiative in redemption. . . . Christians today are heirs of an answer given long ago. In 451 C.E., representatives of the churches still in communion with one another gathered at Chalcedon and hammered out a formula that was supposed to answer these persistent questions: There is one person, Jesus, who is truly of the same being as God the Father and creator in his divine aspect and truly of the same being as we are in his human aspect; when Jesus acts it is always God acting and man acting. Almost all the Christian churches still consider this the orthodox formula of Christian faith.

—*Monika K. Hellwig, 20th century*

Jesus Christ: Savior

Next to the doctrine of the person of Jesus Christ, no theological issue is more important than that which deals with his role as Savior. From before Jesus' birth, when Joseph was instructed to name him Jesus because he would save his people from their sins, until his death when he promised a thief beside him that he would have a place in Paradise, and then through all of the preaching in Acts and the teaching in the epistles, he is seen repeatedly as the Savior. No wonder, then, that theologians, mystics, and poets alike have written about this theme.

140 We speak of Jesus Christ as "the Word," but often we do not put concrete meaning into the term. Ignatius, Bishop of Antioch, makes the term graphic when he describes Jesus as "the original documents," then proceeds to show Christ as Lord of the Old Testament personalities as well as of the church.

I urge you, do not do things in cliques, but act as Christ's disciples. When I heard some people saying, "If I don't find it in the original documents, I don't believe it in the gospel," I answered them, "But it is written there." They retorted, "That's just the question." To my mind it is Jesus Christ who is the original documents. The inviolable archives are his cross and death and his resurrection and the faith that came by him. It is by these things and through your prayers that I want to be justified.

Priests are a fine thing, but better still is the High Priest who was entrusted with the Holy of Holies. He alone was entrusted with God's secrets. He is the door to the Father. Through it there enter Abraham, Isaac, and Jacob, the prophets and apostles and the

Church. All these find their place in God's unity. But there is some-thing special about the gospel—I mean the coming of the Saviour, our Lord Jesus Christ, his Passion and resurrection. The beloved prophets announced his coming; but the gospel is the crowning achievement forever. All these things, taken together, have their value, provided you hold the faith in love.

—Ignatius, c. 35–c. 107

141 John 3:16 probably summarizes better than any other single verse the love that motivated the divine act of saving. Clement of Alexandria, theologian and writer, seeks to examine this love, and sees in it the Mother-quality of divine love.

Consider the mysteries of love, and you will then have a vision of the bosom of the Father, whom the only-begotten God alone has declared. God himself is love, and for the sake of this love he made himself known. And while the unutterable nature of God is Father, his sympathy with us is Mother. It was in his love that the Father became the nature which derives from woman, and the great proof of this is the Son whom he begot from himself, and the love that was the fruit produced from his love. For this he came down, for this he assumed human nature, for this he willingly endured the sufferings of humanity, that by being reduced to the measure of our weakness, he might raise us to the measure of his power. And just before he poured out his offering, when he gave himself as a ran-som, he left us a new testament: "I give you my love" (John 13:34). What is the nature and extent of this love? For each of us he laid down his life, the life which was worth the whole universe, and he requires in return that we should do the same for each other.

—Clement of Alexandria, c. 150–c. 216

142 Melito, Bishop of Sardis, emphasized Christianity's heritage in Judaism in a sermon on the "Pasch," both the Jewish Passover and the Christian Easter. The New Testament pictures Jesus as our eternal Passover lamb; Melito captures this theme in words of holy adoration.

> The mystery of the Pasch
> is new and old,
> eternal and temporal,

corruptible and incorruptible,
mortal and immortal . . .
Born as Son,
led like a lamb,
sacrificed like a sheep,
buried as a man,
he rises from the dead as God,
being by nature both God and man.

He is all things:
when he judges, he is law,
when he teaches, word,
when he saves, grace,
when he begets, father,
when he is begotten, son,
when he suffers, lamb,
when he is buried, man,
when he arises, God.

Such is Jesus Christ!
To him be glory forever! Amen.

—Melito, c. 190

143 Athanasius sees in the sacrificial death of Jesus Christ a tie to the divine-human nature of the Christ. He perceives that it is only because Jesus took on himself "a body capable of death" that he could fully enter into our humanness, and in turn do away with death.

Therefore, assuming a body like ours, because all people were liable to the corruption of death, [the Word] surrendered it to death for all humanity, and offered it to the Father. He presented it to the Father as an act of pure love for humanity, so that by all dying in him the law concerning the corruption of humanity might be abolished (inasmuch as its power was fulfilled in the Lord's body, and no longer has capacity against human beings who are like him), and that he might turn back to a state of incorruption those who had fallen into a state of corruption, and bring them to life by the fact of his death, by the body which he made his own, and by the grace of his resurrection . . . The Word thus takes on a body capable of death, in order that, by partaking in the Word that is above all, this body might be worthy to die instead for all humanity, and remain incorruptible through the indwelling Word, and thus put an end to corruption through the grace of his resurrection . . . Hence he did away with death for all who are like him by the offering of the body which he had taken on himself. The Word, who is above all, offered his own temple and bodily instrument as a ransom for all, and paid their debt through his death. Thus the incorruptible Son of God, being united with all humanity by likeness to them, naturally clothed all humanity with incorruption, according to the promise of the resurrection.

—Athansasius, 296–373

144 Any discussion of Christ as Savior must at some point ask why Jesus was uniquely qualified for this role; why not any good and admirable person? Or to put it another way, how was Jesus different from any earnest martyr? Ambrose, Bishop of Milan and instrumental in the conversion of Augustine, reminds us that only Jesus was free from the bonds of sin, and thus in a position to save others.

Jesus approached the snares, to set Adam free: he came to liberate what had perished. We were all held in the toils; no one could rescue another, for no one could deliver himself. What was needed was one who was not held by the bonds incurred by the sins of human generation; one who had not been caught by avarice, or enslaved by deceit. Jesus alone was that one; for when he encompassed himself with the bonds of this flesh, he was not caught, nor was he ensnared. Rather he broke the bonds and loosed them, and, looking out through the snares, and rising up above the toils, he called to himself the Church, so that the Church also might learn how to escape being held by the bonds. In fact, so far was he from avoiding the bonds that he even submitted to death for our sake. Yet he was not made death's slave; he was 'free among the dead' free, because he had the power to abolish death.

—Ambrose, 339–397

145 Augustine reminds us that the Savior must not only be free from personal sin; he must also have the capacity to be a Mediator between God and our human race, because only someone with a unique tie to God can present the human case to God.

For we could not be redeemed, even through the one Mediator between God and men, the man Christ Jesus, if He were not also God. Now when Adam was created, he, being a righteous man, had no need of a mediator. But when sin had placed a wide gulf between God and the human race, it was expedient that a Mediator, who alone of the human race was born, lived, and died without sin, should reconcile us to God, and procure even for our bodies a resurrection to eternal life, in order that the pride of man might be exposed and cured through the humility of God; that man might be shown how far he had departed from God, when God became incarnate to bring him back; that an example might be set to disobedient man in the life of obedience of the God-Man; that the fountain of grace might be opened by the Only-begotten taking upon Himself the form of a servant, a form which had no antecedent merit; that an earnest of that resurrection of the body which is promised to the redeemed might be given in the resurrection of the Redeemer; that the devil might be subdued by the same nature which it was his boast to have deceived, and yet man not glorified, lest pride should again spring up; and, in fine, with a view to all the advantages which the thoughtful can perceive and describe, or perceive without being able to describe, as flowing from the transcendent mystery of the person of the Mediator.

—Augustine, 354–430

146 Thomas Aquinas, influential theologian of the Middle Ages and a logician at heart, asked questions about the right of God to restore humanity, and from this question led the reader into the necessity that God must become incarnate in a person if there is to be salvation.

The reparation of human nature could not be effected by Adam or by any other purely human being. For no individual man ever occupied a position of preeminence over the whole of nature; nor can any mere man be the cause of grace. . . . Nothing remains, therefore, but that such restoration could be effected by God alone.

But if God had decided to restore man solely by an act of His will and power, the order of divine justice would not have been observed. Justice demands satisfaction for sin. But God cannot render satisfaction, just as He cannot merit. Such a service pertains to one who is subject to another. Thus God was not in a position to satisfy for the sin of the whole of human nature; and a mere man was unable to do so, as we have just shown. Hence divine Wisdom judged it fitting that God should become man, so that thus one and the same person would be able both to restore man and to offer satisfaction. . . .

At the same time, by willing to become man, God clearly displayed the immensity of His love for men, so that henceforth men might serve God, no longer out of fear of death, which the first man had scorned, but out of the love of charity. . . .

Lastly, the Incarnation puts the finishing touch to the whole vast work envisaged by God. For man, who was the last to be created, returns by a sort of circulatory movement to his first beginning, being united by the work of the Incarnation to the very principle of all things.

—Thomas Aquinas, 1225–1274

147 We humans are hard put to find language or concepts that will portray the love of God. It is beyond our vocabulary, so we are forced to find figures of speech that will convey at least some measure of the love that brought about the saving act. Julian of Norwich expressed this love in the role of the mother.

The mother's service is nearest, readiest and surest: nearest because it is most natural, readiest because it is most loving, and surest because it is truest. No one ever might or could perform this office fully, except only him. We know that all our mothers bear us for pain and for death. O, what is that? But our true Mother Jesus, he alone bears us for joy and for endless life, blessed may he be. So he carries us within him in love and travail, until the full time when he wanted to suffer the sharpest thorns and cruel pains that ever were or will be, and at the last he died. And when he had finished, and had borne us so for bliss, still all this could not satisfy his wonderful love. And he revealed this in these great surpassing words of love: If I could suffer more, I would suffer more. He could not die any more, but he did not want to cease working; therefore he must needs nourish us, for the precious love of motherhood has made him our debtor.

The mother can give her child to suck of her milk, but our precious Mother Jesus can feed us with himself, and does, most courteously and most tenderly, with the blessed sacrament, which is the precious food of true life; and with all the sweet sacraments he sustains us most mercifully and graciously, and so he meant in these blessed words, where he said: I am he whom Holy Church preaches and teaches to you. That is to say: All the health and the life of the sacraments, all the power and the grace of my word, all the goodness which is ordained in Holy Church for you, I am he.

—*Julian of Norwich, 1342–after 1416*

148 The biblical formula for communicating faith from one generation to the next is the household, with its parent-child relationship. Not many parents feel ready to take on such a task. Susanna Wesley did so by way of a letter to her daughter. Here she explains the role of Christ as Savior.

Jesus signifies a Saviour, and by that name he was called by the angel Gabriel before his birth, to show us that he came into the world to save us from our sins, and the punishment they justly deserve. And to repair the damage human nature had sustained by the fall of Adam. That, as in Adam all died, so in Christ all should be made alive. And so he became the second general head of all mankind. And as he was promised to our parents in paradise, so was his coming signified by various types and sacrifices under the law and foretold by the prophets long before he appeared in the world. And this Saviour, this Jesus, was the promised messiah, who was so long the hope and expectation of the Jews, the Christ—which in the original signifies anointed.

—*Susanna Wesley, 1670–1742*

149 To experience Christ as Savior is to feel a necessity to tell others of the experience. English hymn writer Charles Wesley, son to Susanna and brother to John, wrote the following poem a year after his conversion experience. In it he draws upon a number of biblical passages.

> And can it be that I should gain
>   An int'rest in the Saviour's blood!
> Dy'd he for me?—who caus'd his pain?
>   For me?—who Him to Death pursued?
> Amazing love! How can it be
> That Thou, my God, shouldst die for me?

'Tis mystery all! th' Immortal dies!
    Who can explore his strange Design?
In vain the first-born Seraph tries
    To sound the Depths of Love divine.
'Tis mercy all! Let earth adore;
Let Angel Minds inquire no more.

He left his Fathers throne above
    (So free, so infinite his grace!)
Empty'd himself of All but Love,
    And bled for *Adam's* helpless Race.
'Tis mercy all, immense and free,
For, O my God! it found out Me!

Long my imprison'd Spirit lay,
    Fast bound in Sin and Nature's Night
Thine Eye diffus'd a quickning Ray;
    I woke; the Dungeon flam'd with Light.
My Chains fell off, my Heart was free,
I rose, went forth, and follow'd Thee.

Still the small inward Voice I hear,
    That whispers all my Sins forgiv'n;
Still the atoning Blood is near,
    That quench'd the Wrath of hostile Heav'n:
I feel the Life his Wounds impart;
    I feel my Saviour in my Heart.

No Condemnation now I dread,
    Jesus, and all in Him, is mine.
Alive in Him, my Living Head,
    And clothed in Righteousness Divine,
Bold I approach th' Eternal Throne,
And claim the Crown, thro' CHRIST my own.
                        —*Charles Wesley, 1707–1788*

150 Our study has separate lessons on salvation, as a doctrine, and on Jesus Christ as Savior. Jeffery Hopper, professor of theology, indicates the relationship between the two, and reminds us that the theological term for the study of salvation, *soteriology,* derives from the Greek word for savior.

Soteriology, from the Greek word *soter* (savior, deliverer), is that focus in Christian theology that seeks to interpret the *saving work* of Jesus Christ, that is, what God has done for us in Jesus Christ. Traditionally it has been distinguished from Christology, which is concerned with clarifying Jesus' "person," that is, who and what Jesus Christ was and is. Most theologians agree that the "person" and the "work" of Jesus Christ must be understood in relation to each other. Serious disputes in the early church led to the decision at Chalcedon (451 C.E.) that Jesus Christ is to be understood as "true God and true man," two natures in one person. This christological decision served for centuries as the presupposition for any understanding of his "person." More recently there has been a growing tendency to give prior attention to the saving work.

The church has never officially sanctioned a particular understanding of the saving work of Jesus Christ. Rather, several different interpretative themes have had power in the thought and worship life of the church. Most of these motifs find a basis among the many titles and terms of the New Testament that suggest but do not develop interpretations of Jesus Christ's saving work.

Prominent among these themes in the early church was the idea of *sacrifice*.

—Jeffery Hopper, 20th century

Atonement

The idea of God's seeking to atone for the sins of the human race and to repair the breach of relationship that sin has brought is an idea so big that we are compelled to use figures of speech to describe it. No single figure of speech is entirely satisfactory. No wonder, then, that the church has never agreed on a single doctrine of atonement. In these readings we see how a variety of theologians over the centuries have approached this subject.

151 Irenaeus gave the church one of the earliest symbolic insights on the Atonement, with what is often called the "ransom theory." This portrays the human race as held captive by sin and Satan, so that a ransom must be paid. In this there is also a concept of justice: Even the devil, so to speak, gets his due.

Thus the powerful Word and true human being, ransoming us by his own blood in a rational manner, gave himself as a ransom for those who have been led into captivity. The apostate one unjustly held sway over us, and though we were by nature the possession of Almighty God, we had been alienated from our proper nature, making us instead his own disciples. Therefore the almighty Word of God, who did not lack justice, acted justly even in the encounter with the apostate one, ransoming from him the things which were his own, not by force, in the way in which [the apostate one] secured his dominion over us at the beginning, by greedily snatching what was not his own. Rather, it was appropriate that God should obtain what he wished through persuasion, not by the use of force, so that the principles of justice might not be infringed, and, at the same time, that God's original creation might not perish. The Lord therefore ransomed us by his own blood, and gave his life for our life, his flesh for our flesh; and he poured out the Spirit of the Father to bring about the union and fellowship of God and humanity, bringing God down to humanity through the Spirit while raising humanity to God through his incarnation, and in his coming surely and truly giving us incorruption through the fellowship which we have with him.

—*Irenaeus, c. 130–c. 200*

152 As we have indicated, different pictures appeal to different generations, and to different persons and cultures within a given time. Rufinus of Aquileia, translator of Greek theological writings, uses a figure of speech that may not appeal to our time, but that is nevertheless interesting for the insights it offers and for its range of imagination.

[The purpose of the Incarnation] was that the divine virtue of the Son of God might be like a kind of hook hidden beneath the form of human flesh . . . to lure on the prince of this world to a contest; that the Son might offer him his human flesh as a bait and that the divinity which lay underneath might catch him and hold him fast with its hook . . . Then, just as a fish when it seizes a baited hook not only fails to drag off the bait but is itself dragged out of the water to serve as food for others; so he that had the power of death seized the body of Jesus in death, unaware of the hook of divinity which lay hidden inside. Having swallowed it, he was immediately caught. The gates of hell were broken, and he was, as it were, drawn up from the pit, to become food for others.

—*Rufinus of Aquileia, 345–411*

153 Sometimes the best way to explain a difficult concept is by an imaginary dialogue, bringing out truth through statement and response. The issue here, as in much discussion of salvation, is the necessity for the Savior to be both God and human, and Anselm employs a kind of conversation to make the point.

A. But this cannot be done unless there is someone to pay to God for human sin something greater than everything that exists, except God.
B. So it is agreed.

A. If he is to give something of his own to God, which surpasses everything that is beneath God, it is also necessary for him to be greater than everything that is not God.

B. I cannot deny it.

A. But there is nothing above everything that is not God, save God himself.

B. That is true.

A. Then no one but God can make this satisfaction.

B. That follows.

A. But no one ought to make it except man; otherwise man does not make satisfaction.

B. Nothing seems more just.

A. If then, as is certain, that celestial city must be completed from among men, and this cannot happen unless the aforesaid satisfaction is made, while no one save God can make it and no one save man ought to make it, it is necessary for a God-Man to make it.

B. "Blessed be God!" We have already found out one great truth about the object of our inquiry. Go on, then, as you have begun, for I hope that God will help us.

—Anselm of Canterbury, 1033–1109

154 One of the best known expositors of the doctrine of atonement was the eleventh-century English theologian, Anselm of Canterbury. He offers a theory that he feels pays proper respect to the character of God.

The problem is, how can God forgive human sin? . . . What is God entitled to? Righteousness, or rectitude of will. Anyone who fails to render this honour to God, robs God of that which belongs to God, and thus dishonours God. . . . It is not enough simply to restore what has been taken away; but, in consideration of the insult offered, more than what was taken away must be rendered back . . . since the only possible way of correcting sin, for which no satisfaction has been made, is to punish it; not to punish it, is to leave it uncorrected. But God cannot properly leave anything uncorrected in His kingdom. Furthermore, to leave sin unpunished would be tantamount to treating the sinful and the sinless alike, which would be inconsistent with God's nature. And this inconsistency is injustice. It is necessary, therefore, that either the honour taken away should be repaid, or punishment should be inflicted.

Otherwise one of two things follows: either God is not just to his own nature; or God is powerless to do what ought to be done, which is a blasphemous supposition. The satisfaction ought to be in proportion to the sin.

—Anselm of Canterbury, 1033–1109

155 When we think of the Atonement, we are inclined to contemplate especially what God has done for our human race in this act of atoning. French theologian and philosopher Peter Abelard (Abailard) reminds us of our response to God's action. We are not only free; we are also made grateful.

Now it seems to us that we have been justified by the blood of Christ and reconciled to God in this way: through this unique act of grace manifested to us—in that his Son has taken upon himself our nature and perservated therein in teaching us by word and example even unto death—he has more fully bound us to himself by love; with the result that our hearts should be enkindled by such a gift of divine grace, and true charity should not now shrink from enduring anything for him.

... Yet everyone becomes more righteous—by which we mean a greater lover of the Lord—after the Passion of Christ than before, since a realized gift inspires greater love than one which is only hoped for. Wherefore, our redemption through Christ's suffering is that deeper affection in us which not only frees us from slavery to sin, but also wins for us the true liberty of sons of God, so that we do all things out of love rather than fear—love to him who has shown us such grace that no greater can be found, as he himself asserts, saying, "Greater love than this no man hath, that a man lay down his life for his friends."

—Peter Abelard (Abailard), 1079–1142/3

156 Martin Luther uses Irenaeus's ransom language in explaining the atonement, and affirms that only God's Son could effect such a price. Luther, who enjoyed vigorous figures of speech, also used the fishhook analogy on occasions.

Because an eternal, unchangeable sentence of condemnation has passed upon sin—for God cannot and will not regard sin with favor, but his wrath abides upon it eternally and irrevocably—redemption was not possible without a ransom of such precious worth as to atone for sin, to assume the guilt, pay the price of wrath and thus abolish sin.

This no creature was able to do. There was no remedy except for God's only Son to step into our distress and himself become man, to take upon himself the load of awful and eternal wrath and make his own body and blood a sacrifice for the sin. And so he did, out of the immeasurably great mercy and love towards us, giving himself up and bearing the sentence of unending wrath and death.

So infinitely precious to God is this sacrifice and atonement of his only begotten Son who is one with him in divinity and majesty, that God is reconciled thereby and receives into grace and forgiveness of sins all who believe in this Son. Only by believing may we enjoy the precious atonement of Christ, the forgiveness obtained for us and given us out of profound, inexpressible love. We have nothing to boast of for ourselves, but must ever joyfully thank and praise him who at such priceless cost redeemed us condemned and lost sinners.

—Martin Luther, 1483–1546

157 We sometimes employ too easily words like *grace* and *mercy*. Thomas Cranmer, Archbishop of Canterbury, puts content into such words by explaining the price of such mercy, "Christ's body and blood."

For all the good works that we can do be unperfect, and therefore not able to deserve our justification: but our justification doth come freely by the mere mercy of God, and of so great and free mercy, that, whereas all the world was not able of theirselves to pay any part towards their ransom, it pleased our heavenly Father of his infinite mercy, without any our desert or deserving, to prepare for us the most precious jewels of Christ's body and blood, whereby our ransom might be fully paid, the law fulfilled, and his justice fully satisfied. So that Christ is now the righteousness of all them that truly do believe in him. He for them paid their ransom by his death. He for them fulfilled the law in his life. So that now in him, and by him, every true Christian man may be called a fulfiller of the law; forasmuch as that which their infirmity lacked, Christ's justice hath supplied.

—Thomas Cranmer, 1489–1556

158 It is implicit in every theory of the Atonement, as the classical writers saw it, that atonement was beyond our human capacity; it must be a God-act. That reasoning is evident in John Calvin's presentation.

[I]t was especially necessary for this cause also that he who was to be our Redeemer should be truly God and man. It was his to swallow up death: who but Life could do so? It was his to conquer sin: who could do so save Righteousness itself? It was his to put to flight the powers of the air and the world: who could do so but the mighty power superior to both? But who possesses life and righteousness, and the dominion and government of heaven, but God alone? Therefore God, in his infinite mercy, having determined to redeem us, became himself our Redeemer in the person of his only-begotten Son.

Another principal part of our reconciliation with God was, that man, who had lost himself by his disobedience, should by way of remedy, oppose to it obedience, satisfy the justice of God, and pay the penalty of sin. Therefore, our Lord came forth very man, adopted the person of Adam, and assumed his name, that he might in his stead obey the Father; that he might present our flesh as the price of satisfaction to the just judgment of God, and in the same flesh pay the penalty which we had incurred. Finally, since as God only he could not suffer, and as man only could not overcome death, he united the human nature with the divine, that he might subject the weakness of the one to death as an expiation of sin, and by the power of the other, maintaining a struggle with death, might gain us the victory.

—John Calvin, 1509–1564

159 A concept as profound as the Atonement inevitably inspires a poetic response, and just as surely calls forth the language of devotion. No one has said it better than some anonymous writer from the Middle Ages, who wrote in Latin. Paul Gerhardt translated the words in 1656, and this familiar form is from James W. Alexander in 1830.

> O sacred Head, now wounded,
> with grief and shame weighed down,
> now scornfully surrounded
> with thorns, thine only crown:

how pale thou art with anguish,
with sore abuse and scorn!
How does that visage languish
which once was bright as morn!

What thou, my Lord, has suffered
was all for sinners' gain;
mine, mine was the transgression,
but thine the deadly pain.
Lo, here I fall, my Savior!
'Tis I deserve thy place;
look on me with thy favor,
vouchsafe to me thy grace.

What language shall I borrow
to thank thee, dearest friend,
for this thy dying sorrow,
thy pity without end?
O make me thine forever;
and should I fainting be,
Lord, let me never, never
outlive my love to thee.

—*Anonymous, Middle Ages*

160 Some modern writers critique Jesus' share in the Atonement in suggesting that he was a helpless victim. Scottish theologian Donald M. Baillie insists that Jesus could have escaped, but that he went into the mission "with His eyes open."

At the same time, it is important to realize, Jesus did not die as a helpless victim: He could have escaped, and He went on with His eyes open. Not only in the Galilean days, but even in Jerusalem almost up to the last, He could have steered clear of the trouble and danger by changing His course. If He had been content to give up His troublesome activities and retire into private life, the authorities would doubtless have been glad to let Him do it: indeed that was precisely what, by opposition and intimidation of various kinds, they tried to make Him do. It would have saved them a great deal of trouble. And He would have saved His life. That was the choice He had to face. But though even His own disciples would have liked Him to take a safe course—which added greatly to the stress of the choice—He could not hesitate. 'He that saveth his life shall lose it': so He had taught. He *could* have saved His own life, but it would have meant the loss of all that He had lived for. So He would not turn aside from the path that was leading Him to suffering, shame and death.

—Donald M. Baillie, 1887–1954

161 Can an idea as complicated as the Atonement be explained to children? C.S. Lewis chose to do so in one of the books from his popular "Chronicles of Narnia" series, resorting (as have most theologians) to the use of figures of speech and parable. What Lewis intended primarily for children makes the concept more accessible for adults too.

The rising of the sun had made everything look so different— all the colours and shadows were changed—that for a moment they didn't see the important thing. Then they did. The Stone Table was broken into two pieces by a great crack that ran down it from end to end; and there was no Aslan.

"Oh, oh, oh!" cried the two girls rushing back to the Table.

"Oh, it's *too* bad," sobbed Lucy; "they might have left the body alone."

"Who's done it?" cried Susan. "What does it mean? Is it more magic?" . . .

"It means," said Aslan, "that though the Witch knew the Deep Magic, there is a magic deeper still which she did not know. Her knowledge goes back only to the dawn of Time. But if she could have looked a little further back, into the stillness and the darkness before Time dawned, she would have read there a different incantation. She would have known that when a willing victim who had committed no treachery was killed in a traitor's stead, the Table would crack and Death itself would start working backwards."

—C.S. Lewis, 1898–1963

Jesus Christ: Lord

In the Christian faith, the gift of salvation waits for a response from the intended recipient, any and every member of the human race. And we intended recipients accept the gift by confessing. Confessing what? That Jesus Christ is our Lord. That phrase is a crucial one throughout the history of the church. Its significance touches upon not only the response of humans to the call of God but to the very structures of the universe. See what theologians have said, from ancient times to the present.

162 The individual believer who accepts the Lordship of Christ may think of the loss suffered by submission. Athanasius considered, rather, that with Christ's Lordship we receive an astonishing new sense of security.

And like as when a great king has entered into some large city and taken up his abode in one of the houses there, such city is at all events held worthy of high honour, nor does any enemy or bandit any longer descend upon it and subject it; but, on the contrary, it is thought entitled to all care, because of the king's having taken up his residence in a single house there: so, too, has it been with the Monarch of all. . . . For now that He has come to our realm, and taken up his abode in one body among His peers, henceforth the whole conspiracy of the enemy against mankind is checked, and the corruption of death which before was prevailing against them is done away. For the race of men had gone to ruin, had not the Lord and Saviour of all, the Son of God, come among us to meet the end of death.

—Athanasius, 296–373

163 Saint John of Damascus resorts to the language of divine conquest. By Jesus' death and resurrection, all of the powers that are antagonistic to our welfare have been brought under the power of Christ.

Every action, therefore, and performance of miracles by Christ are most great and divine and marvellous: but the most marvellous of all is His precious Cross. For no other thing has subdued death, expiated the sin of the first parent, despoiled Hades, bestowed the resurrection, granted the power to us of contemning the present and even death itself, prepared the return to our former blessedness, opened the gates of Paradise, given our nature a seat at the right hand of God, and made us the children and heirs of God, save the Cross of our Lord Jesus Christ. For by the Cross all things have been made right. *So many of us*, the apostle says, *as were baptized into Christ, were baptized into His death*, and *as many of you as have been baptized into Christ, have put on Christ*. Further, *Christ is the power of God and the wisdom of God.* Lo! the death of Christ, that is, the Cross, clothed us with the enhypostatic [subsistent] wisdom and power of God. And the power of God is the Word of the Cross, either because God's might, that is, the victory over death, has been revealed to us by it, or because, just as the four extremities of the Cross are held fast and bound together by the bolt in the middle, so also by God's power the height and the depth, the length and the breadth, that is, every creature visible and invisible, is maintained.

—John of Damascus, c. 655–c. 750

164 We are sometimes too inclined to think of the Lordship of Christ at the moment of surrender or of public commitment. Jeremy Taylor, Anglican bishop and writer, put the divine Lordship in focus by a prayer for a constant sense of Jesus as Lord.

Holy Jesus, make me to acknowledge Thee to be my Lord and Master, and myself a servant and disciple of Thy holy discipline and institution; let me love to sit at Thy feet, and suck in with my ears and heart the sweetness of Thy holy sermons. Let my soul be shod with the preparation of the gospel of peace, with a peaceable and docile disposition. Give me great boldness in the public confession of Thy name and the truth of Thy gospel, in despite of all hostilities and temptations. And grant I may always remember that Thy name is called upon me, and I may so behave myself, that I neither give scandal to others, nor cause disreputation to the honour of religion; but that Thou mayest be glorified in me, and I by Thy mercies, after a strict observance of all the holy laws of Christianity. Amen.

—Jeremy Taylor, 1613–1667

165 Perhaps more people confess their beliefs by their singing than by reciting a creed. Charles Wesley provided a structure for confessing Jesus Christ as Lord in a poem that has been sung by generations of believers around the world.

Jesus! the name high over all,
in hell or earth or sky;
angels and mortals prostrate fall,
and devils fear and fly.

Jesus! the name to sinners dear,
the name to sinners given;
it scatters all their guilty fear,
it turns their hell to heaven.

O that the world might taste and see
the riches of his grace!
The arms of love that compass me
would all the world embrace.

Thee I shall constantly proclaim,
though earth and hell oppose;
bold to confess thy glorious name
before a world of foes.

His only righteousness I show,
his saving truth proclaim:
'tis all my business here below
to cry, "Behold the Lamb!"

Happy, if with my latest breath
I may but gasp his name,
preach him to all and cry in death,
"Behold, behold the Lamb!"

—Charles Wesley, 1707–1788

166 E. Stanley Jones, missionary and writer, reminds us that the earliest Christian creed was the simple statement, "Jesus is Lord." But simple as are the words, the issue is not simple. To declare Jesus as Lord is more than a rote affirmation; it is a declaration of holy submission.

Of all the clarifications that have ever taken place in religion at any time, anywhere, the greatest and the profoundest was in the earliest Christian creed.

Someone has said that all great discoveries are reductions from complexity to simplicity. . . . But of all the reductions from complexity to simplicity the greatest and profoundest was in the earliest Christian creed: "Jesus is Lord." Three words, and yet three worlds are in them—heaven, earth, and hell.

This earliest creed is found in these words: "If you confess . . . that Jesus is Lord . . . , you will be saved" (Rom. 10:9). Again: "Every tongue [should] confess that Jesus Christ is Lord" (Phil. 2:11). And: "No one can say 'Jesus is Lord' except by the Holy Spirit" (I Cor. 12:3). But note that this was not the repetition of a creed; it was a confession—a confession of an attitude: "'Jesus is Lord' to me." It was a committal of life as well as a repeating of a creed.

How did it happen that this phrase arose out of a fiercely monotheistic people whose central confession was: "Hear, O Israel: The Lord our God is one Lord" (Deut. 6:4)? The people who had repeated, "The Lord our God is one Lord," found themselves repeating, "Jesus is Lord." Was Jesus doing something that only God could do? Was His touch upon nature and upon human nature the very touch of God? His impact upon nature and human living was so tremendous that they found their unwilling lips making the most momentous confession that ever fell from human lips anywhere at any time. It was life's central revelation. And the revelation was this: "This Man, who walked our dusty roads, slept upon our hillsides, was crucified on one of our trees, and was laid in one of our rock tombs, was at the right hand of final authority—was Lord and would have the final say in human affairs." That confession was breath-taking.

—E. Stanley Jones, 1884–1973

167 Throughout the nearly twenty centuries of church history, Christians have been compelled on numbers of occasions to confront the claims of a totalitarian state with the claims of Christ as Lord. A group of

German Christians took such a stand in Adolf Hitler's Germany in 1934 with what is known as the Barmen Declaration.

[W]e pledge ourselves to the following evangelical truths: . . .

Jesus Christ, as he is testified to us in the Holy Scripture, is the one Word of God, whom we are to hear, whom we are to trust and obey in life and in death.

We repudiate the false teaching that the church can and must recognize yet other happenings and powers, images and truths as divine revelation alongside this one Word of God, as a source of her preaching.

"But of him are ye in Christ Jesus, who of God is made unto us wisdom, and righteousness, and sanctification, and redemption." (I Cor. 1:30)

Just as Jesus Christ is the pledge of the forgiveness of all our sins, just so—and with the same earnestness—is he also God's mighty claim on our whole life; in him we encounter a joyous liberation from the godless claims of this world to free and thankful service to his creatures.

We repudiate the false teaching that there are areas of our life in which we belong not to Jesus Christ but another lord, areas in which we do not need justification and sanctification through him.

—Barmen Declaration, 1934

168 Perhaps the most visible religious leader in opposition to Hitler was Dietrich Bonhoeffer. He measured discipleship in the language of grace, decrying "cheap grace" and calling for obedience to God that might be costly, as, indeed, was his.

Cheap grace is the deadly enemy of our Church. We are fighting to-day for costly grace. . . .

. . . It is costly because it condemns sin, and grace because it justifies the sinner. Above all, it is *costly* because it cost God the life of his Son: 'ye were bought at a price', and what has cost God much cannot be cheap for us. Above all, it is *grace* because God did not reckon his Son too dear a price to pay for our life, but delivered him up for us. Costly grace is the Incarnation of God.

Costly grace is the sanctuary of God; it has to be protected from the world, and not thrown to the dogs. It is therefore the living word, the Word of God, which he speaks as it pleases him. Costly grace confronts us as a gracious call to follow Jesus, it comes as a word of forgiveness to the broken spirit and the contrite heart. Grace is costly because it compels a man to submit to the yoke of Christ and follow him; it is grace because Jesus says: 'My yoke is easy and my burden is light.'

—Dietrich Bonhoeffer, 1906–1945

169 How is it, however, that the church should declare Jesus Christ as Lord? On what basis is Jesus given such a demanding title? Karl Barth reminds us that Jesus is Lord because he is God. Without divinity, no such claim could honorably be made.

Jesus Christ is Himself God as the Son of God the Father and with God the Father the source of the Holy Spirit, united in one essence with the Father by the Holy Spirit. That is how He is God. He is God as He takes part in the event which constitutes the divine being.

We must add at once that as this One who takes part in the divine being and event He became and is man. This means that we have to understand the very Godhead, that divine being and event and therefore Himself as the One who takes part in it, in the light of the fact that it pleased God—and this is what corresponds outwardly to and reveals the inward divine being and event—Himself to become man. In this way, in this condescension, He is the eternal Son of the eternal Father. This is the will of this Father, of this Son, and of the Holy Spirit who is the Spirit of the Father and the Son. This is how God is God, this is His freedom, this is His distinctness from and superiority to all other reality. It is with this meaning and purpose that He is the Creator and Lord of all things.

—Karl Barth, 1886–1968

170 Karl Barth warned against treating God as an abstraction. He insisted on returning to the crucial word that has always marked the demanding side of the gospel, *Lord,* and with that title, *your,* to be sure that the Lordship is not lost in generality.

'You shall remember the *Lord, your* God!' We are not asked to remember God in general. We are in constant temptation to think of some abstraction when we pronounce or hear the word 'God'....

The *Lord, your* God is a God with a name, a face, a personality. His name, face and personality assure us that he is indeed stern, yet good and faithful, a God whom we used to call as children, and still may call today, a 'dear' God. He is a God who can dispense with, and dispenses us from, the human attempt to form an opinion or elaborate a theory about him. He is indeed the God who has told us long ago and tells us time and again how and what *we shall think of him.* Strangely enough, he does so by revealing what *he thinks of us.* . . . He thinks so highly of us because he is deeply moved by our need of him, our bitter, inescapable need. Is his perhaps the casualness and condescension of a great ruler, occasionally bending down to the man in the street? Not in the least. He takes our place and surrenders himself for us, thereby binding himself to us and compromising himself with us once for all. He is the God of Christmas of whom we sing:

> A tiny child and poor he came
> To give us mercy's blessing.

This is the height and the depth, the ultimate and eternal power and glory of the almighty *Lord*: he has mercy on us. Having mercy on you and on me, he is *your* God and *my* God. Because he is compassionate, it is not particularly difficult, but the most natural thing in the world to believe in him, to hope for him and to love him, and to love our neighbour accordingly. It is he, *this* God who gives you power.

—*Karl Barth, 1886–1968*

171 Our human vision of a lord is one who, to put it in verb form, "lords it over us." The Scriptures give a new definition of the term as Jesus refers to himself as one who came to serve, and particularly as he humbled himself to the task of footwashing. Roman Catholic theologian Edward Schillebeeckx speaks to this insight.

The earliest interpretation [of the footwashing in John's Gospel] is that Jesus gave a model to his disciples: in the Christian community there are not to be any master-slave relationships. . . .

. . . Jesus, recognized by his followers as Lord, was nevertheless doing slave's work. He wants his coming death to be interpreted as his last and greatest work: the service of a spiritual, exalted Lord and Master to earthly men. The footwashing is to prepare the disciples to see that Jesus' coming death is not a fiasco, but a work of liberation, because it reverses all values, even those which are established in society. Just as we heard in the Gospel of John on Palm Sunday that Jesus allowed himself to be hailed as king ... so John wants to impress on us with the footwashing that this man executed on the cross is the true Kyrios, emperor or Lord, the one who is truly great, and not the Roman emperor in whose name Pilate had him crucified. True greatness, royal and human, the greatness of a Son of man, is at the same time both concealed and made manifest in the performing of 'a work': the work of a slave, an action which overthrows all accepted relationships.

—Edward Schillebeeckx, 1914—

172 The New Testament Scriptures, especially in the Gospel of John and in the epistles of Philippians, Ephesians, Colossians, and Hebrews, emphasize the Lordship of Christ over all creation. Gerald O'Collins, a contemporary theologian, declares that emphasis for us.

Christ is understood to share God's lordship over all created beings 'in heaven and on earth or under the earth' (Phil. 2:10). In particular, Christ's lordship makes him sovereign over all angelic beings in heaven (Col. 1:16-17; 2:8-10; I Pet. 3:22). Over and over again the two opening chapters of Hebrews (Heb. 1:1–2:16) insist that Christ is superior to the angels. Unlike them he 'bears the very stamp' of God's nature, upholds 'the universe by his word of power' (Heb. 1:3), and has 'the world to come' subject to him (Heb. 2:5). No wonder then that the angels also bow down before Christ in worship (Rev. 5:11-14). As divine Lord, Christ merits the adoration of all.

—Gerald O'Collins, 20th century

Faith

The concepts that are most difficult to define (and thus to act upon) are those that come to us in familiar words. Having spoken the words, we are likely to think we have grasped the concept. Such is the case with faith. We use the word so easily that we may fail to think what it means. But the word is central to so many other aspects of believing that we need to know how theologians have discussed and defined it over the centuries.

173 Cyril of Jerusalem develops his theology of faith on the basis of the Scriptures. But his explanation also reflects his philosophical insight, as he seeks to break faith into categories of understanding.

For the name of Faith ... has two distinct senses. For there is one kind of faith, the dogmatic, involving an assent of the soul on some particular point: and it is profitable to the soul. . . .

But there is a second kind of faith, which is bestowed by Christ as a gift of grace. *For to one is given through the Spirit the word of wisdom, and to another the word of knowledge according to the same Spirit: to another faith, by the same Spirit, and to another gifts of healing.* This faith then which is given of grace from the Spirit is not merely doctrinal, but also worketh things above man's power. For whosoever hath this faith, *shall say to this mountain, Remove hence to yonder place, and it shall remove.* For whenever any one shall say this in faith, *believing that it cometh to pass, and shall not doubt in his heart,* then receiveth he the grace.

And of this faith it is said, *If ye have faith as a grain of mustard seed.* For just as the grain of mustard seed is small in size, but fiery in its operation, and though sown in a small space has a circle of great branches, and when grown up is able even to shelter the fowls; so, likewise, faith in the swiftest moment works the greatest effects in the soul. . . . Have thou therefore that faith in Him which cometh from thine own self, that thou mayest also receive from Him that faith which worketh things above man.

—Cyril of Jerusalem, 314–386

174 One of Martin Luther's great gifts was his ability to put great concepts of the faith into simple, vigorous language. His explanation of faith both clarifies and inspires, as he wrestles with the relationship between faith and works.

Faith is not the human idea and feeling that some people call faith. People hear and speak a lot about faith. Yet when they see someone whose life is not improving and who performs few good wishes, they are apt to say quite erroneously: "Faith is not enough; a person must do good works in order to be righteous and be saved." They make this error because, when they hear the gospel, they work hard to generate within themselves a mental state in which they can say, "I believe." And they take this to be true faith.

But this kind of belief is a human attitude which can never reach the depths of the heart; so nothing comes of it, and it leads to no improvement of life. True faith is a divine work, by which we are born anew. It kills the old self, and transforms us in heart, soul, mind, and faculties; and it brings with it the Holy Spirit. This faith is a living, busy, active, and powerful thing. It expresses itself constantly in good works.

It does not stop to ask whether good works have to be done; before there is time even to ask the question, it has already performed the good works. Those who do not do good works show that they do not have faith. . . .

Faith is a vibrant and courageous confidence in God's grace. It is so sure and certain that believers would stake their lives on God's grace a thousand times. This confidence makes people joyful, bold, and happy in their relationship with God and with other people.

—Martin Luther, 1483–1546

175 The Bible says simply that faith is the substance of things hoped for, the evidence of things not seen. It remains for the philosophers and theologians to draw distinctions between faith and knowledge, and to show the relationship between the two. John Calvin works to such an end.

We shall now have a full definition of faith if we say that it is a firm and sure knowledge of the divine favour toward us, founded on the truth of a free promise in Christ, and revealed to our minds, and sealed on our hearts, by the Holy Spirit.

... By knowledge we do not mean comprehension, such as that which we have of things falling under human sense. For that knowledge is so much superior, that the human mind must far surpass and go beyond itself in order to reach it. Nor even when it has reached it does it comprehend what it feels, but persuaded of what it comprehends not, it understands more from mere certainty of persuasion than it could discern of any human matter by its own capacity....

We add that it is *sure and firm*, the better to express strength and constancy of persuasion. For as faith is not contented with a dubious and fickle opinion, so neither is it contented with an obscure and ill-defined conception. The certainty which it requires must be full and decisive, as is usual in regard to matters ascertained and proved....

The principal hinge on which faith turns is this: We must not suppose that any promises of mercy which the Lord offers are only true out of us, and not at all in us: we should rather make them ours by inwardly embracing them.

—*John Calvin, 1509–1564*

176 The issue is not simply believing, because we humans are always seeking something to believe; it is believing in God, through Jesus Christ. This is an acknowledgment of our trust in God's mercy, as John Calvin explains.

Free promise we make the foundation of faith, because in it faith properly consists. For though it holds that God is always true, whether in ordering or forbidding, promising or threatening; though it obediently receive his commands, observe his prohibitions, and give heed to his threatenings; yet it properly begins with promise, continues with it, and ends with it. It seeks life in God, life which is not found in commands or the denunciations of punishment, but in the promise of mercy. And this promise must be gratuitous; ... Therefore, when we say, that faith must rest on a free promise, we deny not that believers accept and embrace the word of God in all its parts, but we point to the promise of mercy as its special object. ... We only mean to maintain these two points,— that faith is never decided until it attain to a free promise; and that the only way in which faith reconciles us to God is by uniting us with Christ. Both are deserving of notice. We are inquiring after a faith which separates the children of God from the reprobate, believers from unbelievers. Shall every man, then, who believes that God is just in what he commands, and true in what he threatens, be on that account classed with believers? Very far from it. Faith, then, has no firm footing until it stand in the mercy of God.

—*John Calvin, 1509–1564*

177 The crucial issue of faith as we experience it is in the faith that produces salvation. In most cases, we exercise such faith without analyzing how it is happening. But John Wesley deals with questions that may well arise for those who are more analytical.

Faith in general is defined by the Apostle, ... 'an evidence', a divine 'evidence and conviction' (the word means both), 'of things not seen'—not visible, not perceivable either by sight or by any other of the external senses. It implies both a supernatural *evidence* of God and of the things of God, a kind of spiritual *light* exhibited to the soul, and a supernatural *sight* or perception thereof. Accordingly the Scripture speaks sometimes of God's giving light, sometimes a power of discerning it. So St. Paul: 'God, who commanded light to shine out of darkness, hath shined in our hearts, to give us the light of the knowledge of the glory of God in the face of Jesus Christ.' And elsewhere the same Apostle speaks 'of the eyes of' our 'understanding being opened'. By this twofold operation of the Holy Spirit—having the eyes of our soul both *opened* and *enlightened*—we see the things which the natural 'eye hath not seen, neither the ear heard'. We have a prospect of the invisible things of God. We see the *spiritual world*, which is all round about us, and yet no more discerned by our natural faculties than if it had no being; and we see the *eternal world*, piercing through the veil which hangs between time and eternity. Clouds and darkness then rest upon it no more, but we already see the glory which shall be revealed.

Taking the word in a more particular sense, faith is a divine evidence and conviction, not only that 'God was in Christ, reconciling the world unto himself', but also that Christ 'loved *me*, and gave himself for *me*'.

—*John Wesley, 1703–1791*

178 Discussions of faith so often see faith and reason as being at odds with each other. Trappist monk Thomas Merton insists that this ought not to be so. To do so is to remove faith from the world of issues and importance.

This issue is generally misunderstood, because faith has so often been proposed as alien to reason and even as contrary to it. . . . But if faith has no intellectual reference whatever, it is hardly possible to see how "having faith" can contribute much to your outlook on life or to your behavior. It does not seem to be much more important than having red hair or a wooden leg. It is just something that happened to you, but did not happen to your next-door neighbor.

This false idea of faith . . . barricades itself in the attic, and leaves the rest of the house to reason. Actually, faith and reason are meant to get along happily together. They were not meant to live alone, in divorce or in separation.

—*Thomas Merton, 1915–1968*

179 How does a philosopher discuss faith? Paul Tillich, both philosopher and theologian, places faith in a context of deadly seriousness. In doing so, he reminds us of the courage that faith demands.

An act of faith is an act of a finite being who is grasped by and turned to the infinite. It is a finite act with all the limitations of a finite act, and it is an act in which the infinite participates beyond the limitations of a finite act. Faith is certain in so far as it is an experience of the holy. But faith is uncertain in so far as the infinite to which it is related is received by a finite being. This element of uncertainty in faith cannot be removed, it must be accepted. And the element in faith which accepts this is courage. Faith includes an element of immediate awareness which gives certainty and an element of uncertainty. To accept this is courage. In the courageous standing of uncertainty, faith shows most visibly its dynamic character.

... Where there is daring and courage there is the possibility of failure. And in every act of faith this possibility is present. The risk must be taken. ... The risk to faith in one's ultimate concern is indeed the greatest risk man can run. For if it proves to be a failure, the meaning of one's life breaks down; one surrenders oneself, including truth and justice, to something which is not worth it.

—*Paul Tillich, 1886–1965*

180 H. Richard Niebuhr reminds us that some form of faith is essential to the daily business of living. Thus it is not a matter of whether we will have faith, but of where we will invest it.

Now it is evident, when we inquire into ourselves and into our common life, that without such active faith or such reliance and confidence on power we do not and cannot live. Not only the just but also the unjust, insofar as they live, live by faith. We live by knowledge also, it is true, but not by knowledge without faith. In order to know we must always rely on something we do not know; in order to walk by sight we need to rely on what we do not see. The most evident example of that truth is to be found in science, which conducts its massive campaign against obscurity and error on the basis of a great faith in the intelligibility of things; when it does not know and finds hindrances in the path of knowledge, it asserts with stubborn faith that knowledge nevertheless is possible, that there is pattern and intelligibility in the things which are not yet intelligible. Such faith is validated in practice, yet it evermore outruns practice. Our social life, also, proceeds from moment to moment on the ground of a confidence we have in each other which is distinct from our belief in each other's existence and distinct also from our knowledge of each other's character, though such belief and such knowledge do form the background and the foreground of our faith. How much we live by faith in this area becomes apparent to us when we are deceived or betrayed by those on whom we have relied. When treaties are broken, when bankers embezzle, when marriage partners become disloyal, when friends betray, then doubt of all things invades our minds and we understand how much we have lived by reliance on our fellow men. But we also discover that without some confidence which goes beyond our knowledge we cannot exist at all since we are social persons who cannot live in isolation, and that we are ignorant persons who must in all their living go far beyond their knowledge of each other if they would live at all.

When we inquire into this element of faith or confidence in our life as human beings we become aware of one aspect of it which may above all else be called religious, because it is related to our existence as worshiping beings, even as our faith in the intelligibility of nature is related to our existence as knowing beings and our confidence in each other is related to our moral life. This is the faith that life is worth living, or better, the reliance on certain centers of value as able to bestow significance and worth on our existence. It is a curious and inescapable fact about our lives, of which I think we all become aware at some time or another, that we cannot live without a cause, without some object of devotion, some center of worth, something on which we rely for our meaning. In this sense all men have faith because they are men and cannot help themselves, just as they must and do have some knowledge of their world, though their knowledge be erroneous.

. . . For no man lives without living for some purpose, for the glorification of some god, for the advancement of some cause. If we do not wish to call this faith religion, there is no need to contend about the word. Let us say then that our problem is the problem of faith rather than of religion.

Now to have faith and to have a god is one and the same thing, as it is one and the same thing to have knowledge and an object of knowledge. When we believe that life is worth living by the same act we refer to some being which makes our life worth living. We never merely believe that life is worth living, but always think of it as made worth living by something on which we rely. And this being, whatever it be, is properly termed our god.

—H. Richard Niebuhr, 1894–1962

181 We receive God's grace more easily when we can perceive it more clearly. This is part of the power of the sacraments, as Donald Baillie explains. Through the sacraments, grace is made visible, and faith has a means of taking hold of it.

We cannot create our faith in God, we cannot make ourselves trust in Him. Our faith must be His gift. . . .

God works faith in our hearts. He bestows on us the gift of faith, by winning us, gaining our confidence, not forcing it. His graciousness overcomes our mistrust, His grace creates our faith, so that when we come to Him, it is really our faith, and we come willingly. In order to bring about this end He uses means—words, smiles, gestures, symbolic gifts, which we call sacraments. . . . All such are 'means of grace', methods employed by the graciousness of God to express and develop a gracious personal relationship between Him and us.

—Donald M. Baillie, 1887–1954

182 Because faith, in what might be called its secular form, is so much a part of everyday life, we do well to draw upon such instances of faith in seeking to understand faith in its more spiritual forms. This is the mood of Georgia Harkness in her definition of faith.

Faith, then, does not mean belief without any basis, or intellectual assent to certain ideas, or a leap from solid footing into a chasm of mystery. But what does it mean?

It means, first, *positive trust* in somebody or something, the willingness to commend one's life to another's keeping or to act on some conviction believed to be true. The familiar definition, "Faith is *assurance* of things hoped for, a *conviction* of things not seen," brings out this meaning. . . .

Some analogies on the human level will make clearer what religious faith entails. One does not eat his dinner or lie down on his bed at night without faith that the food will nourish and not poison him, that the bed will support and not suffocate him. One does not usually go to a doctor unless he has faith that the doctor will help him get well. One does not—or ought not—to marry without faith that the other person will co-operate to form a home. In all these instances suspicion can undermine faith, and it ought to undermine it if there are valid grounds for mistrust. Otherwise one is credulous rather than trusting. But if we distrust where we ought to have faith, we not only make ourselves and others unhappy but we cut ourselves off from bodily health and enrichment of spirit. Life could not go on fruitfully without a large-scale exercise of faith in our everyday social relations.

—Georgia Harkness, 1891–1974

183 While the basic quality of faith remains the same generation after generation, the style of description has changed from time to time. So too different generations have given more or less importance to the role of faith. Educator and minister John Dillenberger considers several varying definitions.

In Christian theology, the term "faith" refers to the dynamic and vital stance of the believer's dependence on God. Hence, the term touches the center of Christian life and thought. Naturally, then, expressions such as "the Christian faith" or the "faith of the Church" are used synonymously with that of "faith." But in order to give form to that which is so central and has implications for all facets of life and thought, first it is necessary to provide a succinct definition of faith and then to characterize its relation to other facets of Christian experience.

Fundamentally, faith is a living confidence and trust in God in the experience of knowing God's gracious presence as manifest in Christ. That which has become known has the character of a gift, namely, a reality that one would not have unearthed by oneself but that has come to be present as a sort of miracle, a happening that encompasses but does not seem to be dependent either on one's seeking or on fleeing the divine.

The gift of faith has been variously defined. In the orthodox theologies of the seventeenth century, faith was affirmed by emphasizing the initiative of God apart from the reception of God; that is, God was the all-determining One, and a person's appropriation of God's initiative was secondary. In Protestant liberalism and sometimes in Pietist traditions, the other side of the equation was emphasized. In contrast to faith as a gift, liberals emphasized faith as an individual act of will or as a decision of moral reason. Roman Catholicism, in a more mediational vein, defined faith as the ability to accept the grace or gift by which one is redeemed.

—*John Dillenberger, 1918–*

The Message Behind the Symbols

Holy Spirit: God Present
Holy Spirit: Empowering ♦ The Trinity

The dove as a symbol of the Holy Spirit arises out of John's account of the baptism of Jesus, "I saw the Spirit descending from heaven like a dove" (John 1:32). The descending dove with its three-rayed nimbus symbolizes God's anointing and abiding presence. Closely related to the dove as a symbol of the Holy Spirit is the columbine, which takes its name from the Latin word for dove, *columba*. And the shape of the inverted flower resembles a cluster of doves.

The flame is a symbol of Holy Spirit power and illumination. Divided tongues of fire represent the coming of the Holy Spirit at Pentecost according to the promise of Christ (Acts 1:8).

Equality, unity, and continuity characterize the various symbols of the Trinity: the simple triangle with its three separate but equal sides, symbolizing one God, three Persons; the Triquetra with three arcs representing equality of Father, Son, and Holy Spirit, and interweaving and continuously flowing lines depicting unity and eternity. And finally, a single stem and a leaf of three parts—the mystery of the Trinity in the common shamrock.

Holy Spirit: God Present

The Holy Spirit is the most intimate member of the Trinity, the One promised to dwell in us, yet the One most difficult for us to understand. Pastors sometimes recognize this difficulty simply by avoiding the subject in their preaching. Meanwhile, it has been the work of theologians to clarify teaching on this crucial subject. By doing so, they may help believers experience more of the reality of the Holy Spirit in their lives.

184 When we trace the work of the Holy Spirit through instances in the Old Testament, we can't help but be astonished by the variety of ways in which the Spirit is at work. Basil the Great, Bishop of Caesarea, makes this same point in devout and poetic language.

Through His aid hearts are lifted up, the weak are held by the hand, and they who are advancing are brought to perfection. Shining upon those that are cleansed from every spot, He makes them spiritual by fellowship with Himself. Just as when a sunbeam falls on bright and transparent bodies, they themselves become brilliant too, and shed forth a fresh brightness from themselves, so souls wherein the Spirit dwells, illuminated by the Spirit, themselves become spiritual, and send forth their grace to others. Hence comes foreknowledge of the future, understanding of mysteries, apprehension of what is hidden, distribution of good gifts, the heavenly citizenship, a place in the chorus of angels, joy without end, abiding in God, the being made like to God, and, highest of all, the being made God. Such, then, to instance a few out of many, are the conceptions concerning the Holy Spirit, which we have been taught to hold concerning His greatness, His dignity, and His operations, by the oracles of the Spirit themselves.

—Basil the Great, 330–379

185 Jesus promised his disciples that when the Spirit came to them in fullness, they would enjoy a fuller revelation of himself. This is the point of John Calvin's emphasis.

[S]o long as we are without Christ and separated from him, nothing which he suffered and did for the salvation of the human race is of the least benefit to us. To communicate to us the blessings which he received from the Father, he must become ours and dwell in us. . . . it is true that we obtain this by faith, yet since we see that all do not indiscriminately embrace the offer of Christ which is made by the gospel, the very nature of the case teaches us to ascend higher, and inquire into the secret efficacy of the Spirit, to which it is owing that we enjoy Christ and all his blessings. . . . It is not without cause that the testimony of the Spirit is twice mentioned, a testimony which is engraven on our hearts by way of a seal, and thus seals the cleansing and sacrifice of Christ. . . . The whole comes to this, that the Holy Spirit is the bond by which Christ effectually binds us to himself.

—John Calvin, 1509–1564

186 To speak of the Holy Spirit is, of course, to speak of religious experiences. But such experiences are often so personal and so subjective that it is difficult to get to those matters that have more general, universal significance. John Wesley sought more distinct definitions.

But what is that testimony of God's Spirit which is superadded to and conjoined with this? How does he 'bear witness with our spirit that we are the children of God'? It is hard to find words in the language of men to explain 'the deep things of God'. Indeed there are none that will adequately express what the children of God experience. But perhaps one might say (desiring any who are taught of God to correct, to soften or strengthen the expression), the testimony of the Spirit is an inward impression on the soul, whereby the Spirit of God directly 'witnesses to my spirit that I am a child of God'; that Jesus Christ hath loved me, and given himself for me; that all my sins are blotted out, and I, even I, am reconciled to God.

—John Wesley, 1703–1791

187 The work of the Holy Spirit is nothing if not practical. We see this in so many of the Old Testament accounts, and in the giftedness that marked the early church. Albert Outler brings this concept into the present time.

[F]or historical Christianity, the plainest meaning of the Holy Spirit's 'office' is: God at work in the living present revealing to us the meaning of the Christian past, centered as it is in God's Self-revelation in Jesus Christ. In this representation, the Spirit gives meaning to *that* revelation in the life of the church *today*. The work of the Holy Spirit is to bring men up to date; to make them contemporary witnesses; to transform Christian history into personal faith. It is the Spirit who performs the *actus tradendi* [passing on of the tradition], and so makes Christ our contemporary. This was Jesus' promise of the Paraclete: 'When the Paraclete comes, whom I shall send to you from the Father, even the Spirit of truth, who proceeds from the Father, *He will bear witness to me* (John 15:26) ... He will glorify me, for He will take what is mine and declare it to you' (16:14—but see also 14:16-19; 14:25-29; 15:26–16:1; 16:7-15). And the stretching out of history's time-span, far beyond any expectation in the early church, has not reduced the power of the Spirit to make faith spring forth from the soil of Christian memory. The *medium* of the Holy Spirit's action is—*history!*

—Albert C. Outler, 1908–1989

188 Because the Holy Spirit is difficult to define, Christian preaching and teaching have sometimes tended unconsciously to minimize the Spirit or to make the Spirit something less than God. Karl Barth speaks emphatically to this issue.

[W]hen we speak of the Holy Ghost in the same way as prophets and apostles have done, we are speaking in the same emphatic and complete sense of *God Himself* as when we speak of Jesus Christ. The first centuries after the Apostolic age were longer in reaching clarity about this than in regard to the divinity of Christ.... But the Nicaeno-Constantinopolitan Creed rightly calls Him the "Lord-Spirit" ... Who proceeds from the Father and the Son, Who with the Father and the Son together is worshipped and glorified. That is to say: the Holy Spirit of adoption, of revelation and of witness, the Holy Spirit Who makes us free for the Word of God, is *eternal* Spirit in the same way as the Father is *eternal* Father and as the Son is *eternal* Son. He is of one substance with Father and Son and therefore with Them the one true God, Creator, Reconciler and Redeemer.

—*Karl Barth, 1886–1968*

189 Georgia Harkness helps us see the unique role of the Holy Spirit as the member of the Godhead most accessible to us. Here is a blessed tension of our faith, that God is utterly God and therefore altogether beyond us, yet immediately near to us through the Holy Spirit.

Let us remember that the Holy Spirit means God present with us, God acting for us. Christians believe that God is a majestic Being far above us, and this aspect of God's nature is called the transcendence of God. Yet Christians also believe that God is a loving personal Spirit, concerned about us, very close to us. The belief in the Holy Spirit emphasizes this divine nearness and personal concern, and is the basis of Christian prayer. God as Holy Spirit speaks to us in the deep places of our own spirits, and we can respond to him by our thoughts and lives. We also can speak to him in prayer and feel assured that he hears, and gives to us companionship, guidance, and strength. . . .

Furthermore, the Holy Spirit gives us guidance, with light upon the decisions we must make. The Holy Spirit will not automatically settle our problems for us, for God expects us to use our minds and the best judgment possible about the situation. Yet the Holy Spirit will help us to discover what Paul called "the mind of Christ," that is, the spirit and attitudes of Jesus. . . .

Again, the Holy Spirit supplies strength for daily living. Whether it is in the great crises of life, when sorrow and trouble seem too much to bear in our own human strength, or in the many petty strains that keep us feeling weak and frustrated, the Holy Spirit approached in prayer gives new confidence and strength. The Holy Spirit, coming from God through Christ, forgives the penitent sinner and sets him forward in the way of better and stronger living. What is sometimes called "the witness of the Spirit" gives assurance in the soul that one has been forgiven and accepted by God, and then one can live with an inner peace and a greater strength than would otherwise be possible.

—Georgia Harkness, 1891–1974

190 For those who grasp the work of the Spirit as described in the Old and New Testaments, the Holy Spirit is indeed a source of comfort and power. Theologian Walter Kasper clarifies some of these possibilities.

[T]he Holy Spirit is in a special way a source in the order of grace. He is at work everywhere that human beings seek and find friendship with God. A loving union with God is possible for us only through the Holy Spirit. Through the Spirit we are in God and God is in us. Through him we are God's friends, sons and daughters, who, because we are impelled from within, serve God not as slaves but as free beings and who are filled with joy and consolation by this friendship with God. The grace of the Holy Spirit, which is given through faith in Jesus Christ, is thus ... the law of the new covenant. This law is a law written in the heart, as interior law that moves us from within, and therefore a law of freedom.

... [W]hat has been said of the Spirit has consequences for the understanding of the church. If the Spirit is the authentic presence and realization of the salvation given through Jesus Christ, then whatever is external in the church—scripture and sacraments, offices and certainly the discipline of the church—has for its sole task to prepare men for receiving the gift of the Spirit, to serve in the transmission of this gift, and to enable it to work effectively. This means that the reign of Christ extends beyond and embraces more than the visible church. Wherever there is love, the Spirit of God is at work, and the reign of Christ becomes a reality even without institutional forms and formulas.

—Walter Kasper, 20th century

Holy Spirit: Empowering

J esus made strong claims for the difference the Holy Spirit would make in the lives of his followers. To the point, in fact, of telling his disciples that they would be better off with his going, because then they could receive the full power of the Spirit. So how is it that the Spirit works, and what evidence do we have of the work of the Holy Spirit in our day? A variety of theologians will give us some answers.

191 In a sense, the early church was more in danger of heresy than is the church today, simply because of the difficulties of communication between the leaders and the congregations; after all, news could travel no faster than persons could carry it. Irenaeus emphasized that the Holy Spirit is in the Church, empowering it and keeping it pure.

[T]he preaching of the Church is everywhere consistent, and continues in an even course, and receives testimony from the prophets, the apostles, and all the disciples . . . through [those in] the beginning, the middle, and the end, and through the entire dispensation of God, and that well-grounded system which tends to man's salvation, namely, our faith; which, having been received from the Church, we do preserve, and which always, by the Spirit of God, renewing its youth, as if it were some precious deposit in an excellent vessel, causes the vessel itself containing it to renew its youth also. For this gift of God has been entrusted to the Church, as breath was to the first created man, for this purpose, that all the members receiving it may be vivified; and the [means of] communion with Christ has been distributed throughout it, that is, the Holy Spirit, the earnest of incorruption, the means of confirming our faith, and the ladder of ascent to God. "For in the Church," it is said, "God hath set apostles, prophets, teachers," and all the other means through which the Spirit works; of which all those are not partakers who do not join themselves to the Church, but defraud themselves of life through their perverse opinions and infamous behaviour. For where the Church is, there is the Spirit of God; and where the Spirit of God is, there is the Church, and every kind of grace; but the Spirit is truth.

—*Irenaeus, c. 130–c. 200*

192 The twentieth century was a period of much striving toward church unity. But such a quest has existed in the church through the centuries, as indicated by this reading from Cyril of Alexandria in the early fifth century. Cyril emphasizes, however, that true unity can be achieved only through the Holy Spirit.

All of us who have received the one and the same Spirit, that is, the Holy Spirit, are in a sense merged together with one another and with God. For if Christ, together with the Spirit of the Father and himself, comes to dwell in each one of us, even though there are many of us, then it follows that the Spirit is still one and undivided. He binds together the spirit of each and every one of us . . . and makes us all appear as one in him. For just as the power of the holy flesh of Christ unites those in whom it dwells into one body, I think that, in much the same way, the one and undivided Spirit of God, who dwells in us all, leads us all into spiritual unity.

—*Cyril of Alexandria, died 444*

193 The New Testament makes clear that every believer can enjoy the work of the Holy Spirit. This insight has proved especially true during times of spiritual renewal. John Wesley makes this point in a letter to an eighteenth-century believer, Mary Cooke.

There is an irreconcilable variability in the operations of the Holy Spirit on the souls of men, more especially as to the manner of justification. Many find Him rushing upon them like a torrent, while they experience

The o'erwhelming power of saving grace.
This has been the experience of many; perhaps of more in this late visitation than in any other age since the times of the Apostles. But in others He works in a very different way:

He deigns His influence to infuse,
Sweet, refreshing, as the silent dews.

It has pleased Him to work the latter way in you from the beginning; and it is not improbable He will continue (as He has begun) to work in a gentle and almost insensible manner. Let Him take His own way: He is wiser than you; He will do all things well. Do not reason against Him; but let the prayer of your heart be,

Mould as Thou wilt Thy passive clay!

—*John Wesley, 1703–1791*

194 Both the Hebrew and Greek languages—the original languages of the Old and New Testaments respectively—use the same word for spirit, wind, and breath. Edwin Hatch, Anglican minister and lecturer at Oxford, addresses the Holy Spirit as the "Breath of God" in a prayer-hymn that portrays the transforming power of the Spirit in the life of believers.

Breathe on me, Breath of God,
fill me with life anew,
that I may love what thou dost love,
and do what thou wouldst do.

Breathe on me, Breath of God,
until my heart is pure,
until with thee I will one will,
to do and to endure.

Breathe on me, Breath of God,
till I am wholly thine,
till all this earthly part of me
glows with thy fire divine.

Breathe on me, Breath of God,
so shall I never die,
but live with thee the perfect life
of thine eternity.

—*Edwin Hatch, 1835–1889*

195 Early church councils, and numbers of theologians since, have tried to distinguish between the role of Jesus Christ and the role of the Holy Spirit. The New Testament writings seem plain enough, but individual instances call for more understanding. This is the quest of contemporary theologian Lewis Smedes as he relates the power of Christ and the power of the Spirit.

The gospel is power, but the power is experienced through the Spirit. "Does he who supplies the Spirit to you and works miracles among you do so by works of the law, or by hearing [the gospel] with faith?" (3:5). The power to live a new life, oriented around Jesus Christ, carried on within the new order of the Lord—this is the power of the Spirit at work. The epistle to the Galatians is full of this. God has put His "Spirit into our hearts" (Gal. 4:6) to move and lead us into the new life. By the Spirit, we have real hope for gaining personal righteousness (5:5). Led by the Spirit, we are liberated from the law's indictment against us (5:18). By the work of the Spirit we begin to demonstrate as our own the very characteristics of Jesus (5:22) and so "fulfill the law of Christ" (6:2). Living by the Spirit, we live forever (6:7), for Christ has become the life-giving Spirit. Once again, the Spirit is here, working in power to effect within us the style of the new order in Christ.

—*Lewis B. Smedes, 20th century*

196 When one reads the Old Testament ritual of empowerment for priests, prophets, and rulers, an anointing with oil was included—what would be known in later times as a *charism,* or gift. This Greek word is also the base for the word *charismatic,* a term often used in our day to describe churches that emphasize the gifts of the Spirit. The following reading from the Faith and Order Commission of the World Council of Churches explains some of these connections.

Through the proclamation of the Gospel and the celebration of the sacraments the Holy Spirit is creating and sustaining the faith of God's people. The Spirit pours out an abundance of *charisms.* These charisms are for the building-up of the Church and for service in the world, through teaching, prophecy, healing, miracles, tongues and the discernment of spirits (1 Cor. 12:4-11, 27-30). Since all these gifts are given to individuals for the common good (1 Cor. 12:7) when rightly employed they serve to strengthen the unity of the one body to which we are called in the one baptism (Eph. 4:4-5). . . .

There is broad agreement that the gift of the Spirit is inseparable from faith and baptism. However, some churches specifically associate the gift of charism with the sacrament of chrism [anointing]. Other churches, groups and movements understand the gift of the Spirit to be a separate and distinct work of grace. Hence they look for signs of this gift in special charisms such as speaking in tongues or healing, as the Spirit "completes" the blessing received from God. Although the churches are not yet one in their understanding of the relation of the Spirit's gifts to baptism, all believe that the gifts of the Spirit must not become occasions for church disunity, but are given for the common good of the Church.

—World Council of Churches, 1963–1993

197 Spirit, breath, wind—what is the significance of the interchangeability of these words in both the Old and New Testaments? J. Deotis Roberts, contemporary theologian, explains.

We begin with the etymology of the word "spirit." The Hebrew *ruach,* the Greek *pneuma,* and the Latin *animus* refer to the movement of air. These words are often translated as "wind," "storm," or "breeze." Since the movement of the air may be caused by "breath," the metaphorical meaning shifts from "breath" to the "principle of life" or "vitality." Human beings and animals have *ruach,* but God preeminently has *ruach.* God is a breathing, living, and acting God. In creation, God bestows *ruach* upon the creatures. Human beings receive God's *ruach* to the highest degree— human life results from the breathing of God. Wherever God acts, *ruach* is at work. God's action as the presence and power of *ruach* is prevalent in the Old Testament.

The Greek New Testament continues the same basic meaning of Spirit. *Pneuma* is the sign of human vitality. Greek has two words for the human spirit: *nous,* which refers to "mind" or "intellect," and *pneuma,* which points to the dynamic principle of life. John writes, "The spirit blows (*pneuma pnei*) where it wills . . . ; so it is with every one who is born of the Spirit (*pneumatos*)" (John 3:8).

In sum, we may assert the following: Spirit means that God is a vital, acting God. God grants life and vitality to creation. The human *ruach/pneuma* is God's inspiring breath by which life is given in creation and re-creation. God is in action in human life. The *pneuma* of a human being is his or her *dynamis*—person in action. The *pneuma* of God is God acting in creation, providence, and redemption.

—J. Deotis Roberts, 1927–

198 When the Old Testament prophet Joel promised that the Spirit would fall on all flesh, he introduced the idea of a democracy of the Holy Spirit—that the Spirit would someday be available to all persons, not simply to those with special roles of leadership. Theologian Michael Welker discusses how this is significant in our time.

The Spirit is poured out on "all flesh." According to Joel, this occurs in diverse concretion: men and women, old and young, male and female slaves are touched by the pouring out of the Spirit. Today what initially jumps out at us is the repeatedly emphasized granting of equal status to women and men—in contrast to many other biblical traditions. Hans Walter Wolff has called attention to the fact that the reference in Joel to the pouring out of the Spirit "on all flesh" highlights in general "the weak, the powerless and the hopeless" as "recipients of new life with God." Indeed it is not only female and male slaves, but also the old and the young who are highlighted as recipients of new life. The old women and men are the people who are passing away, who no longer are present in full power, and who will soon belong to the past. Young persons are the people who are not yet powerfully present, whose effective activity lies in the future. Yet it is certain that "sons" and "daughters" mean not only young people, but the old, and to no less of an extent the powerful and hopeful men and women of the generation standing in the middle of life. They, too, are to receive the Spirit and thus "new life with God" and with each other.

—Michael Welker, 20th century

199 Ideally, the church is a body of Spirit-filled persons, and thus a setting for continuing redemption in our world. Is this too ambitious an expectation? Not as Canadian theologian Clark H. Pinnock sees it.

The first act of the risen Lord was to breathe the Spirit on the disciples and send them forth into mission (Jn 20:21-22; Acts 1:8). This alerts us to the fact that the effectiveness of the church is due not to human competency or programming but to the power of God at work. The church rides the wind of God's Spirit like a hawk endlessly and effortlessly circling and gliding in the summer sky. It ever pauses to wait for impulses of power to carry it forward to the nations. What a dynamic and hopeful image to cherish in a day when thinking about the church is often heavy and pessimistic. The main rationale of the church is to actualize all the implications of baptism in the Spirit.

After the resurrection, God's kingdom, which had begun to manifest itself in Jesus himself, would continue to transform the world through the community of empowered disciples. The church is an extension not so much of the incarnation as of the anointing of Jesus. Jesus is the prototype of the church, which now receives its own baptism in the Spirit. Spirit, who maintained Jesus' relationship with the Father and empowered him for mission, now calls the church into that relationship, giving it the power to carry on the mission.

—Clark H. Pinnock, 1937–

The Trinity

While the Trinity is likely to be a remote or mysterious subject to the average layperson, and a difficult one for the parish pastor to address, probably no subject of Christian theology has been discussed more by theologians. This was especially true in the early centuries of the church, as theologians and church councils sought to define the meaning of this most distinctively Christian teaching. By its very nature hard to define, this doctrine has called forth extended discussions in the pursuit of language precise enough to enunciate the doctrine with integrity.

200 Because the doctrine of the Trinity is so difficult to explain, many of the theological writings on this doctrine can easily seem tedious and repetitive. One of the earliest theologians, Gregory of Nyssa, Bishop and Cappodocian Father, carefully finds his way through any possible misunderstandings.

[W]e do not learn . . . that the Father does anything by Himself in which the Son does not work conjointly, or again that the Son has any special operation apart from the Holy Spirit; but every operation which extends from God to the Creation, and is named according to our variable conceptions of it, has its origin from the Father, and proceeds through the Son, and is perfected in the Holy Spirit. For this reason the name derived from the operation is not divided with regard to the number of those who fulfil it, because the action of each concerning anything is not separate and peculiar, but whatever comes to pass, in reference either to the acts of His providence for us, or to the government and constitution of the universe, comes by the action of the Threes, yet what does come to pass is not three things. We may understand the meaning of this from one single instance. From Him, I say, Who is the chief source of gifts, all things which have shared in this grace have obtained their life. When we inquire, then, whence this good gift came to us, we find by the guidance of the Scriptures that it was from the Father, Son, and Holy Spirit. Yet although we set forth Three Persons and three names, we do not consider that we have had bestowed upon us three lives, one from each Person separately; but the same life is wrought in us by the Father, and prepared by the Son, and depends on the will of the Holy Spirit.

—*Gregory of Nyssa, c. 330–c. 395*

201 Augustine was a precise thinker, and it shows in his discussion of the Trinity. As we read Augustine, we see how earnestly he and the other early writers sought to give believers a body of teaching that they could understand and defend, and that would in turn safeguard them against error.

We have already observed that the only terms which can strictly be applied to distinguish the several Persons of the Trinity are those which denote their mutual relations: Father, Son, and Holy Spirit, Gift of both. The Trinity is neither Father nor Son nor Gift. But the terms applicable to the several Persons, regarded in themselves, denote not three beings in the plural, but one, that is, the Trinity itself: thus the Father is God, the Son God, the Holy Spirit God; the Father is good, the Son good, the Holy Spirit good; the Father almighty, the Son almighty, the Holy Spirit almighty; yet there are not three Gods, or three good, or three almighty; but one God, good, almighty—the Trinity itself; and so for every other term which denotes not a mutual relation, but the several Persons regarded in themselves. We may describe such terms as "essential"; for the essence or being of God is the same as his being great, good, wise, and anything else which is true either of each several Person or of the Trinity itself. We use the expression three Persons, or three substances, not to suggest any difference in essence, but to furnish ourselves with some one word by which to answer the question: *What* are these "three"?

In this Trinity there is an absolute equality. In divinity the Father is not greater than the Son; nor are the Father and the Son together greater than the Holy Spirit; nor is any single Person of the three anything less than the Trinity itself.

—*Augustine, 354–430*

202 Although the Apostles' Creed is probably the most familiar statement of faith for the average believer, perhaps the most crucial statement (at least from a historical point of view) is the Nicene-Constantinopolitan Creed. Coming to us from the fourth century, it clarified several crucial issues of church thought and belief, especially regarding the Trinity.

We believe in ONE GOD THE FATHER Almighty,
Maker of heaven and earth,
And of all things visible and invisible.
And in one Lord JESUS CHRIST,
the only-begotten Son of God,
Begotten of the Father before all worlds;
Light of Light,
Very God of very God,
Begotten, not made,
Being of one substance with the Father;
By whom all things were made;
Who, for us men, and for our salvation, came down from heaven,
And was incarnate by the Holy Ghost of the Virgin Mary,
And was made man;
He was crucified for us under Pontius Pilate;
And suffered and was buried;
And the third day he rose again,
According to the Scriptures;
And ascended into heaven,
And sitteth on the right hand of the Father;
And he shall come again, with glory, to judge the quick
    and the dead;
Whose kingdom shall have no end.
And in the HOLY GHOST,
The Lord, and Giver of life;
Who proceedeth from the Father;
Who with the Father and the Son together is worshiped
    and glorified;
Who spake by the Prophets.
And in one holy catholic and apostolic Church;
We acknowledge one baptism for the remission of sins;
And we look for the resurrection of the dead;
And the life of the world to come.

—Nicene-Constantinopolitan Creed, 381

203 In the study of doctrine we are always in danger of analyzing to the point of losing the wonder. The truths of eternity should never be reduced to mathematical formulas. As careful a theologian as Anselm was, he was nevertheless still caught in the wonder of worship, and approached the language of the Trinity with particular awe.

God the Father, you are this good; this good is your word, that is, your Son. For in the word which you yourself utter, there can be nothing other than yourself, or anything greater or less than you. For your word is true just as you are true, and so it is the truth that is you yourself and no other. You are one, and from you nothing can be born except yourself. And this is the one love, between you and your Son—the Holy Spirit which proceeds from you both. This love is nothing less than you and your Son; for your love for him and he for you are as great as you are. That which is no different from you and him is not something other than you and him, for there cannot proceed from the height of your oneness anything that is not yourself. So Father, Son, and Holy Spirit is wholly as Trinity what each is in himself; for each is none other than the highest single unity and the highest unity of persons, which can neither be multiplied nor made other.

'Moreover, one thing is necessary,' This is that one thing necessary, which contains every good, or rather which is wholly, uniquely, entirely, and solely, good.

—Anselm, 1033–1109

204 Hildegard of Bingen was a remarkably learned woman, a theologian, and a composer whose music is still available today. In this piece about the Holy Trinity we see her mystical and poetic nature, and above all, her love for God as Trinity.

Then I saw a most splendid light, and in that light, the whole of which burnt in a most beautiful, shining fire, was the figure of a man of a sapphire colour, and that most splendid light poured over the whole of that shining fire, and the shining fire over all that splendid light, and that most splendid light and shining fire over the whole figure of the man, appearing one light in one virtue and power. And again I heard that living Light saying to me: This is the meaning of the mysteries of God. . . .

. . . On which account thou seest this most splendid Light,

which is without beginning and to Whom nothing can be wanting: this means the Father, and in that figure of a man of a sapphire colour, without any spot of the imperfection of envy and iniquity, is declared the Son, born of the Father, according to the Divinity before all time, but afterwards incarnate according to the humanity, in the world, in time. The whole of which burns in a most beautiful, shining fire, which fire without a touch of any dark mortality shows the Holy Spirit. . . .

. . . [T]his is because the Father, Who is the highest equity, but not without the Son nor the Holy Spirit, and the Holy Spirit who is the kindler of the hearts of the faithful, but not without the Father and the Son, and the Son who is the fullness of virtue, but not without the Father and the Holy Spirit, are inseparable in the majesty of the Divinity; because the Father is not without the Son, neither the Son without the Father, nor the Father and the Son without the Holy Spirit, neither the Holy Spirit without them, and these three Persons exist one God in one whole divinity of majesty.

—Hildegard of Bingen, 1098–1179

205 Part of the significance of the Trinity is that this concept has traditionally provided an understanding of divine love. Richard of St. Victor, theologian and writer on spiritual life, tries to make this rather complex insight accessible to his fellow believers.

If we concede that there exists in the true divinity some one person of such great benevolence that he wishes to have no riches or delights that he does not wish to share with others, and if he is of such great power that nothing is impossible for him, and of such great happiness that nothing is difficult for him, then it is necessary to acknowledge that a Trinity of divine persons must exist. . . .

If there was only one person in the divinity, that one person would certainly not have anyone with whom he could share the riches of his greatness. But on the other hand, the abundance of delights and sweetness, which would have been able to increase for him on account of intimate love, would lack any eternal dimension. But the fulness of goodness does not permit the supremely good One to keep those riches for himself, nor does his fulness of blessedness allow him to be without a full abundance of delights and sweetness. And on account of the greatness of his honour, he rejoices at sharing his riches as much as he glories over enjoying the abundance of delights and sweetness. . . . Only someone who has a partner and a loved one in that love that has been shown to him possesses the sweetness of such delights.

So it follows that such a sharing of love cannot exist except among less than three persons. As we said earlier, there is nothing more glorious and nothing more magnificent than sharing in common whatever is useful and pleasant. This fact can hardly be unknown to the supreme wisdom, nor can it fail to please the supreme benevolence. And as the happiness of the supremely powerful One cannot be lacking in what pleases him, so in the divinity it is impossible for two persons not to be united to a third.

—Richard of St. Victor, died 1173

206 Julian of Norwich, writing from her own devout femininity, was conscious always of those qualities in the Godhead that reflected the qualities of women. Here she expresses, with warmth and piety, the masculine and feminine factors in the Trinity.

God the blessed Trinity, who is everlasting being, just as he is eternal from without beginning, just so was it in his eternal purpose to create human nature, which fair nature was first prepared for his own Son, the second person; and when he wished, by full agreement of the whole Trinity he created us all once. . . .

And so in our making, God almighty is our loving Father, and God all wisdom is our loving Mother, with the love and the goodness of the Holy Spirit, which is all one God, one Lord. . . .

. . . In our almighty Father we have our protection and our bliss, as regards our natural substance, which is ours by our creation from without beginning; and in the second person, in knowledge and wisdom we have our perfection, as regards our sensuality, our restoration and our salvation, for he is our Mother, brother and saviour; and in our good Lord the Holy Spirit we have our reward and our gift for our living and our labour, endlessly surpassing all that we desire in his marvellous courtesy, out of his great plentiful grace. For all our life consists of three: In the first we have our being, and in the second we have our increasing, and in the third we have our fulfillment. The first is nature, the second is mercy, and the third is grace.

As to the first, I saw and understood that the high might of the

Trinity is our Father, and the deep wisdom of the Trinity is our Mother, and the great love of the Trinity is our Lord; and all these we have in nature and in our substantial creation.

—Julian of Norwich, 1342–after 1416

207 Probably the most familiar hymn celebrating the Trinity is "Holy, Holy, Holy," but numbers of others have used the persons of the Trinity as an outline for stanzas of adoration. Here, Charles Wesley devotes a stanza to each person of the Trinity, then calls for praise to the triune Lord.

Father, in whom we live,
In whom we are, and move,
The glory, power and praise receive
Of thy creating love.
Let all the angel throng
Give thanks to God on high;
While earth repeats the joyful song,
And echoes to the sky.

Incarnate Deity,
Let all the ransomed race
Render in thanks their lives to thee
For thy redeeming grace.
The grace to sinners showed
Ye heavenly choirs proclaim,
And cry: Salvation to our God,
Salvation to the Lamb!

Spirit of Holiness,
Let all thy saints adore
Thy sacred energy, and bless
Thine heart-renewing power.
Not angel tongues can tell
Thy love's ecstatic height,
The glorious joy unspeakable,
The beatific sight.

Eternal, triune Lord!
Let all the hosts above,
Let all the sons of men, record

And dwell upon thy love.
When heaven and earth are fled
Before thy glorious face,
Sing all the saints thy love hath made
Thine everlasting praise.
—Charles Wesley, 1707–1788

208 Our generation is blessed with the appearance of theologians in the developing nations of the world. Their theological writings often have a quality reminiscent of the earliest centuries of the church, probably because they are writing under very similar circumstances. Here, African Christopher Mwoleka challenges us regarding the Trinity.

I think we have problems in understanding the Holy Trinity because we approach the mystery from the wrong side. The intellectual side is not the best side to start with. We try to get hold of the wrong end of the stick, and it never works. The right approach to the mystery is to *imitate* the Trinity. . . .

On believing in this mystery, the first thing we should have done was to imitate God, then we would ask no more questions, for we would understand. God does not reveal Himself to us for the sake of speculation. He is not giving us a riddle to solve. He is offering us life. He is telling us: "This is what it means to live, now begin to live as I do." What is the one and only reason why God revealed this mystery to us if it is not to stress that life is not life at all unless it is shared?

If we would once begin to share life in all its aspects, we would soon understand what the Trinity is all about and rejoice.

—Christopher Mwoleka, 20th century

209 Our lesson seeks to trace something of the development of trinitarian belief through the New Testament. Here Robert Jenson, a Lutheran theologian, traces something of that story in the Scriptures, and into the general practice of the church.

So dominant was the use of the name "Jesus" in the religious life of the apostolic church that the whole mission can be described as proclamation "in his name" (Luke 24:47), "preaching good news about the kingdom of God and the name of Jesus

Christ" (Acts 8:12), indeed, as "carrying" Jesus' name to the people (e.g., Acts 9:15). The gatherings of the congregations can be described as "giving thanks . . . in the name of our Lord Jesus Christ" (Ephesians 5:20), indeed, simply as meetings in his name (Matthew 18:20). Where faith must be confessed over against the hostility of society, this is "confession of the name" (e.g., Mark 13:13). The theological conclusion was drawn in such praises as the hymn preserved in Philippians in which God's own eschatological triumph is evoked as cosmic obeisance to the name "Jesus" (Philippians 1:10), or in such formulas as that in Acts which makes Jesus' name the agent of salvation (Acts 4:12). However various groups in the primal church may have conceived Jesus' relation to God, "Jesus" was the way they all invoked God.

One other new naming appears in the New Testament, the triune name: "Father, Son, and Holy Spirit." Its appearance is undoubtedly dependent on naming God by naming Jesus. . . . That the biblical God must have a proper name, we have seen in the Hebrew Scriptures. In the life of the primal church, God is named by uses that involve the name of Jesus. "Father, Son, and Spirit" is the naming of this sort that historically triumphed.

That "Father, Son, and Holy Spirit" in fact occupies in the church the place occupied in Israel by "Yahweh" or, later, "Lord" even hasty observation of the church's life must discover . . . Our services begin and are punctuated with "In the name of the Father, Son, and Holy Spirit." Our prayers conclude, "In his name who with you and the Holy Spirit is . . . Above all, the act by which people are brought both into the fellowship of believers and into their fellowship with God is an initiation "into the name 'Father, Son, and Holy Spirit.' "

The habit of trinitarian naming is universal through the life of the church. How far back it goes, we cannot tell. It certainly goes further back than even the faintest traces of trinitarian reflection, and it appears to have been an immediate expression of believers' experience of God. It is in liturgy, when we talk not *about* God but to and for him, that we need and use God's name, and that is where the trinitarian formulas appear, both initially and to this day. In the immediately postapostolic literature there is no use of a trinitarian formula as a piece of theology or in such fashion as to depend on antecedent development in theology, yet the formula is there. Its home is in the liturgy, in baptism and the eucharist. There its use was regularly seen as the heart of the matter.

—*Robert Jenson, 20th century*

210 Whatever other differences have existed over the centuries between Catholicism and Protestantism, there has been general agreement on the doctrine of the Trinity. Here is the basic dogma of the Trinity as declared in the Catechism of the Roman Catholic Church.

The Trinity is One. We do not confess three Gods, but one God in three persons, the "consubstantial Trinity." The divine persons do not share the one divinity among themselves but each of them is God whole and entire: "The Father is that which the Son is, the Son that which the Father is, the Father and the Son that which the Holy Spirit is, i.e., by nature one God." In the words of the Fourth Lateran Council (1215): "Each of the persons is that supreme reality, viz., the divine substance, essence or nature."

The divine persons are really distinct from one another. "God is one but not solitary." "Father," "Son," "Holy Spirit" are not simply names designating modalities of the divine being, for they are really distinct from one another: "He is not the Father who is the Son, nor is the Son he who is the Father, nor is the Holy Spirit he who is the Father or the Son." They are distinct from one another in their relations of origin: "It is the Father who generates, the Son who is begotten, and the Holy Spirit who proceeds." The divine Unity is Triune.

The divine persons are relative to one another. Because it does not divide the divine unity, the real distinction of the persons from one another resides solely in the relationships which relate them to one another: "In the relational names of the persons the Father is related to the Son, the Son to the Father, and the Holy Spirit to both. While they are called three persons in view of their relations, we believe in one nature or substance.

—*Catechism of the Catholic Church*

The Message Behind the Symbols

The Church: God's Called-Out People
The Church: Body of Christ
Sacraments ◆ Worship

The ship with its cross-shaped mast represents the church and, like the ark before it, offers salvation. The ship of the church has weathered storms of persecution, false teaching, and division. The church is the ship in which Christians navigate the waters of life.

Baptism and Holy Communion are considered sacraments because they can be traced to the Gospels and Jesus' actions. The shell with three drops of water symbolizes the baptism of Jesus and the sacrament of baptism in general. According to tradition, the three drops of water stand for the words used in baptism—in the name of the Father, and of the Son, and of the Holy Spirit. Another interpretation says that in lands where water is scarce, at least three drops of water are necessary for baptism. Grapes and wheat are symbols for Holy Communion. The grape symbolizes the shed blood of Christ; and wheat, the source of flour for the bread that represents Christ's sacrificed body.

The bell is a symbol of worship. It calls all people to come and worship God. Come and be God's people. The sound of the bell carries the message that the things of God take priority over all other interests. In the ritual of some faith communities, the ringing of a bell symbolizes the presence of God in the Eucharist.

The Church: God's Called-Out People

The Western culture, particularly in America, has always prized individualism. As a result, we are poorly equipped to understand the sense of community that prevails throughout the Bible. Nor does it help much to speak of it as the divine community; in a sense, that makes it seem more theoretical and unreal. And yet this is a primary factor in the biblical story of God's purposes for the human race. God works through a community—at first, Israel, and then the church—to bring about the divine purpose.

211 Protestants sometimes feel uncomfortable with the word *catholic* as it appears in the Apostles' Creed, thinking of it as referring to the Roman Catholic Church. But as used in its theological sense, the word has always had more of a spiritual sense than simply an institutional one, meaning "general" in distinction from "particular" and "universal" in contrast with "limited." Cyril of Jerusalem offered a definition of the word *catholic* sixteen or more centuries ago.

The Church, then, is called Catholic because it is spread through the whole world, from one end of the earth to the other, and because it never stops teaching in all its fulness every doctrine that men ought to be brought to know: and that regarding things visible and invisible, in heaven and on earth. It is called Catholic also because it brings into religious obedience every sort of men, rulers and ruled, learned and simple, and because it is a universal treatment and cure for every kind of sin whether perpetrated by soul or body, and possesses within it every form of virtue that is named, whether it expresses itself in deeds or words or in spiritual graces of every description.

—Cyril of Jerusalem, 314–386

212 In every century the people of God have suffered persecution in one part of the world or another. Augustine encourages the faithful to remember that they belong to God's people, and that persecution has been their lot ever since Abel, who could rightly be called the first martyr—not of the Christian faith, but of the people of God.

In this wicked world, in these evil days, when the Church measures her future loftiness by her present humility, . . . there are many reprobate mingled with the good, and both are gathered together by the gospel as in a drag net; and in this world, as in a sea, both swim enclosed without distinction in the net, until it is brought ashore, when the wicked must be separated from the good, that in the good, as in His temple, God may be all in all. . . . This takes place now, since He has spoken, first by the mouth of his forerunner John, and afterward by His own mouth, saying, "Repent: for the kingdom of heaven is at hand." . . . Having sown the holy gospel as much as that behoved to be done by His bodily presence, He suffered, died, and rose again, showing by His passion what we ought to suffer for the truth, and by His resurrection what we ought to hope for in adversity; saving always the mystery of the sacrament, by which His blood was shed for the remission of sins. He held converse on earth forty days with His disciples, and in their sight ascended into heaven, and after ten days sent the promised Holy Spirit.

—Augustine, 354–430

213 With the Protestant Reformation, those persons who became part of the reforming bodies needed a clear doctrine of the community of faith; after all, they were no longer part of the Roman Catholic Church, so how would they now define the church? The Second Helvetic Confession provided a theological answer.

WHAT IS THE CHURCH? The Church is an assembly of the faithful called or gathered out of the world; a communion, I say, of all saints, namely, of those who truly know and rightly worship and serve the true God in Christ the Savior, by the Word and Holy

Spirit, and who by faith are partakers of all benefits which are freely offered through Christ. CITIZENS OF ONE COMMONWEALTH. They are all citizens of the one city, living under the same Lord, under the same laws, and in the same fellowship of all good things. For the apostle calls them "fellow citizens with the saints and members of the household of God" (Eph. 2:19), calling the faithful on earth saints (I Cor. 4:1), who are sanctified by the blood of the Son of God. The article of the Creed, "I believe in the holy catholic Church, the communion of saints," is to be understood wholly as concerning these saints.

—The Second Helvetic Confession, 1566

214 Although the worldwide Methodist movement sprang out of the ministry of John Wesley and his brother Charles, the Wesleys chose to remain in the Anglican Church and had a strong sense of the churchmanship that should mark the community of faith. Here John Wesley defines the people of God.

Here then is a clear unexceptionable answer to that question, What is the church? The catholic or universal church is all the persons in the universe whom God hath so called out of the world as to entitle them to the preceding character; as to be 'one body', united by 'one Spirit'; having 'one faith, one hope, one baptism; one God and Father of all, who is above all, and through all, and in them all.'

That part of this great body, of the universal church, which inhabits any one kingdom or nation, we may properly term a 'national' church, as the Church of France, the Church of England, the Church of Scotland. A smaller part of the universal church are the Christians that inhabit one city or town, as the church of Ephesus, and the rest of the seven churches mentioned in the Revelation. Two or three Christian believers united together are a church in the narrowest sense of the word. Such was the church in the house of Philemon, and that in the house of Nymphas, mentioned Col. 4:15. A particular church may therefore consist of any number of members, whether two or three, or two or three millions. But still, whether they be larger or smaller, the same idea is to be preserved. They are one body, and have one Spirit, one Lord, one hope, one faith, one baptism, one God and Father of all.

—John Wesley, 1703–1791

215 The New Testament speaks of the first believers as "saints." We use this term in a more specialized way. Karl Barth explains the biblical and theological sense of the term as it applies to the people of God.

The Church is the communion of the saints, *communio sanctorum*. Here there is a problem of exegesis: is the nominative *sancti* or *sancta*? I do not wish to decide the dispute, but just to ask whether there is not here intended a remarkable ambiguity in a deeper sense. For only when both interpretations are retained side by side, does the matter receive its full, good meaning. *Sancti* means not specially fine people, but, for example, people like the 'saints of Corinth', who were very queer saints. But these queer folk, to whom we too may belong, are *sancti*, that is, men set apart—for holy gifts and works, for *sancta*. The congregation is the place where God's word is proclaimed and the sacraments are solemnised and the fellowship of prayer takes place, not to mention the inward gifts and works, which are the meaning of these outward ones. So the *sancti* belong to the *sancta* and vice versa.
—*Karl Barth, 1886–1968*

216 Every community has to revolve around some center, whether it be a government, or a social or educational purpose. Ancient Israel was a nation; what is the center for the church, especially since it is a people scattered abroad? H. Richard Niebuhr reminds us that the center is Jesus Christ.

[I]n practice concentration on the Book is ultimately self-corrective since the Bible faithfully studied allows none to make it the highest good or its glorification the final end. It always points beyond itself not so much to its associate, the people, as to the Creator, the suffering and risen Lord and the Inspirer. This is true also of the Church; it loses its character as Church when it concentrates on itself, worships itself and seeks to make love of Church the first commandment. Tension and antagonism between Bible-centered and Church-centered members of the community is being ever-renewed but is also being evermore resolved and their debate is led to higher issues by the witness of the Bible and the Church themselves to that which transcends both. Another long debate has gone on in history and is alive today among those who agree that the chief end of the Church is to gain followers of Jesus Christ or to proclaim his Lordship. . . .

Is not the result of all these debates and the content of the confessions or commandments of all these authorities this: that no substitute can be found for the definition of the goal of the Church as the *increase among men of the love of God and neighbor*? The terms vary; now the symbolic phrase is reconciliation to God and man, now increase of gratitude for the forgiveness of sin, now the realization of the kingdom or the coming of the Spirit, now the acceptance of the gospel. But the simple language of Jesus Christ himself furnishes to most Christians the most intelligible key to his own purpose and to that of the community gathered around him.

—H. Richard Niebuhr, 1894–1962

217 How does the Roman Catholic Church define the people of God today? One leading Catholic theologian, Henri de Lubac, honors the variety of the body, especially its concern for persons society might otherwise ignore.

The Church . . . but when I myself look for her, where will I find her? Of what features is her face composed? . . .

She is both human and divine, given from above, and come from below. Those who belong to her resist, with all the weight of a burdened and wounded nature, the Life with which she tries to permeate them. She is turned toward the past, meditating on a memorial which she knows contains what will never be surpassed; and, at the same time, she looks to the future and rejoices in the hope of an ineffable fulfillment that suffers not even a glimpse. Called, in her present form, to disappear completely like the face of this world, she is destined, in her very essence, to remain whole from the day her innermost being is disclosed. Varied and multiform, she is nonetheless one with the most active and the most demanding unity. She is a people, a huge anonymous crowd, and yet—what other expression is there—the most personal Being. Catholic, that is, universal, she wants her members to be open to all, yet she is only fully herself when she withdraws to the intimacy of her interior life in the silence of adoration. She is both humble and majestic. She claims to assimilate every culture and ennoble its every value; at the same time, she sees herself the home of little ones, the poor, the simple, miserable multitude. Not for a moment does she pause—for this would mean her death, and

she is immortal—in contemplating him who is at once the crucified and the resurrected.

—Henri de Lubac, 1896–1991

218 The most dynamic growth of the church today is in Africa and certain parts of Asia and South America. This makes the sense of the church as
a worldwide body more powerful than it has been since perhaps the early
centuries. Here is a late twentieth-century statement from the World Council
of Churches, a body encompassing most Protestant groups and the Eastern
Orthodox Church.

The unity of the church to which we are called is a koinonia
given and expressed in the common confession of the apostolic
faith; a common sacramental life entered by the one baptism and
celebrated together in one eucharistic fellowship; a common life in
which members and ministries are mutually recognized and reconciled; and a common mission witnessing to the gospel of God's
grace to all people and serving the whole of creation. The goal of
the search for full communion is realized when all the churches
are able to recognize in one another the one, holy, catholic and
apostolic church in its fullness. This full communion will be
expressed on the local and the universal levels through conciliar
forms of life and action. In such communion churches are bound
in all aspects of their life together at all levels in confessing the
one faith and engaging in worship and witness, deliberation and
action.

—World Council of Churches, 1991 Canberra Assembly

219 Our Scripture readings for this lesson emphasize the fact that the
people of God include both ancient Israel and the Church. Henri J.M.
Nouwen, spiritual life writer, brings especially significant understanding
to this whole concept.

The basis of the Christian community is not the family tie, or
social or economic equality, or shared oppression or complaint, or
mutual attraction . . . but the divine call. The Christian community
is not the result of human efforts. God has made us into his people
by calling us out of "Egypt" to the "New Land," out of the desert
to fertile ground, out of slavery to freedom, out of our sin to sal-

vation, out of captivity to liberation. All these words and images give expression to the fact that the initiative belongs to God and that he is the source of our new life together. By our common call to the New Jerusalem, we recognize each other on the road as brothers and sisters. Therefore, as the people of God, we are called *ekklesia* (from the Greek *kaleo*=call; and *ek*=out), the community called out of the old world into the new....

It is quite understandable that in our large anonymous cities we look for people on our "wave length" to form small communities. ... But sometimes a false type of like-mindedness can narrow our sense of community. ... There is a great wisdom hidden in the old bell tower calling people with very different backgrounds away from their homes to form one body in Jesus Christ. It is precisely by transcending the many individual differences that we can become witnesses of God who allows his light to shine upon poor and rich, healthy and sick alike.

—Henri J.M. Nouwen, 20th century

220 When we speak of the community of faith, we can easily resort to such spiritual terms that we forget the very human factors that go into any institution. Theologian James Gustafson is straightforward in dealing with this spiritual-institutional dichotomy.

The Church is both a fellowship and an institution. These two aspects of its life are necessary to each other and to the whole for the continuation of the Church and its social unity. ... The Bible is the most important objectification of the meaning of Jesus Christ and life in relation to him. Indeed, both the Old and New Testaments are expressions of the common life of a people who understand themselves and all events of history to be related to God. The Bible in its various types of literature carries in a relatively stable form the meanings that mark the Christian community in distinction from other human groups. It bears the possibility of those meanings becoming the center of life for individual persons, and remaining the center of life for the whole Church. It is not sufficient in and of itself, however, and therefore other institutional forms are necessary. The communication and interpretation of its meaning depend upon the existence of certain offices and rites. The ministry exists in part to make living and internal the meanings carried externally and objectively in the

Bible. The Lord's Supper is a rite in which the significance of the death of Jesus Christ is remembered again. Liturgies as a whole carry out for each congregation a pattern of meaning in which men can participate.

—*James M. Gustafson, 1925–*

221 A contemporary theologian, Christos Yannaras, brings us back to the classical definitions of the church, and of the community of faith, as a people "called out" to be God's people.

The first community of Christ's disciples appear in history with the name "ecclesia". By this word it declared its identity and its truth.

"Ecclesia" (from a Greek verb "to call out") means the gathering which is a result of a call or invitation. It is a gathering or assembling of those called. The first disciples of Christ had the consciousness that they were "called", called by him to an assembly of unity, to an ecclesia. Not to be faithful to a new "religion", nor to be partisans of a new ideology or social teaching. What united them was not the reception of some theoretical "principles" or "axioms", but the reception of the call which radically changed their lives: It transformed individuals, detached units, into a single body, the Church. Their gathering is not exhausted in a simple meeting together; it is not a passing, casual event. They live as a church, as a single body of life, they share life as "brothers"—just like brothers who draw their existence from the same womb—they are "members" of an organic, living "body". . . .

The Church is also this one chosen people, the "new Israel", with a new historical mission: to reveal to the world God's new relationship and covenant with mankind "in Christ Jesus". The unity of this new "people of God" no longer depends at all, on tribal elements. To the contrary, it is a community open "to all nations". It is founded on a new "Covenant" with God, sealed by the blood of Christ's sacrifice on the cross. For you to share in this people, for you to be a member of the body of the Church, is an act of accepting the "New Covenant": the act of "breaking bread" and "blessing the cup", the participation in the Eucharistic meal.

—*Christos Yannaras, 20th century*

The Church:
Body of Christ

When we read some of the New Testament descriptions of the church, we might easily wonder if any church could ever fulfill such a grand standard. On the other hand, when we read, in the epistles, what the church was like in the first century, we realize how human a body it was and is. Theologians have had to work with the same ambivalence—a body that is intended to be God's holy people, made perfect by divine expectations, but in actual fact painfully human. See, then, what theologians of the ages have said about the church.

222 One of the primary characteristics of the church was to be its unity. But how is one to describe a unity that encompasses so many different kinds of persons, scattered over so many nations of the earth? In what shall their unity be found? Cyprian of Carthage, North African bishop, found a useful analogy to provide an answer.

The Church also is one, which is spread abroad far and wide into a multitude by an increase of fruitfulness. As there are many rays of the sun, but one light; and many branches of a tree, but one strength based in its tenacious root; and since from one spring flow many streams, although the multiplicity seems diffused in the liberality of an overflowing abundance, yet the unity is still preserved in the source. Separate a ray of the sun from its body of light, its unity does not allow a division of light; break a branch from a tree,—when broken, it will not be able to bud; cut off the stream from its fountain, and that which is cut off dries up. Thus also the Church, shone over with the light of the Lord, sheds forth her rays over the whole world, yet it is one light which is everywhere diffused, nor is the unity of the body separated. Her fruitful abundance spreads her branches over the whole world. She broadly expands her rivers, liberally flowing, yet her head is one, her source one; and she is one mother, plentiful in the results of fruitfulness; from her womb we are born, by her milk we are nourished, by her spirit we are animated.

—Cyprian, died 258

223 When we speak of the church as the body of Christ, it is possible to use the term in a quite poetic or spiritual way. But in truth, the concept is intensely practical, as Cyril of Alexandria points out. For if we believers are indeed the body of Christ, then we are "already one," since Christ is the "bond of unity."

We too then are to be combined and commingled into a unity with God and with one another, in spite of our observable separation as individuals distinct in soul and body. To this end the Only-begotten has found a means devised by the Father's own will and wisdom. With one body, namely his own, he blesses those who believe in him as they partake of the holy mysteries and makes them members of the same body with himself and with one another. . . . For if we all partake of one loaf, then we are all made one body [see 1 Cor. 10:17]; for Christ cannot be divided. And so the Church is also called body of Christ and we individually are limbs, as Paul teaches [see 1 Cor. 12:27]. For we are all united to the one Christ through the holy body, since we receive him who is one and indivisible in our own bodies. Our obligation then as limbs of his is to him rather than to ourselves. The Saviour's role is that of head and the Church is the remainder of the body, made up of the various limbs. . . . So if we are all one body with one another in Christ, not simply with one another but clearly also with him who is in us by virtue of his own flesh, then surely we are all of us already one both in one another and in Christ. For Christ is the bond of unity, being at once both God and man.

—Cyril of Alexandria, died 444

224 Augustine makes a vigorous declaration of the unity of the people of God. When we see how much the early theologians emphasized the issue of unity, we can probably rightly reason that they sensed that this unity was often at risk. They spoke to the subject because it was necessary to do so.

I am not unmindful of the promise by which I pledged myself to deliver a sermon to instruct you, who have just been baptized, on the Sacrament of the Lord's table, which you now look upon and of which you partook last night. . . . If you have received worthily, you are what you have received, for the Apostle says: 'The bread is one; we though many, are one body.' Thus he explained the Sacrament of the Lord's table: 'The bread is one; we though many, are one body.' So, by bread you are instructed as to how you ought to cherish unity. Was that bread made of one grain of wheat? Were there not, rather, many grains? However, before they became bread, these grains were separate; they were joined together in water after a certain amount of crushing. For, unless the grain is ground and moistened with water, it cannot arrive at that form which is called bread. So, too, you were previously ground. . . . Then came the baptism of water; you were moistened, as it were, so as to arrive at the form of bread. But, without fire, bread does not yet exist. What, then, does the fire signify? . . . the fire, that is, the Holy Spirit, comes after the water; then you become bread, that is, the body of Christ. Hence, in a certain manner, unity is signified. . . .

. . . What you see passes; but the invisible, that which is not seen, does not pass; it remains. Behold, it is received; it is eaten; it is consumed. Is the body of Christ consumed? Is the Church of Christ consumed? Are the members of Christ consumed? God forbid! Here they are cleansed; there they will be crowned. Therefore, what is signified will last eternally, even though it seems to pass. Receive, then, so that you may ponder, so that you may possess unity in your heart, so that you may always lift up your heart.

—Augustine, 354–430

225 In practical terms, every generation does some redefining of the church; and in the redefining, some of the integrity of the church's mission is easily lost. Georgia Harkness confronted one of the persistent modern issues, the temptation to make the church simply a social institution.

But if the Church is more than a social group; if it is a worshiping fellowship of those who seek to have the mind of Christ, then the mind of Christ affords a regulative principle by which to judge its action. Any human member of it will fail, and all its members together will sin and fall short of the glory of God, yet still through the miasma of our human frailty will shine the glory of God in the face of Jesus Christ. Christ's true Church, like Christ himself, exists in time yet beyond all time. Because it is more than a human institution, it cannot fail to resist the floods of evil from the gates of hell; because it is more than a human institution it will continue to conserve our Christian heritage and point men forward toward new truth.

—*Georgia Harkness, 1891–1974*

226 Sometimes our perception of doctrine takes on the color of prevailing thought even without our knowing it. In the mid-twentieth century, society wrestled with the ideas of individualism and totalitarianism, and those political philosophies influenced popular understanding of the doctrine of the church. C.S. Lewis set out to show the difference.

Christianity thinks of human individuals not as mere members of a group or items in a list, but as organs in a body—different from one another and each contributing what no other could. When you find yourself wanting to turn your children, or pupils, or even your neighbours, into people exactly like yourself, remember that God probably never meant them to be that. You and they are different organs, intended to do different things. On the other hand, when you are tempted not to bother about someone else's troubles because they are 'no business of yours', remember that though he is different from you he is part of the same organism as you. If you forget that he belongs to the same organism as yourself you will become an Individualist. If you forget that he is a different organ from you, if you want to suppress differences and make people all alike, you will become a Totalitarian. But a Christian must not be either a Totalitarian or an Individualist.

I feel a strong desire to tell you and I expect you feel a strong desire to tell me which of these two errors is the worse. That is the Devil getting at us. He always sends offers into the world in pairs—pairs of opposites. And he always encourages us to spend a lot of time thinking which is the worse. You see why, of course? He relies on your extra dislike of the one error to draw you gradually into the opposite one. But do not let us be fooled. We have to keep our eyes on the goal and go straight through between both errors. We have no other concern than that with either of them.

—*C.S. Lewis, 1898–1963*

227 The basic biblical images of the church have a timelessness that challenges every generation. Thus a modern theologian, John Lawson, reemploys the language of Paul from the First Letter to the Corinthians.

THE BODY OF CHRIST. This doctrine is chiefly associated with the writings of St. Paul. The first stage of his argument is practical. In the passage 1 Corinthians 12:4-31, he is appealing for charity and unity in the congregation at Corinth. He points out that the Christians have a variety of spiritual gifts, some more prominent than others. However, all are necessary for the fulfilling of God's plan through the Church. The different members are like the various limbs and organs of the human body; of very different function, and some apparently more important or more dignified in use than others, yet every one necessary to the health of the body. Therefore the Christians with prominent gifts must be humble-minded, and those with only modest gifts must guard against both envy and discouragement. All must cooperate as do the organs of the body, so that the entire Church may be the healthy body of Christ.

—John Lawson, 20th century

228 In the mid-twentieth century, a movement known as liberation theology became a significant force in several developing countries and among many people of color. James H. Cone explains the meaning of the church in the system of liberation theology.

In the New Testament the church *(ecclesia)* is the community that has received the Holy Spirit and is now ready to do what is necessary to live out the gospel. It is the assembly of those who have become heirs of the promises of God; and because they have experienced what that means for humanity, they cannot accept the world as it is. They must rebel against evil so all citizens may know that they do not have to behave according to unjust societal laws.

Participation in the historical liberation spearheaded by God is the defining characteristic of the church. The task of the church is threefold. First, it proclaims the reality of divine liberation. This is what the New Testament calls preaching the gospel. The gospel is the proclamation of God's liberation as revealed in the event of Jesus and the outpouring of the Holy Spirit. It is not possible to receive the good news of freedom *and* keep it to ourselves; it must be told to the whole world. . . .

Secondly, the church not only proclaims the good news of freedom, it actively shares in the liberation struggle. Though the battle against evil has been won, old rulers pretend that they are still in power. . . .

Thirdly, the church as a fellowship is a visible manifestation that the gospel is a reality. If the church is not free, if it is a distorted representation of the irruption of God's kingdom, if it lives according to the old order (as it usually has), then no one will believe its message. If someone tells me that Christ has set us free from all alien loyalties, but he himself obeys the loyalties that he claims Christ has defeated, then I must conclude that he does not really believe what he says. To believe is to live accordingly; the church must live according to its preaching. This is what Bonhoeffer had in mind when he called the church "Christ existing as a community."

—James H. Cone, 1938–

229 In the New Testament, the term *church* sometimes is used to describe a congregation, and sometimes by reference to the larger, mystical body. Roman Catholic theologian Hans Küng seeks to explain something of the relationship between the two uses of the term.

The Church—people of God or body of Christ? The differences between these two conceptions are considerable, as we shall see. In the idea of the "people of God" temporal categories are supremely important; as the people of God the Church is making a journey from Old Testament election through the present towards the future. The notion of the "body of Christ" is dominated by spatial categories: the union of the Church with its glorified Lord as the continuing present.

But the fact that both ideas are typical of Paul's thinking and are integrated in his writings shows that they are not necessarily contradictory. Both concepts of the Church seek to express the union of the Church with Christ and the union of its members among themselves. It is, however, important that in seeing the Church as the body of Christ we should not base our view on an abstract of the body, but see it as the people of God placed by Christ in history. It is fundamental from every point of view to see the Church as the people of God; this idea is found not only in Paul, but is the oldest term to describe the ecclesia, and it emphasizes the crucial continuity between the Church and Israel and the Old Testament. Only by seeing the Church as the people of God can we understand the idea of the Church as the body of Christ; then we shall see that the concept "body of Christ" describes very fittingly the new and unique nature of this new people of God. The Church is only the body of Christ insofar as it is the people of God; but by being the new people of God constituted by Christ it is truly the body of Christ. The two concepts of the Church are linked precisely through their Jewish roots.

—*Hans Küng, 1928–*

230 Here a contemporary theologian, Marjorie Hewitt Suchocki, pictures the church as a grand, extended family.

Consider the unity that is created if many people share in an identity formed through faith in Christ. The unity we see in a family group stems from its past: brothers and sisters, by sharing the same parents, share the same family identity. Their common past, whether by birth or adoption, defines them as family. For the family that is the Christian church, unity comes primarily from a shared future. Just as the sharing of a past creates a real kinship, even so the sharing of a future creates a real kinship. If John's identity is formed through Christ, and if Kwasi's identity is formed through Christ, and if Ti-Fam's identify is formed through Christ, then all three share in the same identity and become brothers and sisters to one another even though they live so widely scattered in the world. Christ, as the source of their identity, is also the ground of their unity, creating in them a bond as real and as close as family, creating them as the community of church. . . .

Suppose that John meets another Christian, and they wish to experience their common bond, their unity as members of the one body of Christ. . . . In an orientation toward service, unity will become apparent, almost as a byproduct of responsiveness to the one God, leading us in ways of well-being. The future, not the past, clarifies the unity of the church.

—*Marjorie Hewitt Suchocki, 20th century*

Sacraments

It is in the celebration of the sacraments that typical believers have the most tangible experience of faith. Most other faith celebrations are internal, spiritual, or intellectual. But the sacraments, by definition, involve physical elements. Not surprisingly, these physical elements themselves have sometimes been controversial for theologians. But more often the issues have had to do with the role of the celebrant, the response of the worshiper, and the significance of the sacrament itself.

231 Because Holy Communion (like baptism) is celebrated frequently, we are in danger of treating it with inappropriate familiarity. Paul warned the Corinthians against this danger, and one of the earliest church writings, the Didache, reinforced the profound sacredness of this simple ceremony.

On the Lord's own day come together and break bread and give thanks, after first confessing your sins, so that your sacrifice may be pure.

Let no one who has a dispute with a fellow Christian assemble with you until they are reconciled, so that your sacrifice may not be defiled. For this is the sacrifice spoken of by the Lord: " 'In every place and at all times offer me a pure sacrifice, for I am a great King,' says the Lord, 'and my name is the wonder of the nations.' "

—Didache 14, c. 60

232 Some bodies of Christendom intentionally immerse, sprinkle, or pour three times, to emphasize the role of the Trinity in baptism. In reading Hippolytus of Rome, writer and theologian, we learn the questions that accompanied each of the three acts, questions reflecting portions of the Apostles' Creed.

And when he who is to be baptised goes down to the water, let him who baptises lay hand on him saying thus:
Dost thou believe in God the Father Almighty? And he who is being baptised shall say: I believe. Let him forthwith baptise him once, having his hand laid upon his head.
And after this let him say:
Dost thou believe in Christ Jesus, the Son of God,
Who was born of the Holy Spirit and the Virgin Mary,
Who was crucified in the days of Pontius Pilate,
And died and was buried
And He rose the third day living from the dead
And ascended into heaven,
And sat down at the right hand of the Father,
And will come to judge the living and the dead?
And when he says: I believe, let him baptise the second time.
And again let him say:
Dost thou believe in the Holy Spirit in the Holy Church
And the resurrection of the flesh?
And he who is being baptised shall say: I believe.
And so let him baptise him the third time.

—*Hippolytus of Rome, c. 170–c. 236*

233 Part of the power of a sacrament is the imagery that physical elements evoke. Augustine takes full advantage of these images as he explains something of the meaning and significance of the bread, the cup, and the grapes.

What you see is bread and a cup; that is what your eyes tell you. But what your faith (as yet uninstructed) insists is that the bread is the body of Christ and the cup the blood of Christ. That can briefly be stated and it may be all that faith needs. Yet faith does crave instruction. . . .

These things, my brothers, are called sacraments because there is a difference between their appearance and their true meaning. In appearance they have a physical form; in their true meaning they have a spiritual effect. If you want to understand what is meant by 'the body of Christ', you must attend to the words of the apostle: 'You are the body of Christ and his members' [1 Cor. 12:27]. So then if you are the body of Christ and his members it is the mystery of yourselves that is placed on the Lord's table; it is the mystery of yourselves that you receive. It is to what you are that you make the response 'Amen', and in making that response you give your personal assent. You hear 'the body of Christ' and you answer 'Amen'. Be a member of Christ's body and make your 'Amen' true. . . .

What about the meaning of the cup? . . . Remember, my brothers, how wine is made. There are many grapes hanging on the vine, but the juice of the grapes is mixed up together in unity. In this the Lord Christ was giving us a picture of ourselves. He wanted us to belong to him; at his table he consecrated the mystery of our peace and of our unity. He who receives the mystery of unity but does not keep the bond of peace, receives not a mystery that will profit him but a testimony that will witness against him.

—Augustine, 354–430

234 Sacraments are often defined as "outward and visible signs of inward and spiritual grace." Hugh of Saint Victor, known for his writings on the sacraments, seeks to put further content into this idea.

The doctors have designated with a brief description what a sacrament is: "A sacrament is the sign of a sacred thing." For just as in man there are two things, body and soul, and in one Scripture likewise two things, letter and sense, so also in every sacrament there is one thing which is treated visibly without and is seen, and there is another which is believed invisibly within and is received. What is visible without and material is a sacrament, what is invisible within and spiritual is the thing or virtue of the sacrament; the sacrament, however, which is treated and sanctified without is a sign of spiritual grace and this is the thing of the sacrament and is received invisibly. . . . Now if anyone wishes to define more fully and more perfectly what a sacrament is, he can say: "A sacrament is a corporeal or material element set before the senses without, representing by similitude and signifying by institution and containing by sanctification some invisible and spiritual grace." This definition is recognized as so fitting and perfect that it is found to befit every sacrament and a sacrament alone. For every thing that has these three is a sacrament, and everything that lacks these three can not be properly called a sacrament.

—Hugh of Saint Victor, died 1141

235 Although the sacraments are outward signs of inward grace, their picture language is not to be separated from the specific content of Scripture. Martin Luther's *Small Cathechism* makes a constant tie between the sacrament of baptism and the Word of the Scriptures.

What is baptism?

Baptism is not simply common water, but it is the water comprehended in God's command, and connected with God's Word.

What is this Word of God?

It is that which our Lord Christ speaks in the last chapter of Matthew [xxviii.19]:

'Go ye [into all the world], and teach all nations, baptizing them in the name of the Father, and of the Son, and of the Holy Ghost.'

What does Baptism give, or of what use is it?

It worketh forgiveness of sins, delivers from death and the devil, and gives everlasting salvation to all who believe, as the Word and promise of God declare.

What are such words and promises of God?

Those which our Lord Christ speaks in the last chapter of Mark:

'He that believeth and is baptized shall be saved; but he that believeth not, shall be damned.'

How can water do such great things?

It is not water, indeed, but the Word of God which is with and in the water, and faith, which trusts in the Word of God in the water. For without the Word of God the water is nothing but water, and no baptism; but with the Word of God it is a baptism—that is, a gracious water of life and a washing of regeneration in the Holy Ghost. . . .

What does such baptizing with water signify?

It signifies that the old Adam in us is to be drowned by daily sorrow and repentance, and perish with all sins and evil lusts; and that the new man should daily come forth again and rise, who shall live before God in righteousness and purity forever.

—*Martin Luther, 1483–1546*

236 Those saintly persons who, through the ages, have sought for experiences that make the presence of God penetratingly real, have often found special grace in the sacrament of Holy Communion. Teresa of Avila reflects on how this has worked in her experience.

If our nature or health doesn't allow us to think always about the [Lord's] passion, since to do so would be arduous, who will prevent us from being with him in his risen state? We have him so near in the blessed sacrament, where he is already glorified and where we don't have to gaze upon him as being so tired and worn out, bleeding, wearied by his journeys, persecuted by those for whom he did so much good, and not believed in by the apostles. Certainly there is no one who can endure thinking all the time about the many trials he suffered. Behold him here without suffering, full of glory, before ascending into heaven, strengthening some, encouraging others, our companion in the most blessed sacrament; it doesn't seem it was in his power to leave us for a moment. And what a pity it was for me to have left you, my Lord, under the pretext of serving you more! When I was offending you I didn't know you; but how, once knowing you, did I think I could gain more by this path! Oh, what a bad road I was following, Lord! Now it seems to me I was walking on no path until you brought me back, for in seeing you at my side I saw all blessings. There is no trial that it wasn't good for me to suffer once I looked at you as you were, standing before the judges. Whoever lives in the presence of so good a friend and excellent a leader, who went ahead of us to be the first to suffer, can endure all things. The Lord helps, strengthens us, and never fails; he is a true friend. And I see clearly, and I saw afterward, that God desires that if we are going to please him and receive his great favors, we must do so through the most sacred humanity of Christ, in whom he takes his delight. Many, many times have I perceived this truth through experience. The Lord has told it to me. I have definitely seen that we must enter by this gate if we desire his sovereign majesty to show us great secrets.

—Teresa of Avila, 1515–1582

237 Something about us human beings likes to give magical significance to special objects. Some early Swiss theologians recognized this danger, and in the First Helvetic Confession made clear that the power of the sacraments is due to God alone, and has nothing to do with the elements or proceedings themselves.

The signs . . . , which are called sacraments, are two, namely, Baptism and the Lord's Supper. These sacraments are significant, holy signs of elevated and secret things.... However, they are not merely empty signs, but consist of both the sign and substance. For in baptism the water is the sign, but the substance and spiritual thing is rebirth and admission into the people of God. In the Lord's Supper the bread and wine are the signs, but the spiritual substance is the communion of the body and blood of Christ, the salvation acquired on the cross, and forgiveness of sins. As the signs are physically received, so these substantial, invisible and spiritual things are received in faith. In addition, the entire power, efficacy and fruit of the sacraments lies in these spiritual and substantial things. For this reason, we confess that the sacraments are not simply outward signs of Christian fellowship. On the contrary, we confess them to be signs of divine grace by which the ministers of the Church work with the Lord for the purpose and to the end which He Himself promises, offers, and efficaciously provides. We confess, however, that all sanctifying and saving power is to be ascribed to God, the Lord alone.

—First Helvetic Confession, 1536

238 The Anglican Church retained the classical teachings of the Christian faith, while rejecting what it perceived to be accretions in Roman Catholicism. When John Wesley, himself an Anglican cleric, provided the Methodist movement in America with a doctrinal basis, he stayed with the Anglican Articles of Religion, in most cases revising them only to fit the American scene. The Methodist statement of the sacraments is therefore nearly identical to the Anglican.

Sacraments ordained of Christ are not only badges or tokens of Christian men's profession, but rather they are certain signs of grace, and God's good will toward us, by which he doth work invisibly in us, and doth not only quicken, but also strengthen and confirm, our faith in him.

There are two Sacraments ordained of Christ our Lord in the Gospel; that is to say, Baptism and the Supper of the Lord....

The Sacraments were not ordained of Christ to be gazed upon, or to be carried about; but that we should duly use them. And in such only as worthily receive the same, they have a wholesome effect or operation; but they that receive them unworthily, purchase to themselves condemnation, as St. Paul saith.

—Articles of Religion, 1784

239 So many of the first generation in the Methodist movement were persons with very limited church background. Their knowledge of the sacraments was often sparse. John Wesley worked faithfully not only to instruct but also to make the sacraments an effective means of grace.

[B]efore you use any means [of grace], let it be deeply impressed on your soul: There is no *power* in this. It is in itself a poor, dead, empty thing: separate from God, it is a dry leaf, a shadow. Neither is there any *merit* in my using this, nothing intrinsically pleasing to God, nothing whereby I deserve any favour at His hands, no, not a drop of water to cool my tongue. But, because God bids, therefore I do; because he directs me to wait in this way, therefore here I wait for his free mercy, whereof cometh my salvation....

Remember also to use all means *as means*; as ordained, not for their own sake, but in order to the renewal of your soul in righteousness and true holiness. If therefore they actually tend to this, well; but, if not, they are dung and dross.

—John Wesley, 1703–1791

240 The "real presence" of Christ is one of the most significant teachings in the sacrament of Communion, but also one of the most controversial. Donald M. Baillie explains the meaning and the significance of this teaching.

[W]hat do we mean by Real Presence? Is it different in the sacrament from the kind of divine presence we can have at any time when we draw near to God?

It is important to note that even apart from the sacrament we are bound to distinguish several degrees or modes of the divine presence. To begin with the most general, we believe in the *omnipresence* of God. He is everywhere present. And yet we also say that God is with those who trust and obey Him in a way in which He is not with others. We say, God is with them. And we say that God's presence is with us *more* at some times than at others. We speak of entering into His presence in worship, and we ask Him to come and be with us and grant us His presence. We say that wherever two or three are gathered together in His name, He is there in the midst of them. And then in apparently a still further sense we speak of the Real Presence in the sacrament. What does all that mean?

Surely the first thing we have to remember is that God's presence is not strictly speaking a *local* or *spatial* presence at all, but a spiritual personal relationship which we have to symbolise by spatial metaphors. When we say that God is everywhere present, that does not mean that He fills every portion of space. For God is not in space at all. Space is part of His creation, and He Himself transcends it. And His omnipresence, as a Christian doctrine, means that wherever we are in this world of space and time, we are not away from God, and He is not absent. What then of His special presence with certain people on certain occasions? Surely that is a spiritual relationship, not less real on that account: we might even say *more real*, because this presence is something much greater, more besetting, more penetrating than any merely local or spatial presence could be. But there are degrees in this relationship. God has a certain spiritual relation to His whole creation, even the material world, in the sense that its very existence and functioning from moment to moment depend upon His will. There is a further degree of this presence in the relationship between God and man, because now there is the beginning of a personal relationship, in the sense that it is only through being *addressed* by God that man is man at all as a personal responsible being. There is a still further stage when man responds to that divine address by personal faith and obedience; so that God is specially present to the faith of the believer or, better still, to the faith of a fellowship of believers in worship, where two or three are gathered together in His name.

—*Donald M. Baillie, 1887–1954*

241 When we are told that one of the words for sacrament infers "mystery," we are too likely to let our popular meaning of that word confuse rather than enlighten us. Thomas C. Oden relates the word to its classical meaning, to show us the depth of meaning for our understanding of the sacraments.

The idea of mystery (from *mueō*, "to instruct in sacred things"), was never meant to suggest incomprehensibility or absurdity, but rather the teaching of spiritual meaning that was as yet not fully revealed for all to see, yet anticipatively revealed, at least in its basic direction, for those who have eyes to see. In the New Testament *mustērion* refers to the divine plan of salvation hidden in past ages, but now brought to light in Jesus Christ (Eph. 1:2). The mystery was not that God was wholly unrevealed, but that his holy will had now at long last become manifest, that his governance was already present in the community of faith, and that the banquet of the end time was in anticipation already being set with bread and wine as lively indications of God's own real presence. . . .

Through these visible re-enactments, God's grace is awakening and empowering our participation in the life of Christ. We are born in Christ in baptism, and through Holy Communion we are nurtured, sustained, and, it is hoped, eventually sanctified (made mature in holy living) in Christ. . . .

The sacraments presuppose that God has met us in history and that this meeting calls us to regular recollection and re-enactment in order to experience God's real presence in our midst. The grace of God is offered in and through these sacraments in a way that we cannot grasp by our own moral efforts. . . . grace is being offered and, by faith, communicated to the believer in baptism and Holy Communion by Christ's own ordinance. They are means of grace. . . .

Water, bread, and wine express promises, not that we make to God but that God makes to us, to which we may respond in obedient faith. They are signs of God's mercy to us and of God's immediate presence in our midst. We are cleansed through water and fed through bread. We are brought into the community by baptism and sustained in the community by communion.

—Thomas C. Oden, 1931–

Worship

The creeds include no statements regarding worship and prayer, nor have these matters been issues for church councils. But from the point of view of the average believer, nothing could be closer to the daily experience of the Christian life. So what do theologians have to say?

242 Some inner qualities of worship are the same from generation to generation. But worshipers must be reminded of these qualities, or they can easily be neglected or obscured. Irenaeus reminds his generation of some of these principles.

Again, giving directions to His disciples to offer to God the first-fruits of His own created things—not as if He stood in need of them, but that they might be themselves neither unfruitful nor ungrateful—He took that created thing, bread, and gave thanks, and said, "This is My body." And the cup likewise, which is part of that creation to which we belong, He confessed to be His blood, and taught the new oblation of the new covenant; which the Church receiving from the apostles, offers to God throughout all the world, to Him who gives us as the means of subsistence the first-fruits of His own gifts in the New Testament. . . .

. . . We are bound, therefore, to offer to God the first-fruits of His creation, as Moses also says, "Thou shalt not appear in the presence of the Lord thy God empty;" so that man, being accounted as grateful, by those things in which he has shown his gratitude, may receive that honour which flows from Him.

. . . For it behoves us to make an oblation to God, and in all things to be found grateful to God our Maker, in a pure mind, and in faith without hypocrisy, in well-grounded hope, in fervent love, offering the first-fruits of His own created things. And the Church alone offers this pure oblation to the Creator, offering to Him, with giving of thanks, [the things taken] from His creation.

—*Irenaeus, c. 130–c. 200*

243 We can rightly reason, from our reading of the New Testament, that early Christian worship followed at least some of the patterns of Judaism for that period; nothing could have been more natural. But not until Christian apologist Justin Martyr, in the middle of the second century, do we have some clear record of how our Christian predecessors conducted public worship.

And on the day called Sunday there is a meeting in one place of those who live in cities or the country, and the memoirs of the apostles or the writings of the prophets are read as long as time permits. When the reader has finished, the president in a discourse urges and invites [us] to the imitation of these noble things. Then we all stand up together and offer prayers. And, as said before, when we have finished the prayer, bread is brought, and wine and water, and the president similarly sends up prayers and thanksgivings to the best of his ability, and the congregation assents, saying the Amen; the distribution, and reception of the consecrated [elements] by each one, takes place and they are sent to the absent by the deacons. Those who prosper, and who so wish, contribute, each one as much as he chooses to. What is collected is deposited with the president, and he takes care of orphans and widows, and those who are in want on account of sickness or any other cause, and those who are in bonds, and the strangers who are sojourners among [us], and, briefly, he is the protector of all those in need. We all hold this common gathering on Sunday, since it is the first day, on which God transforming darkness and matter made the universe, and Jesus Christ our Saviour rose from the dead on the same day.

—*Justin Martyr, c. 100–c. 165*

244 The Psalms urge us to worship God with all sorts of musical instruments. A detached observer might see such use of instruments as being nothing more than a natural development. Hildegard of Bingen saw it as an expression of earnest worship.

I received a word from the living light regarding the diverse kinds of musical instruments that praise God. For it was of these that

David speaks: "Praise him with trumpet sound; praise him with lute and harp." etc. to "Let everything that breathes praise the Lord!" (Psalm 150)

In these words we are taught about inner matters through external ones, namely, how we, according to the material and character of our instruments, should do our best to bring our inner devotion to the praise of the Creator and give it full expression. When we lovingly engage ourselves in this way, we are doing it with rememberance of the way humankind went in search of the voice of the living Spirit. Adam had lost it through his disobedience. Because he lost his innocence, his voice in no way harmonized with the voices of the angels who sing God's praise. . . .

The holy prophets, taught by the same Spirit they too had received, composed not only psalms and hymns to increase the devotion of their hearers, but also invented various musical instruments as sonorous accompaniments. . . .

Zealous and wise people have imitated these prophets, and they too, through their human ingenuity, have developed a variety of musical instruments in order to be able to sing in joyfulness of heart.

—Hildegard of Bingen, 1098–1179

245 Because we humans are, by nature, worshiping creatures, we will find an object for our worship—if not a good one, whatever is appealing and available. Martin Luther deals with the hazards in this human instinct.

"You shall have no other gods."

That is, you shall regard me alone as your God. What does this mean, and how is it to be understood? What is it to have a god? What is God?

Answer: A god is that to which we look for all good and in which we find refuge in every time of need. To have a god is nothing else than to trust and believe him with our whole heart. As I have often said, the trust and faith of the heart alone make both God and an idol. If your faith and trust are right, then your God is the true God. On the other hand, if your trust is false and wrong, then you have not the true God. For these two belong together, faith and God. That to which your heart clings and entrusts itself is, I say, really your God.

—Martin Luther, 1483–1546

246 What elements ought to be present in corporate worship? John Calvin, one of the great Reformers, insisted that two marks of the true church are the preaching of the Word of God and a proper use of the sacraments. This preaching should be "reverently heard," for preaching that is not effectively received does not fulfill its mission.

We have said that the symbols by which the Church is discerned are the preaching of the word and the observance of the sacraments, for these cannot anywhere exist without producing fruit and prospering by the blessing of God. I say not that wherever the word is preached fruit immediately appears; but that in every place where it is received, and has a fixed abode, it uniformly displays its efficacy. Be this as it may, when the preaching of the gospel is reverently heard, and the sacraments are not neglected, there for the time the face of the Church appears without deception or ambiguity and no man may with impunity spurn her authority, or reject her admonitions, or resist her counsels, or make sport of her censures, far less revolt from her, and violate her unity.... For such is the value which the Lord sets on the communion of his Church, that all who ... alienate themselves from any Christian society, in which the true ministry of his word and sacraments is maintained, he regards as deserters of religion. So highly does he recommend her authority, that when it is violated he considers that his own authority is impaired.

—John Calvin, 1509–1564

247 The woman of Samaria wanted Jesus to define the proper place to worship (John 4); hers was a reasonable question, since some locations have traditionally been seen as sacred. Richard Hooker, theologian of the Church of England, looks at both sides of this question as he considers that proper worship can be pursued anywhere, but that there is something particular to be said for the designated place.

The true worship of God is to God in itself acceptable, who respects not so much in what place as with what affection he is served; and therefore Moses in the midst of the sea, Job on the dunghill, Ezekiel in bed, Jeremiah in mire, Jonah in the whale, Daniel in the den, the children in the furnace, the thief on the cross, Peter and Paul in prison, calling unto God were heard.... Manifest notwithstanding it is, that the very majesty and holiness of the place where God is worshiped has, *in regard of us,* great virtue, force and efficacy, for it serves as a sensible help to stir up devotion, and *in that respect* no doubt *betters* even our holiest and best actions in this kind. As therefore we every where exhort all men to worship God, even so for performance of this service of the people of God assembled, we think not any place *so good* as the church, neither any exhortation so fit as that of David, "O worship the Lord in the beauty of holiness."

—Richard Hooker, 1554–1600

248 Because worship is so natural to us human beings, we rarely try to define it; and when we do, we hardly know where to find the right words. Few people have been more effective at putting the essence of worship into significant form than Evelyn Underhill, writer on the spiritual life.

Worship, in all its grades and kinds, is the response of the creature to the Eternal: nor need we limit this definition to the human sphere. There is a sense in which we may think of the whole life of the Universe, seen and unseen, conscious and unconscious, as an act of worship, glorifying its Origin, Sustainer, and End. Only in some such context, indeed, can we begin to understand the emergence and growth of the spirit of worship in men, or the influence which it exerts upon their concrete activities. Thus worship may be overt or direct, unconscious or conscious. Where conscious, its emotional colour can range from fear through reverence to self-oblivious love. But whatever its form of expression may be, it is always a subject-object relationship; and its general existence therefore constitutes a damaging criticism of all merely subjective and immanental explanations of Reality. For worship is an acknowledgment of Transcendence; that is to say, of a Reality independent of the worshipper, which is always more or less deeply coloured by mystery, and which is there first.... it at least points to man's profound sense of dependence upon "the spiritual side of the unknown".

So, directly we take this strange thing Worship seriously, and give it the status it deserves among the various responses of men to their environment, we find that it obliges us to take up a particular attitude towards that environment....

It is true that from first to last self-regarding elements are mixed with human worship; but these are no real part of it. Not man's needs and wishes, but God's presence and incitement, first evoke it. As it rises towards purity and leaves egotistic piety behind, He becomes more and more the only Fact of existence, the one Reality; and the very meaning of Creation is seen to be an act of worship, a devoted proclamation of the splendour, the wonder, and the beauty of God. In this great *Sanctus*, all things justify their being and have their place. God alone matters, God alone Is—creation only matters because of Him. "Wherein does your prayer consist?" said St John of the Cross to one of his penitents. She replied: "In considering the Beauty of God, and in rejoicing that He has such beauty."

—*Evelyn Underhill, 1875–1941*

249 We experience worship so differently, because God graciously engages us at our own levels of perception. For that reason, worship is difficult to define. William Temple, Archbishop of Canterbury in the twentieth century, has given us what is probably as comprehensive and memorable a definition of worship as we are likely to find.

Worship is the submission of all our nature to God. It is the quickening of conscience by his holiness; the nourishment of mind with his truth; the purifying of the imagination by his beauty; the opening of the heart to his love; the surrender of will to his purpose—and all of this gathered up in adoration, the most selfless emotion of which our nature is capable and therefore the chief remedy of that self-centredness which is our original sin and the source of all actual sin.

—*William Temple, 1881–1944*

250 Music has been part of worship for the people of God since early in the history of Israel; one thinks of Miriam, leading the women of the nation in song after the people had gone through the Red Sea. But the quality of worship doesn't come to music without a spirit of dedication. Fred Pratt Green speaks as musician and worshiper.

When in our music God is glorified,
and adoration leaves no room for pride,
it is as though the whole creation cried
Alleluia! Alleluia!

How often, making music, we have found
a new dimension in the world of sound,
as worship moved us to a more profound
Alleluia! Alleluia!

So has the church in liturgy and song,
in faith and love, through centuries of wrong,
borne witness to the truth in every tongue,
Alleluia! Alleluia!

And did not Jesus sing a psalm that night
when utmost evil strove against the light?
Then let us sing, for whom he won the fight:
Alleluia! Alleluia!

Let every instrument be tuned for praise!
Let all rejoice who have a voice to raise!
And may God give us faith to sing always
Alleluia! Alleluia!

—*Fred Pratt Green, 1903–*

251 Although, as we have noted, the pattern of Christian worship began with its Hebrew antecedents, somewhere it began to take on qualities of its own. We see the beginning of this process already in the New Testament, in what happened in the church in the very first century. Educator David L. Bartlett helps us trace this process.

For Christians, worship is both the praise that people owe God and the means by which God's grace strengthens and guides people. Christians believe that they praise God through Christ and that God's grace has been given them in Christ. Although prayer and devotion may be individual, worship is the work of the church community.

Earliest Christian worship was influenced by worship in the synagogue, but very soon Christian worship began to take on its own distinctive shape. In I Corinthians, Paul describes the nature of worship in a predominantly Gentile congregation. He talks of the practice of the Lord's Supper (I Corinthians 11), indicating that for some, at least, it includes a communal meal, and insisting that for all it should include taking of bread and wine "in remembrance" of Christ's death. Paul also says that the assembly of Christians includes hymns, lessons, speaking in tongues, and interpretation of tongues (I Corinthians 14).

Very early on, the central worship of the congregations took place on Sunday in celebration of Christ's resurrection on the first day of the week. Almost from the beginning, Sunday worship included both the Lord's Supper and some kind of prophecy or proclamation.

—David L. Bartlett, 20th century

252 Because we humans have an insistent capacity for selfishness, we can easily turn even the beauty of worship into self-centering channels. To do so is to miss the essence of what worship means, Leander E. Keck, biblical theologian, reminds us.

[A]uthentic praise of God acknowledges what is true about God; it responds to qualities that are "there" and not simply "there for me." This is true generically of praise, not just of God-oriented praise. The person who praises an athlete's achievement, a work of art, the manifestation of a person's virtue, affirms that these are indeed praiseworthy, and that something would be wrong with a beholder who did not acknowledge them. In other words, God is to be praised because God is God, because of what God is and does, quite apart from what God is and does for me. Anyone can, and should, praise God when the Lord blesses one and keeps one, when the Lord makes his face to shine upon one and is gracious to one, when the Lord lifts up his countenance upon one and grants peace (Num. 6:24-26). Gratitude is indeed often expressed as praise, and rightly. But that does not make praise and gratitude identical. Or does God cease to be praiseworthy when gratitude has fled because the Lord seems to withhold blessing, when the divine face appears to be set against us, and when agony drives out peace? If God is indeed praiseworthy, must God earn our praise?

If this Reality is the Creator to whom we trace our existence but who does not trace its existence to us, then it has an integrity of its own, an integrity whose ways are not our ways, and whose ends cannot be conflated with ours. Only such a Reality is worthy of praise, inherently.

—Leander E. Keck, 1928–

The Message Behind the Symbols

The Christian Life
Sanctification/Holiness

Symbols of the faithful, fruitful Christian life appropriately include the fish as the symbol of the believer whose life is meant to imitate Jesus Christ—whose symbol is also the fish.

The ivy vine symbolizes the relationship between Christian believers and God through Christ. Jesus said, "I am the vine, you are the branches" (John 15:5). Vital Christian living has its source in the connection of the branch to the vine.

Sheep, known for their fidelity in following their shepherd, represent followers of Jesus Christ the Good Shepherd—always attuned to his call and his leading. Both the fig and the strawberry, with their tiny but numerous seeds, symbolize righteous, holy living, rich with the fruit of good deeds. The torch with its vigorous, light-casting flame, represents the passion and the warmth with which the Christian witnesses for Christ in a dark but expectant world.

The crown symbolizes the crown of life, the mark of victory, the reward for faithful Christian living. "Be faithful until death, and I will give you the crown of life" (Revelation 2:10).

The Christian Life

In some ways the Christian life is very simple; all we have to do is to "take up the cross" and follow Jesus. But we soon discover that cross-bearing and following Jesus can be very complex. How do we maintain the inner quality of life that will sustain true discipleship? And if we find rules that will help, might those rules also tend to a kind of legalism that will be very un-Christlike? Saints and teachers over the ages have given counsel for this wondrous journey.

253 Over the centuries numbers of Christian movements have sought to identify themselves as God's people by particular forms of speech or dress. But very early in the history of the church the Letter to Diognetus noted that Christian distinctiveness is not that easily achieved. Christians follow the customs of the world around them, yet have a special quality.

For Christians cannot be distinguished from the rest of the human race by country or language or customs. They do not live in cities of their own; they do not use a peculiar form of speech; they do not follow an eccentric manner of life. This doctrine of theirs has not been discovered by the ingenuity or deep thought of inquisitive men, nor do they put forward a merely human teaching, as some people do. Yet, although they live in Greek and barbarian cities alike, as each man's lot has been cast, and follow the customs of the country in clothing and food and other matters of daily living, at the same time they give proof of the remarkable and admittedly extraordinary constitution of their own commonwealth. They live in their own countries, but only as aliens. They have a share in everything as citizens, and endure everything as foreigners. Every foreign land is their fatherland, and yet for them every fatherland is a foreign land.

—*Letter to Diognetus, 2nd century*

254 Effective Christian living demands an amount of introspection, else we will become superficial. But the introspection can easily lead to a kind of spiritual paralysis, where we're afraid to do anything lest our motives be wrong, or results go astray. Francis of Assisi dealt thoughtfully with such concerns.

Great grace cannot be possessed in peace, because many conflicts always arise against it. The more grace a man has, the more the devil attacks him. But a man should not on that account stop being guided by his grace, because the harder the battle, the greater will his crown be, if he wins. . . .

Again someone said to him: "What can I do? For if I do any good, I become vain about it, and if I do bad, I am depressed and almost fall into despair." The holy Brother Giles answered: "You do right in grieving for your sin. However, I advise you to grieve moderately. For you must always believe that God's power to forgive is greater than your power to sin. If God has mercy on some great sinner, do you think He abandons a smaller sinner? But don't stop doing good because of the temptation to vanity. For if a farmer wishing to throw seed on the ground says to himself: 'I don't want to sow this year because, if I sow, birds may come and eat that seed,' and if therefore he does not sow, he would not have any produce from his land to eat. But if he sows, although some of the seed perishes, still he will have most of it. That is the way it is with the man who is tempted to vanity and fights against it."

—Francis of Assisi, 1181–1226

255 Few followers of Christ have seemed to fulfill the teachings of their Master in truer fashion than Francis of Assisi. His prayer of total commitment is a succinct commentary on Jesus' call to take up the cross.

> Lord, make me an instrument of thy peace;
> where there is hatred, let me sow love;
> where there is injury, pardon;
> where there is doubt, faith;
> where there is despair, hope;
> where there is darkness, light;
> and where there is sadness, joy.

> O Divine Master,
> grant that I may not so much seek
> to be consoled as to console;
> to be understood, as to understand;
> to be loved, as to love;
> for it is in giving that we receive,
> it is in pardoning that we are pardoned,
> and it is in dying that we are born to eternal life.
>
> *—Francis of Assisi, 1181–1226*

256 Abraham, the father of the faithful, became a pilgrim in order to follow his call. The New Testament pictured the Christian life as one of an earthly pilgrimage. Martin Luther used this same theme to describe the Christian life to his generation of believers.

Every Christian, be he lord or servant, prince or subject, should conduct himself as befits his station, using in trust whatever God has given him—dominion and subjects, house and home, wife and children, money and property, meat and drink. He is to regard himself solely as a guest of earth, as one eating his morsel of bread or taking his lunch in an inn; he must conduct himself in this earthly harbor as a pious guest. Thus may he actually be a king reigning with fidelity, or a lord faithful to his office, and at the same time declare: "I count nothing on this life. I do not expect to remain here. This is but a strange country to me. True, I am seated in the uppermost place at table in this inn; but the occupant of the lowest seat has just as much as I, here or yonder. For we are alike guests. But he who assigned my duty, whose command I execute, gave me orders to conduct myself piously and honorably in this inn, as becomes a guest." . . .

. . . At the same time, we are to regard this life as a journey through a country where we have no citizenship—where we are not at home; to think of ourselves as travelers or pilgrims occupying for a night the same inn, eating and drinking there and then leaving the place.

—Martin Luther, 1483–1546

257 Those outside the company of believers always look for consistency between the Christian profession and the Christian life. Thomas Cranmer made a passionate appeal for such consistency.

Let us therefore, good Christian people, try and examine our faith, what it is: let us not flatter ourselves, but look upon our works, and so judge of our faith what it is. Christ himself speaketh of this matter, and saith: "The tree is known by the fruit" (Luke 6:44). Therefore let us do good works, and thereby declare our faith to be the lively Christian faith....

If these fruits do not follow, we do but mock with God, deceive ourselves, and also other men. Well may we bear the name of Christian men, but we do lack the true faith that doth belong thereunto.... Thy deeds and works must be an open testimonial of thy faith: otherwise thy faith, being without good works, is but the devils' faith, the faith of the wicked, a phantasy of faith, and not a true Christian faith.

—Thomas Cranmer, 1489–1556

258 From the first century on, Christians have been urged to be in the world yet not of the world, to use its resources yet not be possessed by them. It is a difficult assignment; no wonder some religious movements have simply sought to absent themselves from the world. But English spiritual writer William Law insisted that the Christian life has to be lived out right where we are.

For as all men and all things in the world as truly belong unto God as any places, things, or persons that are devoted to divine service, so all things are to be used, and all persons are to act in their several states and employments, for the glory of God.

Men of worldly business therefore must not look upon themselves as at liberty to live to themselves, to sacrifice to their own humors and tempers because their employment is of a worldly nature. But they must consider that as the world and all worldly professions as truly belong to God as persons and things that are devoted to the altar, so it is as much the duty of men in worldly business to live wholly unto God as 'tis the duty of those who are devoted to divine service.

As the whole world is God's, so the whole world is to act for God. As all men have the same relation to God, as all men have all their powers and faculties from God, so all men are obliged to act for God with all their powers and faculties.

As all things are God's, so all things are to be used and regarded as the things of God. For men to abuse things on earth and live to themselves is the same rebellion against God as for angels to abuse things in heaven, because God is just the same Lord of all on earth as he is the Lord of all in heaven.

Things may and must differ in their use, but yet they are all to be used according to the will of God.

—*William Law, 1686–1761*

259 Dedication, consecration, and commitment have always been key words in the vocabulary of Christian discipleship. But John Wesley, building on materials from other communions, puts new content into these words as he spells out some of the possibilities.

[M]ake me what you will, Lord, and set me where you will: let me be a vessel of silver or gold, or a vessel of wood or stone, so I be a vessel of honor: of whatsoever form or metal, whether higher or lower, finer or coarser, I am content; if I be not the head, or the eye, or the ear, one of the nobler and more honorable instruments you will employ, let me be the hand, or the foot, one of the most laborious, and lowest, and most contemptible of all the Servants of my Lord, let my dwelling be upon the dunghill, my portion in the wilderness, my name and lot among the hewers of wood, or drawers of water, among the doorkeepers of your house; anywhere, where I may be serviceable; I put myself wholly into your hands: put me to what you will, rank me with whom you will; put me to doing, put me to suffering, let me be employed for you, or laid aside for you, exalted for you, or trodden under foot for you; let me be full, let me be empty, let me have all things, let me have nothing, I freely and heartily resign all to your pleasure and disposal.

—*John Wesley, 1703–1791*

260 Through the centuries believers have sung their commitments, as well as their hopes and petitions, in the hymnody of faith. One of Charles Wesley's hymns puts Christian discipleship into everyday language.

> Forth in thy name, O Lord, I go,
> My daily labor to pursue,
> Thee, only thee resolved to know
> In all I think, or speak, or do.

The task thy wisdom has assigned
Oh, let me cheerfully fulfill,
In all my works thy presence find,
And prove thy acceptable will.

Thee may I set at my right hand
Whose eyes my inmost substance see,
And labor on at thy command,
And offer all my works to thee.

Give me to bear thy easy yoke,
And every moment watch and pray,
And still to things eternal look,
And hasten to thy glorious day;

For thee delightfully employ
Whate'er thy bounteous grace hath given,
And run my course with even joy,
And closely walk with thee to heaven.

—Charles Wesley, 1707–1788

261 Ultimately our doctrines are proved or disproved by the quality of our lives. American social reformer Lucretia Mott was angered by the inconsistencies she so often found between belief and practice, and in a period shortly before the American Civil War challenged Christians to live up to their professions.

It is time that Christians were judged more by their likeness to Christ than their notions of Christ. Were this sentiment generally admitted we should not see such tenacious adherence to what men deem the opinions and doctrines of Christ while at the same time in every day practise is exhibited anything but a likeness to Christ. . . .

Instead of going about doing good as was his wont, instead of being constantly in the exercise of benevolence and love as was his practice, we find the disposition too generally to measure the Christian by his assent to a creed which had not its sign with him nor indeed in his day. Instead of engaging in the exercise of peace, justice and mercy, how many of the professors are arrayed against him in opposition to those great principles even as were his opposers in his day. Instead of being the bold nonconformist (if I may so speak) that he was, they are adhering to old church usages, and worn-out forms and exhibiting little of a Christ like disposition and character. Instead of uttering the earnest protests against wickedness in high places, against the spirit of proselytism and sectarianism as did the blessed Jesus—the divine, the holy, the born of God, there is the servile accommodation to this sectarian spirit and an observance of those forms even long after there is any claim of virtue in them.

—*Lucretia Mott, 1793–1880*

262 Whenever we discuss discipleship, we are in danger of becoming overly theoretical. Two twentieth-century writers who have been especially active in the day-by-day renewal of the church, Robert H. Ramey, Jr., and Ben Campbell Johnson, have spelled out the nature of our Christian life and experience in practical, understandable terms.

Those who now come into the church, as well as those who have been involved for some time, will benefit from examining the meaning of Christian commitment and the Christian life. Being a Christian can be summed up in the following statements:

1. To be a Christian is to be awakened to the goodness and mercy of God through the proclamation of the gospel of Jesus Christ.

2. To be a Christian is to recognize that you are a sinner before God and need God's grace in order to be saved from the power and guilt of sin.

3. To be a Christian is to place your faith in Jesus Christ as Lord and Savior and to repent of sin.

4. To be a Christian is to intend to be Christ's faithful disciple, obeying his word and showing his love to your life's end.

5. To be a Christian is to belong to the church, Christ's Body, and to participate actively and responsibly in its worship and mission.

—*Robert H. Ramey, Jr., and Ben Campbell Johnson, 20th century*

Sanctification/Holiness

No ancient church councils ever met to settle definitions of holiness, yet the pursuit of holiness has driven and inspired the best of believers in every century. Along the way, whole movements have developed around this pursuit, and in some cases religious denominations. Our sources of readings include both professional theologians and earnest practitioners.

263 The work of salvation is of such grand dimensions that we break it into manageable parts, one of which is sanctification. In John Calvin's view, these various parts are, however, inseparable, since they are all part of the person and work of our Lord Christ.

Why, then, are we justified before God by faith? Because by faith we grasp Christ's righteousness, through which we are reconciled to God. Yet you could not grasp this righteousness without at the same time grasping sanctification. . . . Christ justifies no one who he does not also sanctify.

These benefits are joined together by a permanent and indissoluble bond, so that those whom he illumines with his wisdom, he also redeems; those whom he redeems, he justifies; those whom he justifies, he sanctifies. But since our question concerns only righteousness and sanctification, let us dwell on these. Although we may distinguish them, Christ contains both of them inseparably in himself.

Do you wish to attain righteousness in Christ? You must first possess Christ. Yet you cannot possess Christ without first sharing his sanctification, because Christ cannot be divided into pieces. Christ sacrificed himself that we might enjoy his benefits; hence he bestows both of them at the same time, never giving one without the other. Thus it is clear that we are justified not without good works, yet not through good works. By becoming part of Christ, we are justified before God; and in the process we are sanctified also.

—John Calvin, 1509–1564

264 Jonathan Edwards holds a unique place in American history as a philosopher and preacher, but biographers note that his wife, Sarah Pierrepont Edwards, may well have been equally outstanding. Here she recounts her own experience of holiness.

About 11 o'clock, as I accidentally went into the room where Mr. Buell was conversing with some of the people, I heard him say, "that we, who are the children of God, should be cold and lifeless in religion!" and I felt such a sense of the deep ingratitude manifested by the children of God, in such coldness and deadness, that my strength was immediately taken away, and I sunk down on the spot.... After I had lain a while, I felt more perfectly subdued and weaned from the world, and more fully resigned to God, than I had ever been conscious of before. I felt an entire indifference to the opinions, and representations, and conduct of mankind respecting me.... At the same time, I felt a far greater love to the children of God, than ever before. I seemed to love them as my own soul; and when I saw them, my heart went out towards them, with an inexpressible endearedness and sweetness.... This was accompanied with a ravishing sense of the unspeakable joys of the upper world. They appeared to my mind in all their reality and certainty, and as it were in actual and distinct vision; so plain and evident were they to the eye of my faith, I seemed to regard them as begun....

My soul remained in a kind of heavenly elysium. So far as I am capable of making a comparison, I think that what I felt each minute, during the continuance of the whole time, was worth more than all the outward comfort and pleasure, which I had enjoyed in my whole life put together. It was a pure delight, which fed and satisfied the soul.

—Sarah Pierrepont Edwards, 1710–1758

265 Much of the impetus in the Wesleyan (Methodist) revival came from the search for a deeper, more fulfilling Christian life. Charles Wesley put this search into words in many of his hymns, most notably the following one.

Love divine, all loves excelling,
joy of heaven, to earth come down;
fix in us thy humble dwelling;
all thy faithful mercies crown!
Jesus, thou art all compassion,
pure, unbounded love thou art;
visit us with thy salvation;
enter every trembling heart.

Breathe, O breathe thy loving Spirit
into every troubled breast!
Let us all in thee inherit;
let us find that second rest.
Take away our bent to sinning;
Alpha and Omega be;
end of faith, as its beginning,
set our hearts at liberty.

Come, Almighty to deliver,
let us all thy life receive;
suddenly return and never,
nevermore thy temples leave.
Thee we would be always blessing,
serve thee as thy hosts above,
pray and praise thee without ceasing,
glory in thy perfect love.

Finish, then, thy new creation;
pure and spotless let us be.
Let us see thy great salvation
perfectly restored in thee;
changed from glory into glory,
till in heaven we take our place,
till we cast our crowns before thee,
lost in wonder, love, and praise.
—Charles Wesley, 1707–1788

266 Jesus insisted, in the Sermon on the Mount, that we should be perfect even as our heavenly Father is perfect. But how is such perfection to be defined? For John Wesley, it is to be made perfect in love.

From the time of our being 'born again' the gradual work of sanctification takes place. We are enabled 'by the Spirit' to 'mortify the deeds of the body', of our evil nature. And as we are more and more dead to sin, we are more and more alive to God. We go on from grace to grace, while we are careful to 'abstain from all appearance of evil', and are 'zealous of good works', 'as we have opportunity doing good to all men'; while we walk in all his ordinances blameless, therein worshipping him in spirit and in truth; while we take up our cross and deny ourselves every pleasure that does not lead us to God.

It is thus that we wait for entire sanctification, for a full salvation from all our sins, from pride, self-will, anger, unbelief, or, as the Apostle expresses it, 'Go on to perfection.' But what is perfection? The word has various senses: here it means perfect love. It is love excluding sin; love filling the heart, taking up the whole capacity of the soul. It is love 'rejoicing evermore, praying without ceasing, in everything giving thanks.'

—John Wesley, 1703–1791

267 The end of the Christian life has never been simply that persons should be saved from judgment, but that they should become exemplary followers of their Lord. This was one of the strongest convictions of John Wesley, and he spoke vigorously against any theology that was content with less.

[H]ere let no man deceive his own soul. It is diligently to be noted, the 'faith which bringeth not forth repentance' and love, and all good works, is not that 'right living faith' which is here spoken of, 'but a dead and devilish one. . . . For even the devils believe that Christ was born of a virgin, that he wrought all kind of miracles, declaring himself very God; that for our sakes he suffered a most painful death, to redeem us from death everlasting; that he rose again the third day; that he ascended into heaven and sitteth at the right hand of the Father, and at the end of the world shall come again to judge both the quick and the dead. These articles of our faith the devils believe, and so they believe all that is written in the

Old and New Testament. And yet for all this faith, they be but devils. . . .'

'The right and true Christian faith is' (to go on in the words of our own Church) 'not only to believe that Holy Scripture and the articles of our faith are true, but also to have a sure trust and confidence to be saved from everlasting damnation by Christ'—it is a 'sure trust and confidence' which a man hath in God 'that by the merits of Christ his sins *are* forgiven, and he reconciled to the favour of God'—'whereof doth follow a loving heart to obey his commandments.'

Now whosoever has this faith which 'purifies the heart', by the power of God who dwelleth therein, from pride, anger, desire, 'from all unrighteousness', 'from all filthiness of flesh and spirit'; which fills it with love stronger than death both to God and to all mankind—love that doth the works of God, glorying to spend and to be spent for all men, and that endureth with joy, not only the reproach of Christ, the being mocked, despised, and hated of all men, but whatsoever the wisdom of God permits the malice of men or devils to inflict; whosoever has this faith, thus 'working by love', is not *almost* only, but *altogether* a Christian.

—John Wesley, 1703–1791

268 Those who wrote about holiness and sanctification moved easily from the theory to the practice. They developed a full theological position, but were ready always to put the theory into expressions of daily living. Phoebe Palmer, a highly popular nineteenth-century teacher and preacher, was especially effective in this manner.

Gospel holiness is that *state* which is attained by the believer when, through *faith* in the infinite merit of the Saviour, body and soul, with every ransomed faculty, are ceaselessly presented, a living sacrifice, to God; the purpose of the soul being steadily bent to know nothing among men, save Christ and Him crucified, and the eye of faith fixed on "the Lamb of God which taketh away the sin of the world." In obedience to the requirement of God, the sacrifice is presented *through* Christ, and the soul at once proves that "He is able to save them to the *uttermost* that come unto God by Him."

Holiness implies salvation from sin, a redemption from *all* iniquity. The soul, through faith, being laid upon the *altar* that *sancti-*

fieth the gift, experiences *constantly* the all-cleansing efficacy of the blood of Jesus.

—Phoebe Palmer, 1807–1874

269 A freed slave, Amanda Berry Smith, became a popular preacher and evangelist. Part of her transforming strength came from an experience of sanctification that she described in this way:

"There are a great many persons who are troubled about the blessing of sanctification; how they can keep it if they get it."

"Oh!" I said, "he means me, for that is just what I have said. With my trials and peculiar temperament and all that I have to contend with, if I could get the blessing how could I keep it? Now, some one has told him, for he is looking right at me and I know he means me." And I tried to hide behind the post, and he seemed to look around there. Then I said, "Well, he means me, and I will just take what he says." He used this illustration: "When you work hard all day and are very tired,—"Yes," I said, and in a moment my mind went through my washing and ironing all night,—"When you go to bed at night you don't fix any way for yourself to breathe,"—"No," I said, "I never think about it,"—"You go to bed, you breathe all night, you have nothing to do with your breathing, you awake in the morning, you had nothing to do with it."

"Yes, yes, I see it."

He continued: "You don't need to fix any way for God to live in you; get God in you in all His fullness and He will live Himself."

"Oh!" I said, "I see it." . . . "God in you, God in you," and I thought doing what? Ruling every ambition and desire, and bringing every thought unto captivity and obedience to His will. How I have lived through it I cannot tell, but the blessedness of the love and the peace and power I can never describe. O, what glory filled my soul!

—Amanda Berry Smith, 1837–1915

270 A sometimes neglected aspect of sanctification is the potential it sees in every human being. We are not simply souls to be saved, but persons of unimaginable possibilities. Reinhold Niebuhr explores this aspect and its challenge.

A new synthesis is therefore called for. It must be a synthesis which incorporates the twofold aspects of grace of Biblical religion, and adds the light which modern history, and the Renaissance and Reformation interpretations of history, have thrown upon the paradox of grace. Briefly this means that on the one hand life in history must be recognized as filled with indeterminate possibilities. There is no individual or interior spiritual situation, no cultural or scientific task, and no social or political problem in which men do not face new possibilities of the good and the obligation to realize them. It means on the other hand that every effort and pretension to complete life, whether in collective or individual terms, that every desire to stand beyond the contradictions of history, or to eliminate the final corruptions of history must be disavowed....

The double aspect of grace, the twofold emphasis upon the obligation to fulfill the possibilities of life and upon the limitations and corruptions in all historic realizations, implies that history is a meaningful process but is incapable of fulfilling itself and therefore points beyond itself to the judgment and mercy of God for its fulfillment.

—Reinhold Niebuhr, 1892–1971

271 From a theologian's point of view, sanctification is one part of the larger doctrine of salvation. In this reading, Karl Barth speaks of the relationship between justification and sanctification.

Under the title "sanctification" we take up the theme which constitutes the particular scope of this second part of the doctrine of reconciliation. The divine act of atonement accomplished and revealed in Jesus Christ does not consist only in the humiliation of God but in and with this in the exaltation of man. Thus it does not consist only in the fact that God offers Himself up for men; that He, the Judge, allows Himself to be judged in their place, in this way establishing and proclaiming among sinners, and in defiance of their sin, His divine right which is as such the basis of a new right of man before Him. It does not consist, therefore, only in the justification of man. It consists also in the sanctification which is indissolubly bound up with his justification, i.e., in the fact that as He turns to man in defiance of his sin He also, in defiance of his sin, turns man to Himself. The reconciliation of man with God takes place also in the form that He introduces as a new man the one in relation to whom He has set Himself in the right and whom He has set in the right in relation to Himself. He has introduced him in the new form of existence of a faithful covenant-partner who is well-pleasing to Him and blessed by Him. "I will be your God" is the justification of man. "Ye shall be my people" is his sanctification. . . .

What is meant by sanctification (*sanctificatio*) might just as well be described by the less common biblical term regeneration (*regeneratio*) or renewal (*renovatio*), or by that of conversion (*conversio*), or by that of penitence (*poenitentia*) which plays so important a role in both the Old and New Testaments, or comprehensively by that of discipleship which is so outstanding especially in the synoptic Gospels. The content of all these terms will have to be brought out under the title of sanctification. But there is good reason to keep the term sanctification itself in the foreground. It includes already, even verbally, the idea of the "saint," and therefore in contradistinction to the other descriptions of the same matter it shows us at once that we are dealing with the being and action of God, reminding us in a way which is normative for the understanding of the other terms as well of the basic and decisive fact that God is the active Subject not only in reconciliation generally but also in the conversion of man to Himself. Like His turning to man, and man's justification, this is His work, His *facere*. But it is now seen and understood, not as his *iustificare*, but as his *sanctificare*.

—*Karl Barth, 1886–1968*

272 Anything so wonderful as true holiness must, of course, come at a price. C.S. Lewis explains the price in direct, down-to-earth fashion.

Christ says "Give me All. I don't want so much of your time and so much of your money and so much of your work: I want You. I have not come to torment your natural self, but to kill it. No half-measures are any good. I don't want to cut off a branch here and a branch there. I want to have the whole tree down. . . .

" . . . The moment you put yourself in My hands, that is what you are in for. Nothing less, or other, than that. You have free will, and if you choose, you can push Me away. But if you do not push Me away, understand that I am going to see this job through. Whatever suffering it may cost you in your earthly life, whatever inconceivable purification it may cost you after death, whatever it costs Me, I will never rest, nor let you rest, until you are literally perfect—until my Father can say without reservation that He is well pleased with you, as He said He was well pleased with me. This I can do and will do. But I will not do anything less."

—*C.S. Lewis, 1898–1963*

273 One of the most significant religious movements in late eighteenth and nineteenth century America was the pietistic revival among German immigrants. Out of this movement came, eventually, the Evangelical United Brethren Church, whose doctrinal standard includes a clear statement about the nature of sanctification and perfection.

We believe sanctification is the work of God's grace through the Word and the Spirit, by which those who have been born again are cleansed from sin in their thoughts, words and acts, and are enabled to live in accordance with God's will, and to strive for holiness without which no one will see the Lord.

Entire sanctification is a state of perfect love, righteousness and true holiness which every regenerate believer may obtain by being delivered from the power of sin, by loving God with all the heart, soul, mind and strength, and by loving one's neighbor as one's self. Through faith in Jesus Christ this gracious gift may be received in this life both gradually and instantaneously, and should be sought earnestly by every child of God.

We believe this experience does not deliver us from the infirmities, ignorance, and mistakes common to man, nor from the possibilities of further sin. The Christian must continue on guard against spiritual pride and seek to gain victory over every temptation to sin. He must respond wholly to the will of God so that sin will lose its power over him; and the world, the flesh, and the devil are put under his feet. Thus he rules over these enemies with watchfulness through the power of the Holy Spirit.

—*Confession of Faith of The Evangelical United Brethren Church, 1962*

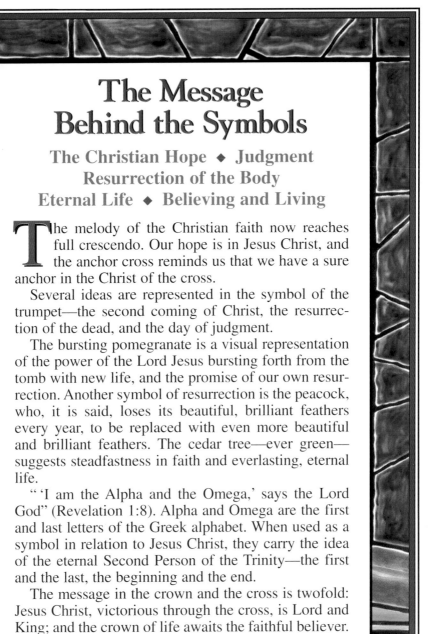

The Message Behind the Symbols

The Christian Hope ◆ Judgment
Resurrection of the Body
Eternal Life ◆ Believing and Living

The melody of the Christian faith now reaches full crescendo. Our hope is in Jesus Christ, and the anchor cross reminds us that we have a sure anchor in the Christ of the cross.

Several ideas are represented in the symbol of the trumpet—the second coming of Christ, the resurrection of the dead, and the day of judgment.

The bursting pomegranate is a visual representation of the power of the Lord Jesus bursting forth from the tomb with new life, and the promise of our own resurrection. Another symbol of resurrection is the peacock, who, it is said, loses its beautiful, brilliant feathers every year, to be replaced with even more beautiful and brilliant feathers. The cedar tree—ever green—suggests steadfastness in faith and everlasting, eternal life.

"'I am the Alpha and the Omega,' says the Lord God" (Revelation 1:8). Alpha and Omega are the first and last letters of the Greek alphabet. When used as a symbol in relation to Jesus Christ, they carry the idea of the eternal Second Person of the Trinity—the first and the last, the beginning and the end.

The message in the crown and the cross is twofold: Jesus Christ, victorious through the cross, is Lord and King; and the crown of life awaits the faithful believer.

The Christian Hope

The apostle Paul said that faith, hope, and love abide, and that the greatest of these is love. Love has rightly become a dominant word in the Christian message. And yet, no word is more dramatically Christian than *hope*. But what, exactly, is that hope? See what theologians have said.

274 The Hebrew prophets envisioned a world in which all nature would be in harmony, so that lion and lamb can lie down together. Augustine portrays such harmony in other terms: a world where, with evil absent and good dominant, all of life will show beauty.

How great shall be that felicity, which shall be tainted with no evil, which shall afford leisure for the praises of God, who shall be all in all! For I know not what other employment there can be where no lassitude shall slacken activity, nor any want stimulate to labor. . . . All the members and organs of the incorruptible body, which now we see to be suited to various necessary uses, shall contribute to the praises of God; for in that life necessity shall have no place, but full, certain, secure, everlasting felicity. . . .

True honor shall be there, for it shall be denied to none who is worthy, nor yielded to any unworthy; neither shall any unworthy person so much as sue for it, for none but the worthy shall be there. True peace shall be there, where no one shall encounter opposition either from himself or any other. God Himself, who is the Author of virtue, shall there be its reward; for, as there is nothing greater or better, He has promised Himself. . . . He shall be the end of our desires who shall be seen without end, loved without cloy, praised without weariness. This outgoing of affection, this employment, shall certainly be, like eternal life itself, common to all.

—*Augustine, 354–430*

275 The Advent season in the Christian calendar is meant to review the world's ancient longing for Christ, while also reflecting our continuing longing for the divine consummation of all things. An Advent hymn by Charles Wesley catches up these themes.

> Come, Thou long-expected Jesus,
> Born to set Thy people free;
> From our fears and sins release us;
> Let us find our rest in Thee.
>
> Israel's Strength and Consolation,
> Hope of all the earth Thou art;
> Dear Desire of every nation,
> Joy of every longing heart.
>
> Born Thy people to deliver,
> Born a child, and yet a King,
> Born to reign in us for ever,
> Now Thy gracious kingdom bring.
>
> By Thine own eternal Spirit
> Rule in all our hearts alone;
> By Thine all-sufficient merit
> Raise us to Thy glorious throne.
> —*Charles Wesley, 1707–1788*

276 Over the centuries believers have pictured heaven in ways as diverse as the cultures and circumstances in which they lived. The best insights usually have a basis in the Scriptures, as does this word from John Wesley.

But they shall 'hear a great voice out of heaven, saying, Behold, the tabernacle of God is with men, and he will dwell with them, and they shall be his people, and God himself shall be their God.' Hence will arise an unmixed state of holiness and happiness far superior to that which Adam enjoyed in paradise. In how beautiful and affecting a manner is this described by the Apostle! 'God shall wipe away all tears from their eyes; and there shall be no more death, neither sorrow nor crying, neither shall there be any more pain: for the former things are done away.' As there will be no more death, and no more pain or sickness preparatory thereto; as there will be no more grieving for or parting with friends; so there will be no more sorrow or crying. Nay, but there will be a greater deliverance than all this; for there will be no more sin. And to crown all, there will be a deep, an intimate, an uninterrupted union with God; a constant communion with the Father and his Son Jesus Christ, through the Spirit; a continual enjoyment of the Three-One God, and of all the creatures in him!

—John Wesley, 1703–1791

277 Hope, including the Christian hope, is often seen as something beyond the realm of logic. But Reinhold Niebuhr believed that such a hope was, for the human creature, part of our "norm."

The *eschata* or "last things" in New Testament symbolism are described in three fundamental symbols: the return of Christ, the last judgment and the resurrection....

The idea of the return of the triumphant Christ dominates the other two symbols. The judgment and the resurrection are a part of the vindication of God in the return of Christ. To believe that the suffering Messiah will return at the end of history as a triumphant judge and redeemer is to express the faith that existence cannot ultimately defy its own norm. Love may have to live in history as suffering love because the power of sin makes a simple triumph of love impossible. But if this were the ultimate situation it would be necessary either to worship the power of sin as the final power in the world or to regard it as a kind of second God, not able to triumph, but also strong enough to avoid defeat.

The vindication of Christ and his triumphant return is therefore an expression of faith in the sufficiency of God's sovereignty over the world and history, and in the final supremacy of love over all the forces of self-love which defy, for the moment, the inclusive harmony of all things under the will of God.

—Reinhold Niebuhr, 1892–1971

278 Secular society sometimes says, half-jokingly, that one world at a time is enough. The Christian hope insists that we see our human potential beyond simply this present world. To do otherwise would be a sham, Karl Barth insists.

[I]n the midst of human history and society, in the midst of this all-too-familiar world and time, in the midst of the environment of human existence, the nature of which each in some measure realises best from his own nature, there is sent forth here with the whole force of divine truth a *promise,* a *hope.* It is not possible to receive the Holy Spirit, it is therefore not possible to be in the Church and for Christ's sake obtain forgiveness of sins, without thereby participating also (and that with equal certainty and necessity) in this promise and hope. It is of this promise and hope that the conclusion of the creed speaks: *Carnis resurrectionem, vitam aeternam!* [the resurrection of the body, life everlasting (eternal)] That assuredly means: over against human history and society, time and world, there is a totally different future existence of man. Man as he is to his own self-knowledge has a reflection of himself held up in front of him in which he appears as a completely new man. And he now hears this reflection saying to him: You who here and now are *this,* will then and there be *that.* Your membership of the Church and the forgiveness of your sins for Christ's sake would only be a sham if you did not have standing before you in the same power and truth this future existence of yours.

—*Karl Barth, 1886–1968*

279 The Bible encourages our working to make a better world, but it reminds us that some changes must ultimately require divine intervention. German Reformed theologian Jürgen Moltmann explains why.

The Christian hope is directed towards a *novum ultimum,* towards a new creation of all things by the God of the resurrection of Jesus Christ. It thereby opens a future outlook that embraces all things, including also death, and into this it can and must also take the limited hopes of a renewal of life, stimulating them, relativizing them, giving them direction. It will destroy the *presumption* in these hopes of better human freedom, of successful life, of justice and dignity for our fellow men, of control of the possibilities of nature, because it does not find in these movements the salvation it awaits, because it refuses to let the entertaining and realizing of utopian ideas of this kind reconcile it with existence. It will thus outstrip these future visions of a better, more humane, more peaceable world—because of its own 'better promises' (Heb. 8.6), because it knows that nothing can be 'very good' until 'all things are become new'.

—*Jürgen Moltmann, 1926–*

280 Believers are sometimes accused of being so heavenly-minded as to be of no earthly use. Martin Luther King, Jr., phrased one aspect of the Christian hope as a dream—but one that he expected would someday be fulfilled.

I have a dream that one day on the red hills of Georgia, sons of former slaves and sons of former slave-owners will be able to sit down together at the table of brotherhood.

I have a dream that one day, even the state of Mississippi, a state sweltering with the heat of injustice, sweltering with the heat of oppression, will be transformed into an oasis of freedom and justice.

I have a dream my four little children will one day live in a nation where they will not be judged by the color of their skin but by the content of their character. I have a dream today! . . .

I have a dream that one day every valley shall be exalted, every hill and mountain shall be made low, the rough places shall be made plain, and the crooked places shall be made straight and the glory of the Lord will be revealed and all flesh shall see it together.

This is our hope. This is the faith that I go back to the South with.

With this faith we will be able to hew out of the mountain of despair a stone of hope. With this faith we will be able to transform the jangling discords of our nation into a beautiful symphony of brotherhood.

With this faith we will be able to work together, to pray together, to struggle together, to go to jail together, to stand up for freedom together, knowing that we will be free one day. This will be the day when all of God's children will be able to sing with new meaning—"my country 'tis of thee; sweet land of liberty; of thee I sing; land where my fathers died, land of the pilgrim's pride; from every mountain side, let freedom ring"—and if America is to be a great nation, this must come true.

—Martin Luther King, Jr., 1929–1968

281 What does the book of Revelation mean when it speaks of a new heaven and a new earth? Jürgen Moltmann speculates on the meaning, and in the process enlarges our understanding.

The hope for such a presence of God can be fulfilled, however, only if the negatives of death, suffering, tears, guilt, and evil have disappeared from reality, that is, in a new creation, which, figuratively speaking, is no longer a mixture of day and night, earth and sea, and in which, ontologically speaking, being and nonbeing are no longer intertwined. The hope for the future, in which God is God and a new creation his dwelling place, the expectation of that home of identity in which man is at one with God, nature, and himself radically anew confronts the unfulfilled present with the theodicy question [the question of God's justice in the face of evil]. Where freedom has come near, the chains begin to hurt. Where life is close, death becomes deadly. Where God proclaims his presence, the God-forsakenness of the world turns into suffering. Thus the theodicy question, born of suffering and pain, negatively mirrors the positive hope for God's future. We begin to suffer from the conditions of our world if we begin to love the world. And we begin to love the world if we are able to discover hope for it. And we discover hope for this world if we hear the promise of a future which stands against frustration, transiency, and death. To be sure, we can find certainty only in complete uncertainty. To be sure, we can hope for God only in the pain of the open theodicy question.

—Jürgen Moltmann, 1926–

282 The Christian hope has so many faces—earthly and eternal, personal and social, spiritual and political. Here contemporary American poet Maya Angelou puts hope in personal terms, comparing herself with Job in "Just Like Job."

> My Lord, My Lord,
> Long have I cried out to Thee
> In the heat of the sun,
> The cool of the moon,
> My screams searched the heavens for Thee.
> My God,
> When my blanket was nothing but dew,
> Rags and bones
> Were all I owned.
> I chanted Your name
> Just like Job.

Father, Father,
My life give I gladly to Thee
Deep rivers ahead
High mountains above
My soul wants only Your love
But fears gather round like wolves in the dark
Have You forgotten my name?
Oh, Lord, come to Your child.
Oh, Lord, forget me not.

You said to lean on Your arm
And I'm leaning
You said to trust in Your love
And I'm trusting
You said to call on Your name
And I'm calling
I'm stepping out on Your word.

You said You'd be my protection,
My only and glorious saviour
My beautiful Rose of Sharon,
And I'm stepping out on Your word.
Joy, joy
Your word.
Joy, joy
The wonderful word of the Son of God.

You said that You would take me to glory
To sit down at the welcome table
Rejoice with my mother in heaven
And I'm stepping out on Your word.

Into the alleys
Into the byways
Into the streets
And the roads
And the highways
Past rumor mongers
And midnight ramblers
Past the liars and the cheaters and the gamblers
On Your word

On Your word.
On the wonderful word of the Son of God.
I'm stepping out on Your word.
—*Maya Angelou, 1928–*

283 Our study of the Trinity noted that the Trinity is a revelation of divine love; indeed, of community. João Batista Libânio, a Brazilian professor of theology, sees in this divine community and in Jesus' resurrection a basis for our highest human aspirations.

Utopias are human creations that spring from human longing for a better life in the face of the hard sufferings of the present. It is above all the poor who dream of utopias, because the present is much harder for them. This human character of creating utopias as a spur to political activity, attempting to change things, would remain an enigma, lacking its true meaning, unless theological hope revealed its real origin and final destiny. Human beings were created by a Trinity that is community, the first and most perfect community. Therefore our whole lives are permeated by this deep aspiration toward living together in community.

Hope would also point toward a goal, a destiny which would remain a dark horizon. But Jesus' resurrection fully revealed humanity's utopian structure, its limits, and its anticipatory significance. The resurrection showed that hope in Yahweh does not lead to frustration but to life.

Jesus' resurrection is the prototype, precursor, and anticipation of all resurrections. In it the end of history has already happened. It also shows that only those who give their lives for their brothers and sisters rise again. Lastly, it is the ultimate key to all revelation.

The last word on history has already been said. No human power, no dictator, no ruling power will decide the final destiny of the poor. God's love raised Jesus and will raise all those he loves and who love him. And among these the poor have first place.
—*João Batista Libânio, 20th century*

Judgment

Once we concede that there is such a thing as right and wrong, or good and bad, we acknowledge the importance of some passing of judgment. If the universe has any moral quality, there must be some day or system of reckoning. This is the principle of judgment. If we are thoughtful, we know that judgment must exist. Nevertheless, we are uncomfortable with it. Let's see how theologians over the centuries have dealt with it.

284 The ancient creeds of the church emphasize that judgment is related to Jesus Christ. Martin Luther speaks to this same theme.

Christ is at present not manifest in person, but on the day of judgment he will appear in effulgent splendor, in undimmed honor; a splendor and honor eternally manifest to all creatures. The last day will be an eternal day. Upon the instant of its appearing every heart and all things will stand revealed. . . . Then there will be neither preaching nor faith. To all men everything will be manifest by experience, and by sight as in a clear sky. . . . God has reserved unto the last day the displaying of his greatness and majesty, his glory and effulgence. We behold him now in the Gospel and in faith—a narrow view of him. Here he is not great because but slightly comprehended. But in the last appearing he will permit us to behold him in his greatness and majesty.

—Martin Luther, 1483–1546

285 Jesus Christ is the Lord of judgment, but he is also our human hope when facing judgment. George Herbert describes this dichotomy in poetry, and in it finds peace.

JUDGMENT

Almighty Judge, how shall poor wretches brook
   Thy dreadful look,
Able a heart of iron to appall,
   When thou shalt call
For ev'ry man's peculiar book?

What others mean to do, I know not well;
   Yet I hear tell,
That some will turn thee to some leaves therein
   So void of sin,
That they in merit shall excel.

But I resolve, when thou shalt call for mine,
   That to decline,
And thrust a Testament into thy hand:
   Let that be scann'd.
There thou shalt find my faults are thine.
            —George Herbert, 1593–1633

286 Hell is perhaps the most difficult of all subjects for a preacher or teacher; who, after all, is in a position to describe this strange and fearful prospect? Jonathan Edwards, leading American theologian during the colonial period (who preached much of love) is remembered for a passionate sermon on hell.

The God that holds you over the pit of hell, much as one holds a spider, or some loathsome insect over the fire, abhors you, and is dreadfully provoked: his wrath towards you burns like fire; he looks upon you as worthy of nothing else, but to be cast into the fire; he is of purer eyes than to bear to have you in his sight; you are ten thousand times more abominable in his eyes, than the most hateful venomous serpent is in ours. You have offended him infinitely more than ever a stubborn rebel did his prince; and yet it is nothing but his hand that holds you from falling into the fire every moment. . . .

O sinner! Consider the fearful danger you are in: it is a great furnace of wrath, a wide and bottomless pit, full of the fire of wrath, that you are held over in the hand of that God, whose wrath is provoked and incensed as much against you, as against many of the damned in hell. You hang by a slender thread, with the flames of divine wrath flashing about it, and ready every moment to singe it, and burn it asunder; and you have no interest in any Mediator, and nothing to lay hold of to save yourself, nothing to keep off the flames of wrath, nothing of your own, nothing that you ever have done, nothing that you can do, to induce God to spare you one moment.

—Jonathan Edwards, 1703–1758

287 It is easy to push aside Jonathan Edwards's passionate words about hell as overly dramatic and perhaps even gruesome. We should remember, however, that they sprang from Edwards's belief in the absolute greatness and holiness of God, and that while his words are severe, they are prompted by a passion for God and for the souls of his hearers.

There is no want of *power* in God to cast wicked men into hell at any moment. Men's hands cannot be strong when God rises up. The strongest have no power to resist him, nor can any deliver out of his hands. He is not only able to cast wicked men into hell, but he can most easily do it. Sometimes an earthly prince meets with a great deal of difficulty to subdue a rebel, who has found means to fortify himself, and has made himself strong by the numbers of his followers. But it is not so with God. There is no fortress that is any defence from the power of God. Though hand join in hand, and vast multitudes of God's enemies combine and associate themselves, they are easily broken in pieces. They are as great heaps of light chaff before the whirlwind; or large quantities of dry stubble before devouring flames. We find it easy to tread on and crush a worm that we see crawling on the earth; so it is easy for us to cut or singe a slender thread that any thing hangs by: thus easy is it for God, when he pleases, to cast his enemies down to hell. What are we, that we should think to stand before him, at whose rebuke the earth trembles, and before whom the rocks are thrown down? . . .

They are now the objects of that very same *anger* and wrath of God, that is expressed in the torments of hell. And the reason why they do not go down to hell at each moment, is not because God, in whose power they are, is not then very angry with them; as he is with many miserable creatures now tormented in hell, who there feel and bear the fierceness of his wrath. Yea, God is a great deal more angry with great numbers that are now on earth: yea, doubtless, with many that are now in this congregation, who it may be are at ease, than he is with many of those who are now in the flames of hell.

—*Jonathan Edwards, 1703–1758*

288 We think of Jesus Christ as the voice of love and mercy, and we are right. But he is also the one before whom we must stand in judgment, John Wesley reminds us. There we must give an accounting.

[W]e shall all, I that speak and you that hear, 'stand at the judgment seat of Christ'.... There we are to give an account of all our works, from the cradle to the grave: of all our words; of all our desires and tempers, all the thoughts and intents of our hearts; of all the use we have made of our various talents, whether of mind, body, or fortune, till God said, 'Give an account of thy stewardship; for thou mayest be no longer steward.' In this [earthly] court it is possible some who are guilty may escape for want of evidence. But there is no want of evidence in that court. All men with whom you had the most secret intercourse, who were privy to all your designs and actions, are ready before your face. So are all the spirits of darkness, who inspired evil designs, and assisted in the execution of them. So are all the angels of God—those 'eyes of the Lord that run to and fro over all the earth'—who watched over your soul, and laboured for your good so far as you would permit. So is your own conscience, a thousand witnesses in one, now no more capable of being either blinded or silenced, but constrained to know and to speak the naked truth touching all your thoughts and words and actions. And is conscience as a thousand witnesses? Yea, but God is as a thousand consciences! O who can stand before the face of 'the great God, even our Saviour, Jesus Christ'!

—*John Wesley, 1703–1791*

289 From a philosophical point of view, one of the issues of judgment is the principle of end, or purpose. Is there any end to history, any reason or purpose to the human story? If so, there must also be judgment, a time of reckoning. See how Reinhold Niebuhr confronts this issue.

The symbol of the last judgment in New Testament eschatology contains three important facets of the Christian conception of life and history. The first is expressed in the idea that it is Christ who will be the judge of history. Christ as judge means that when the historical confronts the eternal it is judged by its own ideal possibility, and not by the contrast between the finite and the eternal character of God. The judgment is upon sin and not finiteness. This idea is in logical accord with the whole Biblical conception of life and history, according to which it is not the partial and particular character of human existence which is evil, but rather the self-love by which men disturb the harmony of creation as it would exist if all creatures obeyed the divine will.

The second facet in the symbol of the last judgment is its emphasis upon the distinction between good and evil in history. When history confronts God the differences between good and evil are not swallowed up in a distinctionless eternity. All historical realities are indeed ambiguous. Therefore no absolute distinction between good and evil in them is possible. But this does not obviate the necessity and possibility of a *final* judgment upon good and evil. . . .

The third facet in the symbol of the last judgment is to be found in its locus at the "end" of history. There is no achievement or partial realization in history, no fulfillment of meaning or achievement of virtue by which man can escape the final judgment. The idea of a "last" judgment expresses Christianity's refutation of all conceptions of history, according to which it is its own redeemer and is able by its process of growth and development, to emancipate man from the guilt and sin of his existence, and to free him from judgment.

—*Reinhold Niebuhr, 1892–1971*

290 It is often said that the modern mind finds hell repugnant. In a sense, there's a strange inconsistency in this, since violence is such a popular commodity in movies and television. One twentieth-century writer, C.S. Lewis, makes a case for judgment.

Some moderns talk as though duties to posterity were the only duties we had. I can imagine no man who will look with more horror on the End than a conscientious revolutionary who has, in a sense sincerely, been justifying cruelties and injustices inflicted on millions of his contemporaries by the benefits which he hopes to confer on future generations: generations who, as one terrible moment now reveals to him, were never going to exist. Then he will see the massacres, the faked trials, the deportations, to be all ineffaceably real, an essential part, his part, in the drama that has just ended: while the future Utopia had never been anything but a fantasy.

Frantic administration of panaceas to the world is certainly discouraged by the reflection that 'this present' might be 'the world's last night'; sober work for the future, within the limits of ordinary morality and prudence, is not. For what comes is Judgement: happy are those whom it finds labouring in their vocations, whether they were merely going out to feed the pigs or laying good plans to deliver humanity a hundred years hence from some great evil. The curtain has indeed now fallen. Those pigs will never in fact be fed, the great campaign against White Slavery or Governmental Tyranny will never in fact proceed to victory. No matter: you were at your post when the Inspection came.

Our ancestors had a habit of using the word 'Judgement' in this context as if it meant simply 'punishment': hence the popular expression, 'It's a judgement on him'. I believe we can sometimes render the thing more vivid to ourselves by taking a judgement in a stricter sense: not as the sentence or award, but as the Verdict. Some day (and 'What if this present were the world's last night?') an absolutely correct verdict—if you like, a perfect critique—will be passed on what each of us is.

—*C.S. Lewis, 1898–1963*

291 When we read history, we may well wonder if justice can ever finally triumph. Christian theology, as the Scriptures declare it, sees a final end to injustice in God's judgment. So Marjorie Hewitt Suchocki reasons.

In the Old Testament, the judgment of God always thundered down against the wayward nation for the sole sake of calling that nation to justice, to the establishment of the kingdom of God. In this last chapter of the New Testament, we finally read, "There shall no more be anything accursed." The purging, saving judgment of God, bringing about justice, will finally triumph over all injustice, and God's kingdom will finally be established.

Clearly, the kingdom is God's triumph of goodness over evil in the ultimacy of justice. This triumph of the good is given two dimensions: the temporal and the eternal. Temporally, the kingdom of God is realized in our openness to modes of justice in our daily lives. These modes of justice must relate to the well-being of all peoples, both personally and societally; justice will bring about a positive relationship to the natural world around us, and an inclusiveness to the nations. Eternally, the kingdom relates to a resurrection of the dead, brought about solely through the power of God. . . . Immortality is for the sake of judgment and transformation, as all things are made new. And this transformation brings about the final establishment of a kingdom of justice where all evil is overcome, the kingdom of God.

—Marjorie Hewitt Suchocki, 20th century

292 The purposes of God are expressed—especially in the teachings of Jesus in the Gospels—in the kingdom of God. The coming of God's kingdom is the great hope of the human race; but it is also, by its very nature, an act of judgment. Teacher and theologian Jerald C. Brauer explains.

The kingdom of God is one of the most fruitful yet controversial concepts in Christian theology. It has been employed to uphold the status quo, and it has been a revolutionary ideal used to break social forms and customs. Although appropriated from Judaism, it was radically transformed by Jesus and so reinterpreted by the early Christian community.

In the New Testament the concept signifies the sovereignty or kingly rule of God. Its basic intent is to affirm the fact that God reigns in all aspects of personal and social life. It is not a general, but a unique, kind of rule or reign. Whereas Judaism encountered the rule of God through obedience to the Law and looked forward to the complete establishment of God's rule, the New Testament asserted that in a new and peculiar way the kingdom of God had already come.

Jesus said that if he cast out demons through the power of God, "then the kingdom of God has come upon you." The Gospel of Mark takes its departure from the assertion that the time has reached fulfillment and that the kingdom of God has come— "repent and believe the good news." This claim is not merely a statement of living under God's commandments and so living under godly rule. Rather, it is a new manifestation of God's power and sovereignty in which God's nature, power, and will are brought to bear.

The early Christian community believed that in Jesus of Nazareth the Christ (or Messiah) was encountered and that God's kingdom was made manifest. People could either repent and believe or they could reject it, but regardless of human response, the Kingdom had come.

—*Jerald C. Brauer, 20th century*

293 Because contemporary churches do not often preach or teach about final judgment, believers may wonder how the doctrines of typical Protestant bodies compare. In truth, their historic positions are quite similar, Ted A. Campbell, church historian, points out.

The traditional doctrinal standards of [Protestant] churches reflect the view that beyond death and the final judgment, believers will share fellowship with Christ and with one another through eternity, and those who reject faith in Christ will be cut off from Christ and will suffer eternal punishment. In formal doctrine there is very little speculation on what heaven (eternal fellowship with Christ) or hell (eternal punishment) will be like. All Reformation churches (Lutheran, Reformed, and Anglican) reject the notion of purgatory as a place in which the prayers of those on earth may help those who have died. The Westminster Confession makes it clear that human bodies perish at death, believers go to be with Christ in heaven and unbelievers are tormented, then at the final judgment believers are reunited with their "redeemed" bodies and share eternity with Christ. The belief in a particular state between death and the final judgment was sometimes identified as an "intermediate state," and although in the 1500s Protestants distinguished this clearly from Catholic notions of purgatory then popular, clarification of Catholic teaching since that time has suggested that these ideas may not be so far separate.

—*Ted A. Campbell, 20th century*

Resurrection of the Body

Our generation is ambivalent about the body. On one hand, we give it more attention than has any previous generation in human history, as evidenced by our diet programs, our health clubs, and our glorifying of the well-formed body. But at the same time, we have lost much of what some other generations felt of reverence for the body as the habitation of God's Spirit. Centuries of theologians help to clarify our contemporary thinking.

294 When reading the apostle Paul's explanation of the resurrection of the body to the Corinthians, one senses that people had probably asked questions that were childlike in their simplicity. Scholar and theologian Origen seems to have been dealing with similar questions in his generation.

Now we ask how can anyone imagine that our animal body is to be changed by the grace of the resurrection and become spiritual? ...It is clearly absurd to say that it will be involved in the passions of flesh and blood...By the command of God the body which was earthly and animal will be replaced by a spiritual body, such as may be able to dwell in heaven; even on those who have been of lower worth, even of contemptible, almost negligible merit, the glory and worth of the body will be bestowed in proportion to the deserts of the life and soul of each. But even for those destined for eternal fire or for punishment there will be an incorruptible body through the change of the resurrection.

—Origen, 185–254

295 It is probably quite impossible to explain the resurrection of the body in fully satisfactory fashion, but if any success is to be attained, it will probably be through analogies. An early believer, Macrina, older sister to Basil the Great and Gregory of Nyssa, does an artful and imaginative job.

Grant it possible, then, in the art of painting not only to mix opposite colours, as painters are always doing, to represent a particular tint, but also to separate again this mixture and to restore to each of the colours its natural dye. . . . we suppose that our artist will none the less remember the actual nature of that colour, and that in no case will he show forgetfulness . . . if after having become quite a different colour by composition with each other they each return to their natural dye. . . . Now, if reason can see any analogy in this simile, we must search the matter in hand by its light. Let the soul stand for this Art of the painter; and let the natural atoms stand for the colours of his art; and let the mixture of that tint compounded of the various dyes, and the return of these to their native state . . . represent respectively the concourse, and the separation of the atoms. . . . so, we assert, does the soul know the natural peculiarities of those atoms whose concourse makes the frame of the body . . . even after the scattering of those atoms. . . . none the less will the soul be near each by its power of recognition, and will persistently cling to the familiar atoms, until their concourse after this division again takes place in the same way, for that fresh formation of the dissolved body which will properly be, and be called, resurrection.

—Macrina, 327–380

296 Paul's description of the resurrection body in First Corinthians challenged and inspired early theologians. Rufinus rises to that challenge in a vigorous way.

[W]hen the Apostle says, "This corruptible must put on incorruption, and this mortal must put on immortality," are not his words those of one who in a manner touches his body and places his finger upon it? This body then, which is now corruptible, will by the grace of the resurrection be incorruptible, and this which is now mortal will be clothed with virtues of immortality, that, as "Christ, rising from the dead dieth no more, death hath no more dominion over Him," so those who shall rise in Christ shall never again feel corruption or death, not because the nature of flesh will have been cast off, but because its condition and quality will have been changed. There will be a body, therefore, which will rise from the dead incorruptible and immortal, not only of the righteous, but also of sinners; of the righteous that they may be able ever to abide with Christ, of sinners that they undergo without end the punishment due to them.

—Rufinus, 345–411

297 How important is the resurrection of the body? Some might think it almost incidental. Not Saint John of Damascus. He saw it as an evidence of God's justice and righteousness, and logically compelling.

We believe in the resurrection of the dead. For there will be in truth, there will be, a resurrection of the dead, and by resurrection we mean resurrection of bodies. For resurrection is the second state of that which has fallen. For the souls are immortal, and hence how can they rise again? For if they define death as a separation of soul and body, resurrection surely is the re-union of soul and body, and the second state of the living creature that has suffered dissolution and downfall. It is, then, this very body, which is corruptible and liable to dissolution, that will rise again incorruptible. For He, who made it in the beginning of the sand of the earth, does not lack the power to raise it up again after it has been dissolved again and returned to the earth from which it was taken, in accordance with the reversal of the Creator's judgment.

For if there is no resurrection, let us eat and drink: let us pursue a life of pleasure and enjoyment.... If there is no resurrection, neither is there any God nor Providence, but all things are driven and borne along of themselves. For observe how we see most righteous men suffering hunger and injustice and receiving no help in this present life, while sinners and unrighteous men abound in riches and every delight. And who in his senses would take this for the work of a righteous judgment or a wise providence? There must be, therefore, there must be, a resurrection. For God is just and is the rewarder of those who submit patiently to Him.

—John of Damascus, c. 655–c. 750

298 Sometimes the greatest truths are delivered best by way of analogy and imagination, rather than by sheer analysis. John Bunyan, author of *The Pilgrim's Progress,* gives us such a picture in the homegoing of his Pilgrim.

Now I further saw, that betwixt them and the Gate was a River, but there was no Bridge to go over; the River was very deep; at the sight therefore of this River, the Pilgrims were much stounded, but the men that went with them, said, You must go through, or you cannot come at the Gate.

The Pilgrims then began to enquire if there was no other way to the Gate; to which they answered, Yes; but there hath not any, save two, to wit, *Enoch* and *Elijah*, been permitted to tread that path, since the foundation of the World, nor shall, untill the last Trumpet shall sound. The Pilgrims then, especially *Christian*, began to dispond in his mind, and looked this way and that, but no way could be found by them, by which they might escape the River. Then they asked the men if the Waters were all of a depth. They said no; yet they could not help them in that Case; for said they, *You shall find it deeper or shallower, as you believe in the King of the place.*

They then addressed themselves to the Water; and entring, *Christian* began to sink, and crying out to his good friend *Hopeful*; he said, I sink in deep Waters, the Billows go over my head, all his Waves go over me, *Selah.*

Then said the other, Be of good chear, my Brother, I feel the bottom, and it is good. Then said *Christian*, Ah my friend, the sorrows of death have compassed me about, I shall not see the Land that flows with Milk and Honey....

Then I saw in my Dream that *Christian* was as in a muse a while; to whom also *Hopeful* added this word, *Be of good cheer, Jesus Christ maketh thee whole:* And with that, *Christian* brake out with a loud voice, Oh I see him again! and he tells me, *When thou passest through the waters, I will be with thee, and through the Rivers, they shall not overflow thee.* Then they both took courage, and the enemy was after that as still as a stone, until they were gone over. *Christian* therefore presently found ground to stand upon; and so it followed that the rest of the River was but shallow. Thus they got over. Now upon the bank of the River, on the other side, they saw the two shining men again, who there waited for them. Wherefore being come up out of the River, they saluted them, saying, *We are ministring Spirits, sent forth to minister for those that shall be Heirs of Salvation.* Thus they went along towards the Gate.

—*John Bunyan, 1628–1688*

299 What did the apostle Paul mean when he referred to our resurrection bodies as immortal and incorruptible? John Wesley explains some of the implications as he perceives them.

The body that we shall have at the resurrection, shall be immortal and incorruptible: "For this corruptible must put on incorruption, and this mortal must put on immortality." Now these words, *immortal* and *incorruptible,* not only signify, that we shall die no more, (for in that sense the damned are immortal and incorruptible,) but that we shall be perfectly free from all the bodily evils which sin brought into the world; that our bodies shall not be subject to sickness, or pain, or any other inconveniences we are daily exposed to. This the Scripture calls "the redemption of our bodies,"—the freeing them from all their maladies. Were we to receive them again, subject to all their frailties and miseries which we are forced to wrestle with, I much doubt whether a wise man, were he left to his choice, would willingly take his again;—whether he would not choose to let his still lie rotting in the grave, rather than to be again chained to such a cumbersome clod of earth. Such a resurrection would be, as a wise Heathen calls it, "A resurrection to another sleep." It would look more like a redemption to death again, than a resurrection to life. . . .

Our bodies shall be raised in glory. "Then shall the righteous shine as the sun in the kingdom of their Father." A resemblance of this we have in the lustre of Moses's face, when he had conversed with God on the mount.

—John Wesley, 1703–1791

300 Secular thought perceives eternal life, if it accepts the idea at all, as a continuation of influence or something similar. But the Christian belief in the resurrection goes much further, Karl Barth insists.

And now the Christian man looks forward. What is the meaning of the Christian hope in this life? A life after death? An event apart from death? A tiny soul which, like a butterfly, flutters away above the grave and is still preserved somewhere, in order to live on immortally? That was how the heathen looked on the life after death. But that is not the Christian hope. 'I believe in the resurrection of the body.' Body in the Bible is quite simply man, man, moreover, under the sign of sin, man laid low. And to this man it is said, Thou shalt rise again. Resurrection means not the continuation of this life, but life's completion. To this man a 'Yes' is spoken which the shadow of death cannot touch. In resurrection our life is involved, we men as we are and are situated. *We* rise again, no one else takes our place. 'We shall be changed' (I Cor. 15); which does not mean that a quite different life begins, but that '*this* corruptible must put on incorruption, and this mortal put on immortality'. Then it will be manifest that 'death is swallowed up in victory'. So the Christian hope affects our whole life: this life of ours will be completed. That which is sown in dishonour and weakness will rise again in glory and power. The Christian hope does not lead us away from this life; it is rather the uncovering of the truth in which God sees our life. It is the conquest of death, but not a flight into the Beyond. The reality of this life is involved. Eschatology, rightly understood, is the most practical thing that can be thought. In the eschaton the light falls from above into our life. We await this light. 'We bid you hope', said Goethe. Perhaps even he knew of this light. The Christian message, at any rate, confidently and comfortingly proclaims hope in this light.

—Karl Barth, 1886–1968

301 Sometimes persons wonder how the resurrection of Jesus—which is a precursor of the resurrection promised to all believers—is different from, say, the resurrection of Lazarus. Here is an insight from C.S. Lewis.

[T]he Resurrection was not regarded simply or chiefly as evidence for the immortality of the soul. It is, of course, often so regarded today: I have heard a man maintain that 'the importance of the Resurrection is that it proves *survival*. Such a view cannot at any point be reconciled with the language of the New Testament. On such a view Christ would simply have done what all men do when they die: the only novelty would have been that in His case we were allowed to see it happening. But there is not in Scripture the faintest suggestion that the Resurrection was new evidence for something that had *in fact* been always happening. The New Testament writers speak as if Christ's achievement in rising from the dead was the first event of its kind in the whole history of the universe. He is the 'first fruits', the 'pioneer of life'. He has forced open a door that has been locked since the death of the first man. He has met, fought, and beaten the King of Death.

Everything is different because He has done so. This is the beginning of the New Creation: a new chapter in cosmic history has opened.

—C.S. Lewis, 1898–1963

302 Nature provides us with analogies of resurrection, though doctrine should never be content to stop there. So hymn writer Natalie Sleeth, in the midst of personal loss, begins with the language of nature but continues into the specific declaration of biblical resurrection faith.

In the bulb there is a flower;
in the seed, an apple tree;
in cocoons, a hidden promise:
butterflies will soon be free!
In the cold and snow of winter
there's a spring that waits to be,
unrevealed until its season,
something God alone can see.

There's a song in every silence,
seeking word and melody;
there's a dawn in every darkness,
bringing hope to you and me.
From the past will come the future;
what it holds, a mystery,
unrevealed until its season,
something God alone can see.

In our end is our beginning;
in our time, infinity;
in our doubt there is believing;
in our life, eternity.
In our death, a resurrection;
at the last, a victory,
unrevealed until its season,
something God alone can see.

—Natalie Sleeth, 1930–1992

HYMN OF PROMISE
Words & Music: Natalie Sleeth
Copyright © 1986 by Hope Publishing Co., Carol Stream, IL 60188.
All rights reserved. Used by permission.

303 The Christian belief in the resurrection of our Lord, and ultimately of believers, must always be distinguished from the more common idea of the immortality of the soul. This is a point at which the belief in the resurrection of the body is so significant, as contemporary theologian Otto Hentz indicates.

The notion of resurrection differs significantly from the notion of immortality of the soul. The basic difference lies in an understanding of the person that comes from the biblical tradition. The biblical notion of the person does not involve a distinction of body and soul as two disparate parts, but as two dimensions of a single reality. When Scripture uses the word for one of the two dimensions, it nonetheless refers to the whole person. When, for example, Paul distinguishes flesh and spirit, he is not distinguishing body and soul within a person. Rather, he contrasts a person who is mortal, weak, and sinful with a person graced by God. Flesh refers to the whole human person, a unity that, taken by itself, is weak, mortal, sinful. Spirit is the life of grace bestowed by God on the whole person (flesh). Resurrection, therefore, means God's granting of life beyond death to the whole person, in both its spiritual and bodily dimensions. . . .

In the notion of the resurrection as the summons to everlasting life of the whole person, not a disembodied soul, a great deal is at stake. The issue is not fidelity to traditional teaching, but what is at stake in the traditional teaching: our understanding of ourselves as persons, of our relationships with one another, of our world, of what we accomplish in history. If we imagine life beyond death as immortality of the soul, then our ultimate hope is not salvation of the world, of the history, of the community we have shaped, but salvation *out of* the world, beyond a history, with others left apart. The dualism that focuses on the immortality of the soul begets a disdain for the world, indifference to accomplishment in history, and a radical individualism that fractures the fundamental connection by which we were made to be ourselves precisely with one another in a shared history. But the resurrection of Jesus inaugurates the transformation of the whole of creation. Hence, resurrection hope means hope for society and the world. And, more than signaling a future destiny, it shapes life now.

—Otto Hentz, 20th century

Eternal Life

We humans have in our souls an eternal hopefulness. We see our bodies waste away yet sense that they are made for eternity. And nowhere is this expectation of hope more gladly affirmed than in the Scriptures. Theologians have tried through the centuries to refine our understanding of eternal life—including statements in the major creeds and in continuing church documents. Here is part of the story.

304 Some words become familiar to us without our really knowing what the words mean. This can be especially true of cherished religious terms. Here Calvinist theologian Zacharias Ursinus helps us understand familiar words having to do with eternal life.

That is called *everlasting,* 1. Which is without beginning or end, as God is. 2. That which is without a beginning, but which has an end, as the decrees of God. 3. That which has a beginning, but will have no end, as the angels, &c. It is in this third sense that our heavenly life is called everlasting, by which we mean, that whilst it has a beginning, it will have no end. The everlasting life of man, then, is the eternal being of man, regenerated and glorified, which will consist in having the image of God perfectly restored in him, as it was when he was first created, having perfect wisdom, righteousness, and happiness, or being endowed with the true knowledge and love of God, in connection with eternal joy....

The beginning of everlasting life is given already in this world; but the consummation of it, is reserved for the life to come, which none receive, but those in whom it is here begun.

—Zacharias Ursinus, 1534–1583

305 The Apostles' Creed speaks of "the life everlasting." Is this simply an extension of days far beyond what medical science has so far been able to develop, or are other elements involved? Susanna Wesley explains the term in a letter to her young daughter. Susanna's letter draws on a work by Bishop John Pearson.

By everlasting life is not only meant that we shall die no more, for in this sense the damned shall have everlasting life as well as the saints: they shall always have a being, though in intolerable torments, which is infinitely worse than none at all. But we are to understand by it full and perfect enjoyment of solid inexpressible joy and felicity. "Eye hath not seen, nor ear heard, neither hath it entered into the heart of man to conceive what God hath prepared for those that love him." The soul shall be perfectly renewed and sanctified, nor shall it be possible to sin any more. All its faculties shall be purified and exulted: the understanding shall be filled with the beatific vision of the adorable Trinity, shall be illuminated, enlarged and eternally employed and satisfied in the contemplation of the sublimest truths. Here we see as in a glass, have dark and imperfect perceptions of God, but there we shall behold him as he is, shall know as we are known. Not that we shall fully comprehend the divine nature as he doth ours—that is impossible, for he is infinite and incomprehensible and we, though in heaven, shall be finite still—but our apprehensions of his being and perfections shall be clear, just, true; we shall see him as he is, shall never be troubled with misapprehensions or false conceptions of him more.

—*Susanna Wesley, 1670–1742*

306 The biblical descriptions of heaven and of eternal life seem open-ended, as if encouraging succeeding generations of believers to exercise their own faith-imagination. When John Wesley was near his death, he looked toward the future with exultant hope.

In a short time I am to quit this tenement of clay, and to remove into another state. . . . What kind of existence shall I then enter upon? When my spirit has launched out of the body, how shall I feel myself? Perceive my own being? How shall I discern the things that are round about me, either material or spiritual objects? When my eyes no longer transmit the rays of light, how will the naked spirit *see?* When the organs of hearing are mouldered into dust, in what manner shall I *hear?* When the brain is of no farther use, what means of *thinking* shall I have? When my whole body is resolved into senseless earth, what means shall I have of gaining *knowledge?* ...

... What astonishing scenes will then discover themselves to our newly opening senses! ... shall we not be able to move, quick as thought, through the wide realms of uncreated night? Above all, the moment we step into eternity, shall we not feel ourselves swallowed up of him who is in this and every place, who filleth heaven and earth? It is only the veil of flesh and blood which now hinders us from perceiving that the great Creator cannot but fill the whole immensity of space. He is every moment above us, beneath us, and on every side. Indeed in this dark abode, this land of shadows, this region of sin and death, the thick cloud which is interposed between conceals him from our sight. But the veil will disappear, and he will appear in unclouded majesty, God over all, blessed for ever!

—John Wesley, 1703–1791

307 The belief in a world to come has been a source of strength to generations of believers. Writing at the time of the American Civil War, William W. How, Anglican Bishop of Wakefield, caught up some of the grand expectations of faith with expressions that encompassed the ages.

> For all the saints, who from their labors rest,
> who thee by faith before the world confessed,
> thy name, O Jesus, be forever blest.
> Alleluia, Alleluia!
>
> Thou wast their rock, their fortress, and their might;
> thou, Lord, their captain in the well-fought fight;
> thou, in the darkness drear, their one true light.
> Alleluia, Alleluia!
>
> O may thy soldiers, faithful, true, and bold,
> fight as the saints who nobly fought of old,
> and win with them the victor's crown of gold.
> Alleluia, Alleluia!

O blest communion, fellowship divine!
We feebly struggle, they in glory shine;
yet all are one in thee, for all are thine.
Alleluia, Alleluia!

And when the strife is fierce, the warfare long,
steals on the ear the distant triumph song,
and hearts are brave again, and arms are strong.
Alleluia, Alleluia!

From earth's wide bounds, from ocean's farthest coast,
through gates of pearl streams in the countless host,
singing to Father, Son, and Holy Ghost:
Alleluia, Alleluia!

—William W. How, 1823–1897

308 Because we humans understand length more easily than we do quality, our vision of heaven is often limited to time measurements. Nothing could be further from the point, as John Baillie, a Scottish theologian, explains.

The first thing to be noted is that eternal life stands primarily not for a greater length of life but for a new depth of it. This has emerged very clearly from our historical survey. The soul's hope has not been for more of the same, but for something altogether higher and better. The shortness of the present life is very far from being its most unsatisfying feature. And we are left in no doubt as to how much interest those who have hoped most for immortality would have retained in the prospect of it, had they been told it was to mean only an endless prolongation of the common life of earth. So far from being elated, they would have been crushed and terrified. . . . *Nobody ever wanted an endless quantity of life until discovery had been made of a new and quite particular and exceptional quality of life. . . .*

It comes, then, to this—that the only knowledge we can have of eternal life is that which comes to us through our present foretasting of its joys. All that we know of the other life *there* is what we know of it *here*. For even here there is *another* life that may be lived, a life wholly other than that which commonly bears the name and yet one which may be lived out in this very place where

I now am, be it desert or tilled field, office or market-place, study or sick-bedroom—and may be begun to-day. This other life is the life everlasting.

—John Baillie, 1886–1960

309 No doubt there are times when believers have looked to heaven as an escape from this world, especially in times when this world has been dominated by suffering. But at its best, as Karl Barth demonstrates, belief in eternal life ought to energize and fortify life on this earth.

Eternal life was the destination of Christ's journey. It is the destination of our journey as well, since the Easter story happened for us. No backing out, dear brothers and sisters! No return to a life where we once again would labour in the service of sin, of our evil defiance, only to earn and to receive death as the wages of sin! No, forward, into life eternal! Eternal life is man's life when God has spoken his 'yes' upon it, once for all, unconditionally and unreservedly, not to be changed any more. Eternal life is man's life lived with God, in his bright light, nourished and sustained by his own life. Eternal life is man's life committed to the service of God and thereby to the service of the neighbour, a life which certainly also serves him best who is allowed to live it. Eternal life is a strong and no longer weak life; joyous and no longer sad; true and no longer deceitful. Eternal life is man's indestructible life because it comes from God and is sustained by him. It is life everlasting, extending beyond any natural end which now can no longer be death.

—Karl Barth, 1886–1968

310 It is sometimes said that we are as unprepared to comprehend the world to come as an unborn infant is to understand the world outside the womb. In truth, we simply have nothing in our experience that equips us to comprehend heaven. C.S. Lewis reasons with some of our problems of understanding.

Our notion of Heaven involves perpetual negations: no food, no drink, no sex, no movement, no mirth, no events, no time, no art. Against all these, to be sure, we set one positive: the vision and enjoyment of God. And since this is an infinite good, we hold (rightly) that it outweighs them all. That is, the reality of the

Beatific Vision would or will outweigh, would infinitely out-weigh, the reality of the negations. But can our present notion of it outweigh our present notion of them? That is quite a different question. And for most of us at most times the answer is No. . . .

Thus the negatives have, so to speak, an unfair advantage in every competition with the positive. What is worse, their presence—and most when we most resolutely try to suppress or ignore them—vitiates even such a faint and ghostlike notion of the positive as we might have had. . . .

We must not allow this to happen if we can possibly prevent it. We must believe—and therefore in some degree imagine—that every negation will be only the reverse side of a fulfilling. And we must mean by that the fulfilling, precisely, of our humanity; not our transformation into angels nor our absorption into Deity. For though we shall be 'as the angels' and made 'like unto' our Master. I think this means 'like with the likeness proper to men': as different instruments that play the same air but each in its own fashion. How far the life of the risen man will be sensory, we do not know. But I surmise that it will differ from the sensory life we know here, not as emptiness differs from water or water from wine but as a flower differs from a bulb or a cathedral from an architect's drawing.

—C.S. Lewis, 1898–1963

311 Quite naturally, most of our thinking about heaven involves questions concerning what heaven will mean to us. But what about God? C.S. Lewis reminds us of that divine dimension.

We were made for God. Only by being in some respect like Him, only by being a manifestation of His beauty, lovingkindness, wisdom or goodness, has any earthly Beloved excited our love. It is not that we have loved them too much, but that we did not quite understand what we were loving. It is not that we shall be asked to turn from them, so dearly familiar, to a Stranger. When we see the face of God we shall know that we have always known it. He has been a party to, has made, sustained and moved moment by moment within, all our earthly experiences of innocent love. All that was true love in them was, even on earth, far more His than ours, and ours only because His. In Heaven there will be no anguish and no duty of turning away from our earthly Beloveds.

First, because we shall have turned already; from the portraits to the Original, from the rivulets to the Fountain, from the creatures he made lovable to Love Himself. But secondly, because we shall find them all in Him. By loving Him more than them we shall love them more than we now do.

—*C.S. Lewis, 1898–1963*

312 Time and again we see in this world beauty such as our hearts can hardly contain. The further prospect of heaven ought to inspire us to make better use of the world we now have, and to appreciate more than ever its wonder and glory. Karen Baker-Fletcher and Garth KASIMU Baker-Fletcher, contemporary writers on theology, urge us to that end.

We are called into the apocalyptic vision of New Creation, a moment-by-moment, day-by-day, generation-by-generation process of earthly and spiritual renewal. The creation of a new heaven and a new earth requires that the people of God, who is Spirit, more fully embody Spirit, which is found in the dust of the earth as well as in the invisible breath of life that is the Gift of Spirit to all of creation. To love Spirit we must, then, more fully love one another and the environment that sustains us physically. . . . it involves putting our hands both in the generating dust of the earth that produces food and in the dust that threatens to bury the poor, the hungry, the homeless, the ill, the dying, the mourning, and the weeping, a dust which needs to be removed. By the Spirit, we are called to realize the apocalyptic vision of a new heaven and a new earth by being wise stewards of body, dust, and spirit, employing each in the task of healing and wholeness. The creation of a new heaven and a new earth need not be a violent, destructive, fiery event. If enough people choose to act in harmony with God as Spirit who loves its creation, the creation of a new heaven and a new earth can be a gradual, life-affirming, reviving, and replenishing process in which God's original intention for the freedom to live abundantly and for the equality of the well-being of all is fulfilled.

—*Karen Baker-Fletcher and Garth KASIMU Baker-Fletcher, 20th century*

Believing and Living

A pragmatic kind of person is likely to say that it doesn't matter what you believe, only what you do. But in truth, our conduct rarely strays far from our beliefs. Indeed, our conduct is likely to reveal what we truly believe, which may not be what we profess to believe. The Scriptures are insistent about right believing because of the way our beliefs eventually shape our conduct. See what centuries of theologians have said about this matter.

313 The majority of Christians live out their discipleship in rather common and uneventful ways. But vast thousands have died for their faith, and continue to do so. The story of one of these martyrs, Polycarp, Bishop of Smyrna in the first half of the second century, has been recorded for us in majestic and poignant language.

The proconsul was insistent and said: "Take the oath, and I shall release you. Curse Christ."

Polycarp said: "Eighty-six years I have served him, and he never did me any wrong. How can I blaspheme my King who saved me?"

And upon his persisting still and saying, "Swear by the fortune of Caesar," he answered, "If you vainly suppose that I shall swear by the fortune of Caesar, as you say, and pretend that you do not know who I am, listen plainly: I am a Christian. . . ."

And again [he said] to him, "I shall have you consumed with fire, if you despise the wild beasts, unless you change your mind."

But Polycarp said: "The fire you threaten burns but an hour and is quenched after a little; for you do not know the fire of the coming judgment and everlasting punishment that is laid up for the impious. But why do you delay? Come, do what you will." . . .

. . . Straightway then, they set about him the material prepared for the pyre. . . .

...And with his hands put behind him and tied, like a noble ram out of a great flock ready for sacrifice, a burnt offering ready and acceptable to God, he looked up to heaven and said:

"Lord God Almighty, Father of thy beloved and blessed Servant Jesus Christ, through whom we have received full knowledge of thee, 'the God of angels and powers and all creation' and of the whole race of the righteous who live in thy presence: I bless thee, because thou hast deemed me worthy of this day and hour, to take my part in the number of the martyrs, in the cup of thy Christ, for 'resurrection to eternal life' of soul and body in the immortality of the Holy Spirit; among whom may I be received in thy presence this day as a rich and acceptable sacrifice, just as thou hast prepared and revealed beforehand and fulfilled, thou that art the true God without any falsehood. For this and for everything I praise thee, I bless thee, I glorify thee, through the eternal and heavenly High Priest, Jesus Christ, thy beloved Servant, through whom be glory to thee with him and Holy Spirit both now and unto the ages to come. Amen."

And when he had concluded the Amen and finished his prayer, the men attending to the fire lighted it.

—Martyrdom of Polycarp, February 23, 155/6

314 Jesus warned that no one can serve two masters. Gregory of Nyssa, looking at the example of Moses, challenged that we must have "one purpose" in life, if we are to be servants of God.

This truly is the vision of God: never to be satisfied in the desire to see him. But one must always, by looking at what he can see, rekindle his desire to see more. Thus, no limit would interrupt growth in the ascent to God, since no limit to the Good can be found nor is the increasing of desire for the Good brought to an end because it is satisfied. . . .

What does the history say about this? That *Moses the servant of Yahweh died as Yahweh decreed, and no one has ever found his grave, his eyes were undimmed, and his face unimpaired.* From this we learn that, when one has accomplished such noble actions, he is considered worthy of this sublime name, to be called *servant of Yahweh*, which is the same as saying that he is better than all others. For one would not serve God unless he had become superior to everyone in the world. This for him is the end of the virtuous life, an end wrought by the word of God. History speaks of "death," a living death, which is not followed by the grave, or fills the tomb, or brings dimness to the eyes and aging to the person.

What then are we taught through what has been said? To have but one purpose in life: to be called servants of God by virtue of the lives we live. For when you conquer all enemies (the Egyptian, the Amalekite, the Idumaean, the Midianite), cross the water, are enlightened by the cloud, are sweetened by the wood, drink from the rock, taste of the food from above, make your ascent up the mountain through purity and sanctity; and when you arrive there, you are instructed in the divine mystery by the sound of the trumpets, and in the impenetrable darkness draw near to God by your faith, and there are taught the mysteries of the tabernacle and the dignity of the priesthood.

—Gregory of Nyssa, c. 330–c. 395

315 The Christian is the only truly free person, yet also the servant of God and of all. How can this be? Martin Luther found the secret in Christ, who is Lord of all, yet who chose to take on himself the form of humanity in order to become a servant.

A Christian is a perfectly free lord of all, and subject to no one. A Christian is a perfectly dutiful servant of all, and subject to all....

Although Christians do not have to prove themselves through good works, they should freely empty themselves and behave like servants. Just as Christ in human form served humanity in every way, so should Christians serve their neighbors....

Just as our heavenly Father in Christ came to our aid, so we ought freely to help those around us, both materially and spiritually. We should, as it were, become Christs to one another, that Christ may be seen in all. We are called Christian not because Christ is absent from us, but because he dwells in us. He transfigures us in his image, that we may act toward others as he acts.

—Martin Luther, 1483–1546

316 The philosopher said that we should know ourselves, and the poet that we should to our own selves be true. John Calvin, the theologian, linked the knowledge of self to the knowledge of God; and all of this, with results in living.

Our wisdom, in so far as it ought to be deemed true and solid wisdom, consists almost entirely of two parts: the knowledge of God and of ourselves. But as these are connected together by many ties, it is not easy to determine which of the two precedes, and gives birth to the other. For, in the first place, no man can survey himself without forthwith turning his thoughts towards the God in whom he lives and moves; because it is perfectly obvious, that the endowments which we possess cannot possibly be from ourselves; nay, that our very being is nothing else than subsistence in God alone.

—John Calvin, 1509–1564

317 A person without deep feelings about God and eternity might well think of each day as an end in itself, or of life as only a matter of survival. The believer senses an eternal importance in what he or she does, as explained by Jeremy Taylor.

God hath given to man a short time here upon earth, and yet upon this short time eternity depends; but so that for every hour of our life, after we are persons capable of laws and know good from evil, we must give account to the great Judge of men and angels. . . .

For we must remember that we have a great work to do, many enemies to conquer, many evils to prevent, much danger to run through, many difficulties to be mastered, many necessities to serve, and much good to do, many children to provide for, or many friends to support, or many poor to relieve, or many diseases to cure, besides the needs of nature and of relation, our private and our public cares, and duties of the world which necessity and the providence of God hath adopted into the family of Religion.

. . . God provides the good things of the world to serve the needs of nature by the labours of the ploughman, the skill and pains of the artisan, and the dangers and traffic of the merchant: these men are in their calling the ministers of the divine providence, and the stewards of the creation, and servants of a great family of God, the world, in the employment of procuring necessaries for food and clothing, ornament and physic. In their proportions also a king and a priest and a prophet, a judge and an advocate, doing the works of their employment according to their proper rules, are doing the work of God, because they serve those necessities, which God hath made.

—Jeremy Taylor, 1613–1667

318 We expect that Christian belief will result in a higher quality of moral conduct. But this does not mean that our conduct will, in itself, save us. John Wesley is emphatic at this point.

From hence we may clearly perceive the wide difference there is between Christianity and morality. Indeed nothing can be more sure than that true Christianity cannot exist without both the inward experience and outward practice of justice, mercy, and truth; and this alone is given in morality. But it is equally certain that all morality, all the justice, mercy, and truth which can possibly exist without Christianity, profiteth nothing at all, is of no value in the sight of God, to those that are under the Christian dispensation. . . . And of consequence, unless those be so changed . . . unless they have new senses, ideas, passions, tempers, they are no Christians! However just, true, or merciful they may be, they are but atheists still.

—John Wesley, 1703–1791

319 Although the Bible emphasizes the importance of the community of faith, from Israel to the church, it just as surely calls each person to a sense of individual responsibility. Selena Hastings, Countess of Huntingdon, who introduced Methodism to English upper classes, was deeply moved by this responsibility, as indicated in a letter to Charles Wesley.

Do aid me in this business with your willing services, your prayers, and your advice. I am but a weak instrument, and need the supporting care of my great Advocate every minute of my existence. Though I am hardly able to hold my pen, yet I am willing, thanks be to God, to be employed in any way that may conduce to the good of others. Pray for me, my good friend, that if it be the will of God and our Lord Jesus Christ, I may be strengthened for the work which is before me, and that which he has appointed for me on earth. I feel that flame still burning within me—the ardent longing to save sinners from the error of their ways. O, how does the zeal of others reprove me! O, that my poor cold heart could catch a spark from others, and be as a flame of fire in the Redeemer's service! Some few instances of success, which God, in the riches of his mercy, has lately favoured me with, have greatly comforted me during my season of affliction; and I have felt the presence of God in my soul in a very remarkable manner, particularly when I have prayed for the advancement of his kingdom amongst men in the world. This revives me, and if God prolongs my poor unprofitable life, I trust it will ever be engaged in one continued series of zealous active services for him, and the good of precious immortal souls.

—Selena Hastings, Countess of Huntingdon, 1707–1791

320 For several centuries, a number of countries have perceived themselves as being "Christian nations." This perception has caused many to judge that they are living exemplary lives simply by virtue of their citizenship. Søren Kierkegaard, a Danish philosopher, vigorously challenged this idea in his day.

We are what is called a "Christian" nation—but in such a sense that not a single one of us is in the character of the Christianity of the New Testament. . . . The illusion of a Christian nation is due doubtless to the power which number exercises over the imagination. I have not the least doubt that every single individual in the nation will be honest enough with God and with himself to say in solitary conversation, "If I must be candid, I do not deny that I am not a Christian in the New Testament sense; if I must be honest, I do not deny that my life cannot be called an effort in the direction of what the New Testament calls Christianity, in the direction of denying myself, renouncing the world, dying from it, etc.; rather the earthly and the temporal become more and more important to me with every year I live." I have not the least doubt that everyone will, with respect to ten of his acquaintances, let us say, be able to hold fast to the view that they are not Christians in the New Testament sense, and that their lives are not even an effort in the direction of becoming so. But when there are 100,000, one becomes confused.

—Søren Kierkegaard, 1813–1855

321 How does one recognize believers? We sometimes wish it were as simple as a style of clothing, a banner, or a bumper sticker. But C.S. Lewis says that they can be recognized; perhaps not easily at first, but in time, persuasively.

The thing has happened: the new step has been taken and is being taken. Already the new men are dotted here and there all over the earth. Some . . . are still hardly recognizable: but others can be recognized. Every now and then one meets them. Their voices and faces are different from ours; stronger, quieter, happier, more radiant. They begin where most of us leave off. They are, I say, recognizable; but you must know what to look for. They will not be very like the idea of 'religious people' which you have formed from your general reading. They do not draw attention to themselves. You tend to think that you are being kind to them when they are really being kind to you. They love you more than other men do, but they need you less. . . . They will usually seem to have a lot of time: you will wonder where it comes from. When you have recognized one of them, you will recognize the next one much more easily. And I strongly suspect (but how should I know?) that they recognize one another immediately and infallibly, across every barrier of colour, sex, class, age, and even of creeds. In that way, to become holy is rather like joining a secret society. To put it at the very lowest, it must be great fun.

—*C.S. Lewis, 1898–1963*

322 The First Epistle of John called upon believers, by sex and age group, to assume their responsibilities. The official report of the World Council of Churches, 1975, follows a similiar pattern in calling children, women, and the oppressed to see their role in God's kingdom.

The gospel is good news from God, our Creator and Redeemer. On its way from Jerusalem to Galilee and to the ends of the earth, the Spirit discloses ever new aspects and dimensions of God's decisive revelation in Jesus Christ. The gospel always includes: the announcement of God's Kingdom and love through Jesus Christ, the offer of grace and forgiveness of sins, the invitation to repentance and faith in him, the summons to fellowship in God's Church, the command to witness to God's saving words and deeds, the responsibility to participate in the struggle for justice and human dignity, the obligation to denounce all that hinders human wholeness, and a commitment to risk life itself. In our time, to the oppressed the gospel may be new as a message of courage to persevere in the struggle for liberation in this world as a sign of hope for God's inbreaking Kingdom. To women the gospel may bring news of a Christ who empowered women to be bold in the midst of cultural expectations of submissiveness. To children the gospel may be a call of love for the "little ones" and to the rich and powerful it may reveal the responsibility to share the poverty of the poor.

—*World Council of Churches Mission Creed, Nairobi, 1975*

323 True believing is set off against heresy. We recognize heresy in the issues of ancient times; does it exist still today—and if so, what difference might it make? C. FitzSimons Allison, Episcopal bishop emeritus, prods us to see the peril of heresy in our own lives.

"What happens to someone who follows heretical teachings?" It became quickly and readily apparent how cruel heretical teachings are and how prevalent the heresies are in contemporary times. Victims of these teachings have been encouraged either to escape the world and their basic humanity into some form of flight and death or to use religion to undergird and isolate further their own self-centered self from the need to be loved and to love....

That the human heart is a "veritable factory of idols" is a truth attributed to various Reformers. The heart is certainly "far gone from original righteousness," and it is a filter through which the gospel must pass in its hearing and its telling. Each heresy in its own way encourages some flaw in our human nature. Without appreciating this human factor one could be led to believe that orthodoxy is a relatively simple matter: the results of proper research and scholarship. The human factor makes us acknowledge that research and scholarship itself must pass through the heart of the researcher and the scholar.

—*C. FitzSimons Allison, 20th century*

Acknowledgments

1 From *Nicene and Post-Nicene Fathers of the Christian Church, Second Series, Vol. VII* (Wm. B. Eerdmans Publishing Co.); p. 32.

3 From *Nicene and Post-Nicene Fathers of the Christian Church, First Series, Vol. I* (Wm. B. Eerdmans Publishing Co.); p. 45.

4 From *Augustine: Earlier Writings,* selected and translated by John H.S. Burleigh (Library of Christian Classics, Ichthus Edition, Westminster Press, 1953); pp. 262–263. Used by permission.

7 From *The Illustrated Book of Christian Literature,* copyright © 1998 Hunt & Thorpe. Text © 1998 Robert Van de Weyer. Abingdon Press edition published 1998; p. 148. Reprinted by permission of Hunt & Thorpe.

8 From *A Compend of Wesley's Theology,* edited by Robert W. Burtner and Robert E. Chiles (Abingdon Press, 1954); p. 30. Copyright 1954 by Pierce & Washabaugh. Used by permission of Abingdon Press.

9 From *The Quest of the Historical Jesus: A Critical Study of Its Progress From Reimarus to Wade,* by Albert Schweitzer (Third Edition, Adam & Charles Black); pages 399–401.

10 From *God and Man,* by Edward Schillebeeckx, translated by Edward Fitzgerald and Peter Tomlinson (Sheed and Ward, 1969); pp. 235–236. Reprinted by permission of Sheed & Ward, an apostolate of the Priests of the Sacred Heart, 7373 South Lovers Lane Road, Franklin, Wisconsin 53132.

11 From *The Christian Tradition: A History of the Development of Doctrine, Vol. 1, The Emergence of the Catholic Tradition (100–600),* by Jaroslav Pelikan (University of Chicago Press, 1971); p. 3. © 1971 by The University of Chicago. Used by permission.

12 From *Essentials of Evangelical Theology, Vol. One* by Donald G. Bloesch. Copyright © 1978 by Donald G. Bloesch. Reprinted by permission of HarperCollins Publishers, Inc.

13 From *The Illustrated Book of Christian Literature,* copyright © 1998 Hunt & Thorpe. Text © 1998 Robert Van de Weyer. Abingdon Press edition published 1998; p. 126. Reprinted by permission of Hunt & Thorpe.

14 From *Luther's Works, Vol. 26.* Copyright, Concordia Publishing House. Used with permission.

15 Reproduced from A COMPEND OF LUTHER'S THEOLOGY edited by H.T. Kerr. Used by permission of Westminster John Knox Press.

16 Reproduced from NATURE AND DESTINY OF MAN by Reinhold Niebuhr. Used by permission of Westminster John Knox Press.

17 Reprinted with the permission of Simon & Schuster from THE MEANING OF REVELATION, by H. Richard Niebuhr. Copyright 1941 by Macmillan Publishing Company; copyright renewed © 1969 by Florence Niebuhr, Cynthia M. Niebuhr, and Richard R. Niebuhr.

18 Reproduced from REVELATION AND REASON, by Emil Brunner, translated by Olive Wyon. © 1946 W.L. Jenkins. Used by permission of Westminster John Knox Press.

19 From *Dogmatics, Vol. I: The Christian Doctrine of God,* by Emil Brunner, translated by Olive Wyon (Westminster Press, 1950); pp. 19–20. © by Theologischer Verlag Zurich. Used by permission.

20 *Foundations of Christian Knowledge,* by Georgia Harkness (Abingdon Press, 1955); pp. 73–74. Copyright 1955 by Pierce & Washabaugh. Used by permission of Abingdon Press.

21 *Church Dogmatics, Vol. I, Part 2: The Doctrine of the Word of God,* by Karl Barth, edited by G.W. Bromiley and T.F. Torrance (T. & T. Clark, 1956); p. 301. Used by permission.

22 Reprinted with the permission of Simon & Schuster from THE MEANING OF REVELATION, by H. Richard Niebuhr. Copyright 1941 by Macmillan Publishing Company; copyright renewed © 1969 by Florence Niebuhr, Cynthia M. Niebuhr, and Richard R. Niebuhr.

23 *Church Dogmatics, Vol. I: The Doctrine of the Word of God,* by Karl Barth, edited by G.W. Bromiley and T.F. Torrance (T. & T. Clark, second edition 1975; p. 111. Used by permission.

26 *Faith Seeking Understanding: An Introduction to Christian Theology,* by Daniel L. Migliore (Wm. B. Eerdmans Publishing Co., 1991); p. 20. Used by permission.

27 From *Ante-Nicene Fathers of the Christian Church, Vol. IV* (Wm. B. Eerdmans Publishing Co., 1963); pp. 349, 353.

28 Quoted in *The Christian Theology Reader,* edited by Alister E. McGrath (Blackwell Publishers, Ltd., 1995); p. 50. Used by permission.

30 Reproduced from ZWINGLI AND BULLINGER translated by G.W. Bromiley (Library of Christian Classics). Used by permission of Westminster John Knox Press.

31 Reproduced from A COMPEND OF LUTHER'S THEOLOGY edited by H.T. Kerr. Used by permission of Westminster John Knox Press.

32 Quoted in *The Christian Theology Reader,* edited by Alister E. McGrath (Blackwell Publishers, Ltd., 1995); p. 60. Used by permission.

34 From *The Works of John Wesley, Vol 1: Sermons I, 1–33,* edited by Albert C. Outler (Abingdon Press, 1984). Copyright © 1984 by Abingdon Press. Used by permission.

36 A PREFACE TO BIBLE STUDY by Alan Richardson (The Westminster Press, 1944); pp. 15–16. Used by permission of Westminster John Knox Press.

37 Reproduced from REVELATION AND REASON, by Emil Brunner, translated by Olive Wyon. © 1946 W.L. Jenkins. Used by permission of Westminster John Knox Press.

38 Karl Barth: THE WORD OF GOD AND THE WORD OF MAN, Peter Smith Publisher, Inc., Gloucester, MA 1978. Used by permission.

39 Quoted in REFORMED READER: A SOURCEBOOK IN CHRISTIAN THEOLOGY, edited by George S. Stroup (Westminster John Knox Press, 1993). Used by permission of Westminster John Knox Press.

40 Quoted in *Ancient Christian Writers: The Works of the Fathers in Translation, No. 16: St. Irenaeus: Proof of the Apostolic Teaching,* edited by Johannes Quasten and Joseph C. Plumpe, translated by Joseph P. Smith (Newman Press, 1978); pp. 50–51. Used by permission of Paulist Press.

41 From *The Works of Saint Augustine,* edited by Edmund Hill and John E. Rotelle (Augustinian Heritage Institute, 1990; published in the United States by New City Press, 1997). Used by permission.

42 From *Nicene and Post-Nicene Fathers of the Christian Church, First Series, Vol. II* (Wm. B. Eerdmans Publishing Co., 1955); pp. 206–207.

43 Quoted in *The Christian Theology Reader,* edited by Alister E. McGrath (Blackwell Publishers, Ltd., 1995); pp. 226–227.

45 From *Susanna Wesley: The Complete Writings,* edited by Charles Wallace, Jr. (Oxford University Press, 1997); p. 385. Used by permission.

46 From *A Compend of Wesley's Theology,* edited by Robert W. Burtner and Robert E. Chiles (Abingdon Press, 1954). Copyright 1954 by Pierce & Washabaugh. Used by permission of Abingdon Press.

47 From *Mere Christianity,* by C.S. Lewis. Reprinted by permission of HarperCollins Ltd.

48 *Church Dogmatics, Vol. III, Part One: The Doctrine of Creation,* by Karl Barth, edited by G.W. Bromiley and T.F. Torrance (T. & T. Clark, 1958); p. 7. Used by permission.

49 From MAKER OF HEAVEN AND EARTH by Langdon Gilkey. Copyright © 1959 by Langdon Gilkey. Used by permission of Doubleday, a division of Random House, Inc.

Acknowledgments

50 From *The Providence of God*, by Georgia Harkness (Abingdon Press, 1960); pp. 65–67.

51 Reprinted from MODELS OF GOD by Sallie McFague, copyright © 1987 Fortress Press. Used by permission of Augsburg Fortress.

52 Adaptation © 1989 The United Methodist Publishing House.

53 From *Cyril of Jerusalem and Nemesius of Emesa*, edited by William Telfer (Library of Christian Classics). Used by permission of Westminster John Knox Press.

54 Julian of Norwich: *The Revelations of Divine Love*, trans. James Walsh s.j., published by Source Books, Trabuco Canyon, California, 1999.

56 From *The Works of John Wesley, Vol. 2: Sermons II, 34–70*, edited by Albert C. Outler (Abingdon Press, 1985). Copyright © 1985 by Abingdon Press. Used by permission.

57 From *The Providence of God*, by Georgia Harkness (Abingdon Press, 1960); p. 18.

58 From *The Providence of God*, by Georgia Harkness (Abingdon Press, 1960); p. 56.

59 From TRUTH AS ENCOUNTER, by Emil Brunner (Westminster Press, 1963); p. 154. Used by permission of Westminster John Knox Press.

60 From *Strength to Love*, by Martin Luther King, Jr. Reprinted by arrangement with The Heirs to the Estate of Martin Luther King, Jr., c/o Writers House, Inc. as agent for the proprietor. Copyright 1963 by Martin Luther King, Jr., copyright renewed 1991 The Estate of Martin Luther King, Jr.

61 From *A Testament of Hope: The Essential Writings and Speeches of Martin Luther King, Jr.*, edited by James Melvin Washington. Reprinted by arrangement with The Heirs to the Estate of Martin Luther King, Jr., c/o Writers House, Inc. as agent for the proprietor. Copyright 1963 by Martin Luther King, Jr., copyright renewed 1991 The Estate of Martin Luther King, Jr.

62 From THE LIVING GOD: SYSTEMATIC THEOLOGY, VOLUME 1 by THOMAS C. ODEN. Copyright © 1987 by Thomas C. Oden. Reprinted by permission of HarperCollins Publishers, Inc.

63 From *God, Creation, and Revelation: A Neo-Evangelical Theology*, by Paul K. Jewett, with sermons by Marguerite Shuster (Wm. B. Eerdmans Publishing Co., 1991); p. 228. Used by permission.

64 Reprinted from MODELS OF GOD by Sallie McFague, copyright © 1987 Fortress Press. Used by permission of Augsburg Fortress.

65 From *Institutes of the Christian Religion*, by John Calvin, translated by Henry Beveridge (Wm. B. Eerdmans Publishing Co., 1989).

66 From *The Illustrated Book of Christian Literature*, copyright © 1998 Hunt & Thorpe. Text © 1998 Robert Van de Weyer. Abingdon Press edition published 1998; p. 148. Reprinted by permission of Hunt & Thorpe.

67 From *The Works of John Wesley, Vol. 2: Sermons II, 34–70*, edited by Albert C. Outler (Abingdon Press, 1985). Copyright © 1985 by Abingdon Press. Used by permission.

69 From *Nature, Man and God*, by William Temple (Macmillan Publishing Co., 1934); pp. 291–292. Used by permission of Macmillan Press Ltd.

70 Reprinted with the permission of Scribner, a Division of Simon & Schuster from THE SHAKING OF THE FOUNDATIONS by Paul Tillich. Copyright 1948 by Charles Scribner's Sons; copyright renewed © 1978 by Hannah Tillich.

71 From *The Providence of God*, by Georgia Harkness (Abingdon Press, 1960); pp. 17, 32–33.

72 From *A Testament of Hope: The Essential Writings and Speeches of Martin Luther King, Jr.*, edited by James Melvin Washington. Reprinted by arrangement with The Heirs to the Estate of Martin Luther King, Jr., c/o Writers House, Inc. as agent for the proprietor. Copyright 1963 by Martin Luther King, Jr., copyright renewed 1991 The Estate of Martin Luther King, Jr.

73 From WHO TRUSTS IN GOD: MUSINGS ON THE MEANING OF PROVIDENCE by Albert C. Outler. Copyright © 1968 by Oxford University Press, Inc. Used by permission of Oxford University Press, Inc.

74 From HERBERT BUTTERFIELD: WRITINGS ON CHRISTIANITY AND HISTORY, by Herbert Butterfield, edited by C. Thomas McIntire. Copyright © 1979 by Oxford University Press, Inc. Used by permission of Oxford University Press, Inc.

75 From *Faith Seeking Understanding: An Introduction to Christian Theology*, by Daniel L. Migliore (Wm. B. Eerdmans Publishing Co., 1991); p. 100. Used by permission.

76 *The Commentary of Dr. Zacharias Ursinus on the Heidelberg Catechism*, translated by G.W. Williard. Quoted in REFORMED READER: A SOURCEBOOK IN CHRISTIAN THEOLOGY, edited by George S. Stroup (Westminster John Knox Press, 1993). Used by permission of Westminster John Knox Press.

77 From *Institutes of the Christian Religion*, by John Calvin, translated by Ford Lewis Battles (Wm. B. Eerdmans Publishing Co., 1986); p. 58. Used by permission.

78 Reprinted from DOCUMENTS OF THE ENGLISH REFORMATION by Gerald Bray, copyright © 1994 Gerald Bray. Used by permission of Augsburg Fortress.

80 From *Nature, Man and God*, by William Temple (Macmillan Publishing Co., 1934); pp. 399–401. Used by permission of Macmillan Press Ltd.

81 From *Dogmatics, Vol. I: The Christian Doctrine of God*, by Emil Brunner, translated by Olive Wyon (Westminster Press, 1950); p. 310. © by Theologischer Verlag Zurich. Used by permission.

82 From *Black Theology and Black Power*, by James H. Cone (Seabury Press, 1969; Orbis Books, 1997); pp. 64–65. Reprinted by permission of Orbis Books.

83 Marjorie Hewitt Suchocki, *God—Christ—Church: A Practical Guide to Process Theology* (The Crossroad Publishing Company, 1986). Copyright © 1982 by Marjorie Hewitt Suchocki. Used by permission of The Crossroad Publishing Company.

84 From *A New Handbook of Christian Theology*, edited by Donald W. Musser and Joseph L. Price. Copyright © 1992 by Abingdon Press. Used by permission.

85 *St. Athanasius on the Incarnation*, translated by A Religious of C.S.M.V. (St. Vladimir's Orthodox Theological Seminary, 1944; revised, 1953; reprinted, 1989); pp. 38, 41. Reprinted by permission of St. Vladimir's Seminary Press, 575 Scarsdale Road, Crestwood, NY 10707.

86 Reproduced from ZWINGLI AND BULLINGER translated by G.W. Bromiley (Library of Christian Classics). Used by permission of Westminster John Knox Press.

87 Reproduced from A COMPEND OF LUTHER'S THEOLOGY edited by H.T. Kerr. Used by permission of Westminster John Knox Press.

88 From *The Works of John Wesley, Vol. 2: Sermons II, 34–70*, edited by Albert C. Outler (Abingdon Press, 1985). Copyright © 1985 by Abingdon Press. Used by permission.

89 From "Quaker's Women's Meetings," SIGNS Magazine (Autumn 1975), edited by Milton Speizman and Jane Kronick; pp. 235–245. Used by permission of The University of Chicago Press.

90 From *Dogmatics, Vol. II: The Christian Doctrine of Creation and Redemption*, by Emil Brunner, translated by Olive Wyon (Westminster Press, 1950); pp. 57–58. © by Theologischer Verlag Zurich. Used by permission.

91 *Church Dogmatics, Vol. III, Part One: The Doctrine of Creation*, by Karl Barth, edited by G.W. Bromiley and T.F. Torrance (T. & T. Clark, 1958); p. 7. Used by permission.

92 From *The Providence of God*, by Georgia Harkness (Abingdon Press, 1960); p. 68.

93 From *A Testament of Hope: The Essential Writings and Speeches of Martin Luther King, Jr.*, edited by James Melvin Washington. Reprinted by arrangement with The Heirs to the Estate of Martin Luther King, Jr., c/o Writers House, Inc. as agent for the proprietor. Copyright 1963 by Martin Luther King, Jr., copyright renewed 1991 The Estate of Martin Luther King, Jr.

94 From *Created in God's Image*, by Anthony A. Hoekema (Wm. B. Eerdmans Publishing Co., 1986); pp. 95–96. Used by permission.

95 From *Not Every Spirit: A Dogmatics of Christian Belief*, by Christopher Morse (Trinity Press International, 1994); p. 256. Used by permission.

Acknowledgments

96 From *Nicene and Post-Nicene Fathers of the Christian Church, First Series, Vol. 3* (Wm. B. Eerdmans Publishing Co.); p. 246.

97 From REVELATIONS OF DIVINE LOVE by Julian of Norwich, translated by Clifton Wolters (Penguin Classics, 1966) copyright © Clifton Wolters, 1966. Reproduced by permission of Penguin Books Ltd.

98 From *Institutes of the Christian Religion,* by John Calvin, translated by Henry Beveridge (Wm. B. Eerdmans Publishing Co., 1989).

99 From *The Complete Works of St. Teresa of Avila,* translated and edited by E. Allison Peers. Reprinted by permission of Sheed & Ward, an apostolate of the Priests of the Sacred Heart, 7373 South Lovers Lane Road, Franklin, Wisconsin 53132.

101 From *The Works of John Wesley, Vol. 2: Sermons II, 34–70,* edited by Albert C. Outler (Abingdon Press, 1985). Copyright © 1985 by Abingdon Press. Used by permission.

102 Reproduced from NATURE AND DESTINY OF MAN by Reinhold Niebuhr. Used by permission of Westminster John Knox Press.

103 From *The Providence of God,* by Georgia Harkness (Abingdon Press, 1960); pp. 82–85.

104 Reprinted with the permission of Scribner, a Division of Simon & Schuster from THE ETERNAL NOW by Paul Tillich. Copyright © 1963 by Paul Tillich, renewed 1991 by Mutie Tillich Farris.

105 From *The Orthodox Way,* by Kallistos Ware (St. Vladimir's Seminary Press, 1990); pp. 75–76. Reprinted by permission of St. Vladimir's Seminary Press, 575 Scarsdale Road, Crestwood, NY 10707.

106 From *Faith Seeking Understanding: An Introduction to Christian Theology,* by Daniel L. Migliore (Wm. B. Eerdmans Publishing Co., 1991); pp. 130–131. Used by permission.

107 From *Augustine: Earlier Writings,* selected and translated by John H.S. Burleigh (Library of Christian Classics, Ichthus Edition, Westminster Press, 1953). Used by permission of Westminster John Knox Press.

108 From *Pseudo-Macarius: The Fifty Spiritual Homilies and the Great Letter,* translated and edited by George A. Maloney (Paulist Press, 1992). Used by permission.

109 From *Luther's Works, Vol. 26.* Copyright, Concordia Publishing House. Used with permission.

110 From *The Works of John Wesley, Vol. 3: Sermons III, 71–114,* edited by Albert C. Outler (Abingdon Press, 1985). Copyright © 1986 by Abingdon Press. Used by permission.

111 From *The Works of John Wesley, Vol. 18: Journals and Diaries I (1735–38),* edited by Richard P. Heitzenrater (Abingdon Press, 1988). Copyright © 1988 by Abingdon Press. Used by permission.

112 From *The Works of John Wesley, Vol. 3: Sermons III, 71–114,* edited by Albert C. Outler (Abingdon Press, 1985). Copyright © 1986 by Abingdon Press. Used by permission.

114 Reprinted with the permission of Simon & Schuster from THE COST OF DISCIPLESHIP by Dietrich Bonhoeffer, translated from the German by R.H. Fuller with some revision by Irmgard Booth. Copyright © 1959 by SCM Press, Ltd.

115 Reprinted with the permission of Scribner, a Division of Simon & Schuster from THE SHAKING OF THE FOUNDATIONS by Paul Tillich. Copyright 1948 by Charles Scribner's Sons; copyright renewed © 1978 by Hannah Tillich.

116 From *The Letter to the Romans: A Commentary,* by Emil Brunner (Westminster Press, 1959); pp. 144–145.

117 From *The Rule of Grace,* by Albert C. Outler (Uniting Church Press, 1982); p. 16.

118 "The Avowal," by Denise Levertov, from OBLIQUE PRAYERS. Copyright © 1984 by Denise Levertov. Reprinted by permission of New Directions Publishing Corp.

120 From *The Constitution of the Presbyterian Church (U.S.A.), Part I: Book of Confessions.* Used by permission of the Office of the General Assembly, Presbyterian Church (U.S.A.).

121 From *George Herbert: The Country Parson, The Temple,* edited by John N. Wall, Jr. (Paulist Press, 1981). Used by permission.

122 From *The Works of John Wesley, Vol. 2: Sermons II, 34–70,* edited by Albert C. Outler (Abingdon Press, 1985). Copyright © 1985 by Abingdon Press. Used by permission.

123 From *The Works of John Wesley, Vol 1: Sermons I, 1–33,*

edited by Albert C. Outler (Abingdon Press, 1984). Copyright © 1984 by Abingdon Press. Used by permission.

124 From *Kerygma and Myth: A Theological Debate,* by Rudolf Bultmann et. al., edited by Hans Werner Bartsch. Translation used by permission of Reginald H. Fuller.

125 DELIVERANCE TO THE CAPTIVES by Karl Barth. Copyright © 1961 by SCM Press Ltd. Copyright renewed. Reprinted by permission of HarperCollins Publishers, Inc.

126 From *Beliefs That Count,* by Georgia Harkness, edited by Henry M. Bullock. Copyright © 1961 by The Graded Press. Used by permission of Abingdon Press.

127 From *A Theology of Liberation: History, Politics, and Salvation,* by Gustavo Gutiérrez, translated and edited by Sister Caridad Inda and John Eagleson (Orbis Books, 1973, revised 1987). Copyright © 1973 Orbis Books, Maryknoll, NY 10545. Used by permission.

128 From *Ante-Nicene Fathers of the Christian Church, Vol. III* (Wm. B. Eerdmans Publishing Co., 1963); p. 624.

129 Quoted in *The Christian Theology Reader,* edited by Alister E. McGrath (Blackwell Publishers, Ltd., 1995); p. 140. Used by permission.

130 From *The Works of Saint Augustine: A Translation for the 21st Century: Vol. I/18: Arianism and Other Heresies,* edited by John E. Rotelle (Augustinian Heritage Institute, 1995; published in the United States by New City Press). Used by permission.

131 From *Nicene and Post-Nicene Fathers of the Christian Church, First Series, Vol. III.* (Wm. B. Eerdmans Publishing Co.); p. 249.

132 "The Definition of Chalcedon," quoted in *Documents of the Christian Church,* edited by Henry Bettenson (Oxford University Press, second edition, 1963); p. 73. Used by permission.

133 "The Person of Christ," by Leo the Great, quoted in *The Later Christian Fathers,* edited and translated by Henry Bettenson (Oxford University Press, 1970); p. 279. Used by permission.

134 From *Nicene and Post-Nicene Fathers of the Christian Church, Second Series, Vol. XII* (Wm. B. Eerdmans Publishing Co.); pp. 142–144.

135 From *Nicene and Post-Nicene Fathers of the Christian Church, Second Series, Vol. XII* (Wm. B. Eerdmans Publishing Co.); p. 130.

136 From *Patrology,* Vol. III, by Johannes Quasten (A Christian Classics Reprint, 1983).

137 From *Nicene and Post-Nicene Fathers of the Christian Church, Second Series, Vol. IX* (Wm. B. Eerdmans Publishing Co.); pp. 47–48.

138 From *Creed or Chaos?* by Dorothy L. Sayers (Harcourt, Brace and Co., 1949). Copyright, 1949, by Dorothy L. Sayers. Reprinted by permission of the Estate of Dorothy L. Sayers and the Watkins / Loomis Agency.

139 From *A New Handbook of Christian Theology,* edited by Donald W. Musser and Joseph L. Price. Copyright © 1992 by Abingdon Press. Used by permission.

140 Reproduced from EARLY CHRISTIAN FATHERS (Library of Christian Classics) edited by Cyril Richardson. Used by permission of Westminster John Knox Press.

141 Quoted in *The Christian Theology Reader,* edited by Alister E. McGrath (Blackwell Publishers, Ltd., 1995); p. 177. Used by permission.

142 Reprinted from *Christian History* Magazine, Issue 37, p. 30, by permission of David F. Wright.

143 Quoted in *The Christian Theology Reader,* edited by Alister E. McGrath (Blackwell Publishers, Ltd., 1995); p. 178. Used by permission.

145 From *Nicene and Post-Nicene Fathers of the Christian Church, First Series, Vol. III* (Wm. B. Eerdmans Publishing Co.); p. 272.

146 Quoted in *Readings in Christian Thought,* edited by Hugh T. Kerr (Abingdon Press, 1966, Second Edition, 1990). Second edition copyright © 1990 by Abingdon Press. Used by permission.

147 From *Showings,* by Julian of Norwich (Paulist Press, 1978). Copyright © 1978 by The Missionary Society of St. Paul the Apostle in the State of New York. Used by permission of Paulist Press.

Acknowledgments

150 From *A New Handbook of Christian Theology,* edited by Donald W. Musser and Joseph L. Price. Copyright © 1992 by Abingdon Press. Used by permission.

151 Quoted in *The Christian Theology Reader,* edited by Alister E. McGrath (Blackwell Publishers, Ltd., 1995); p. 176. Used by permission.

152 Quoted in *The Christian Theology Reader,* edited by Alister E. McGrath (Blackwell Publishers, Ltd., 1995); p. 180. Used by permission.

153 Quoted in *The Christian Theology Reader,* edited by Alister E. McGrath (Blackwell Publishers, Ltd., 1995); p. 182. Used by permission.

154 From *A Scholastic Miscellany: Anselm to Ockham,* edited and translated by Eugene R. Fairweather (Library of Christian Classics, 1956). Used by permission of Westminster John Knox Press.

155 From *A Scholastic Miscellany: Anselm to Ockham,* edited and translated by Eugene R. Fairweather (Library of Christian Classics, 1956). Used by permission of Westminster John Knox Press.

156 Reproduced from A COMPEND OF LUTHER'S THEOLOGY edited by H.T. Kerr. Used by permission of Westminster John Knox Press.

157 From *Certain Sermons or Homilies, Appointed to be read in churches in the time of the late Queen Elizabeth of famous memory* (Oxford University Press, 1832). Used by permission of Oxford University Press.

158 From *Institutes of the Christian Religion,* by John Calvin, translated by Henry Beveridge (Wm. B. Eerdmans Publishing Co., 1989).

160 From *God Was in Christ: An Essay on Incarnation and Atonement,* by D.M. Baillie (Charles Scribner's Sons, 1948); p. 182. Reprinted by permission of Prentice-Hall, Inc., Upper Saddle River, NJ.

161 From *The Lion, the Witch and the Wardrobe,* by C.S. Lewis (Collier Books, Macmillan Publishing Company, 1970). Used by permisssion of HarperCollins Ltd.

162 From *Nicene and Post-Nicene Fathers of the Christian Church, Second Series, Vol. IV* (Wm. B. Eerdmans Publishing Co.).

163 From *Nicene and Post-Nicene Fathers of the Christian Church, Second Series, Vol. XI* (Wm. B. Eerdmans Publishing Co.); p. 80.

164 From *Jeremy Taylor: Selected Works,* edited by Thomas K. Carroll. Copyright © 1990 by The Missionary Society of St. Paul the Apostle in the State of New York. Used by permission of Paulist Press.

166 From *Mastery: The Art of Mastering Life,* by E. Stanley Jones (Abingdon Press, 1955). Copyright © 1955 by Pierce & Washabaugh. Copyright renewal © 1983 by Mrs. Eunice Matthews. Used by permission.

168 Reprinted with the permission of Simon & Schuster from THE COST OF DISCIPLESHIP by Dietrich Bonhoeffer, translated from the German by R.H. Fuller with some revision by Irmgard Booth. Copyright © 1959 by SCM Press, Ltd.

169 *Church Dogmatics, Vol. IV, Part 1,* by Karl Barth, edited by G.W. Bromiley and T.F. Torrance (T. & T. Clark, 1956); p. 129. Used by permission.

170 DELIVERANCE TO THE CAPTIVES by Karl Barth. Copyright © 1961 by SCM Press Ltd. Copyright renewed. Reprinted by permission of HarperCollins Publishers, Inc.

171 *God Among Us: The Gospel Proclaimed,* by Edward Schillebeeckx (The Crossroad Publishing Company, 1987). © Uitgeverij H. Nelissen B.V. 1982. Translation © John Bowden 1983. Used by permission of The Crossroad Publishing Company.

172 From *Christology: A Biblical, Historical, and Systematic Study of Jesus Christ,* by Gerald O'Collins (Oxford University Press, 1995); p. 140. Used by permission of Oxford University Press.

173 From *Nicene and Post-Nicene Fathers of the Christian Church, Second Series, Vol. VII* (Wm. B. Eerdmans Publishing Co.); pp. 31–32.

174 From *The Illustrated Book of Christian Literature,* copyright © 1998 Hunt & Thorpe. Text © 1998 Robert Van de Weyer. Abingdon Press edition published 1998; p. 155. Reprinted by permission of Hunt & Thorpe.

175 From *Institutes of the Christian Religion,* by John Calvin, translated by Henry Beveridge (Wm. B. Eerdmans Publishing Co., 1989).

176 From *Institutes of the Christian Religion,* by John Calvin, translated by Henry Beveridge (Wm. B. Eerdmans Publishing Co., 1989).

177 From *The Works of John Wesley, Vol. 2: Sermons II, 34–70,* edited by Albert C. Outler (Abingdon Press, 1985). Copyright © 1985 by Abingdon Press. Used by permission.

178 Excerpts from THE ASCENT TO TRUTH by Thomas Merton, copyright 1951 by The Abbey of Our Lady of Gethsemani and renewed 1979 by the Trustees of the Merton Legacy Trust, reprinted by permission of Harcourt Brace & Company.

179 From THE DYNAMICS OF FAITH by PAUL TILLICH. Copyright © 1957 by Paul Tillich, renewed © 1985 by Hanna Tillich. Reprinted by permission of HarperCollins Publishers, Inc.

180 From RADICAL MONOTHEISM AND WESTERN CULTURE by H. RICHARD NIEBUHR. Copyright 1943, 1952, 1955, 1960 by H. Richard Niebuhr. Reprinted by permission of HarperCollins Publishers, Inc.

181 Reprinted with the permission of Scribner, a Division of Simon & Schuster from THEOLOGY OF THE SACRAMENTS by Donald M. Baillie. Copyright 1957 by John Baillie; copyright renewed © 1958 by Ian Fowler Baillie.

182 *Understanding the Christian Faith,* by Georgia Harkness (Abingdon Press, 1947); pp. 73–74. Copyright 1947 by Stone & Pierce. Used by permission of Abingdon Press.

183 From *A New Handbook of Christian Theology,* edited by Donald W. Musser and Joseph L. Price. Copyright © 1992 by Abingdon Press. Used by permission.

184 From *Nicene and Post-Nicene Fathers of the Christian Church, Second Series, Vol. VIII* (Wm. B. Eerdmans Publishing Co.); pp. 15–16.

185 From *Institutes of the Christian Religion,* by John Calvin, translated by Henry Beveridge (Wm. B. Eerdmans Publishing Co., 1989).

186 From *The Works of John Wesley, Vol 1: Sermons I, 1–33,* edited by Albert C. Outler (Abingdon Press, 1984). Copyright © 1984 by Abingdon Press. Used by permission.

187 From *The Christian Tradition and the Unity We Seek,* by Albert C. Outler (Oxford University Press, 1957); p. 54. Used by permission of Oxford University Press.

188 From *Credo,* by Karl Barth. Copyright © 1962 Charles Scribner's Sons. Reproduced by permission of Hodder and Stoughton Limited.

189 From *What Christians Believe,* by Georgia Harkness. (Abingdon Press, 1965); pp. 55–56. Copyright © 1965 by Abingdon Press. Used by permission.

190 Walter Kasper, *The God of Jesus Christ,* translated by Matthew J. O'Connell. English translation copyright © 1984 by The Crossroad Publishing Company. Used by permission.

191 From *The Ante-Nicene Fathers, Vol. I,* (Wm. B. Eerdmans Publishing Co.); p. 458.

192 Quoted in *The Christian Theology Reader,* edited by Alister E. McGrath (Blackwell Publishers, Ltd., 1995); pp. 108–109. Used by permission.

193 From *A Compend of Wesley's Theology,* edited by Robert W. Burtner and Robert E. Chiles (Abingdon Press, 1954); p. 30. Copyright 1954 by Pierce & Washabaugh. Used by permission of Abingdon Press.

195 From *Union With Christ,* by Lewis B. Smedes (Wm. B. Eerdmans Publishing Co., 1983); p. 132. Used by permission.

197 From *Black Theology in Dialogue,* by J. Deotis Roberts (Westminster Press, 1987); pp. 54–55. Used by permission of Westminster John Knox Press.

198 Reprinted by permission from GOD THE SPIRIT by Michael Welker, copyright © 1995 Augsburg Fortress.

199 Taken from *Flame of Love* by Clark H. Pinnock. © 1996 by Clark H. Pinnock. Used with permission from InterVarsity Press, P.O. Box 1400, Downers Grove, IL 60515.

200 From *Nicene and Post-Nicene Fathers of the Christian Church, Second Series, Vol. V.* (Wm. B. Eerdmans Publishing Co.); p. 334.

201 From *Augustine: Later Works,* selected and translated by John Burnaby (Library of Christian Classics, Ichthus Edition, Westminster Press, 1980); pp. 38–39.

203 From THE PRAYERS AND MEDITATIONS OF ST. ANSELM translated by Sister Benedicta Ward (Penguin Classics, 1973) copyright © Sister Benedicta Ward, 1973. Reproduced by permission of Penguin Books Ltd.

205 Quoted in *The Christian Theology Reader*, edited by Alister E. McGrath (Blackwell Publishers, Ltd., 1995); pp. 110–111. Used by permission.

206 From *Showings*, by Julian of Norwich (Paulist Press, 1978). Copyright © 1978 by The Missionary Society of St. Paul the Apostle in the State of New York. Used by permission of Paulist Press.

207 From *The Oxford Book of Prayer*, edited by George Appleton (Oxford University Press, 1985); No. 582, p. 183. Used by permission of Oxford University Press.

208 From *Third World Theologies*, edited by Gerald H. Anderson and Thomas F. Stransky (Paulist Press and Wm. B. Eerdmans Publishing Co., 1976); p. 152. Used by permission.

209 Reprinted from CHRISTIAN DOGMATICS, Vol. 1, edited by Carl Braaten and R.W. Jenson, copyright © 1984 Fortress Press. Used by permission of Augsburg Fortress.

210 English translation of the *Catechism of the Catholic Church* for the United States of America copyright © 1994, United States Catholic Conference, Inc.—Libreria Editrice Vaticana.

211 From *Cyril of Jerusalem and Nemesius of Emesa*, edited by William Telfer (Library of Christian Classics). Used by permission of Westminster John Knox Press.

212 From *Nicene and Post-Nicene Fathers of the Christian Church, First Series, Vol. II.* (Wm. B. Eerdmans Publishing Co.); p. 391.

213 From *The Constitution of the Presbyterian Church (U.S.A.), Part I: Book of Confessions.* Used by permission of the Office of the General Assembly, Presbyterian Church (U.S.A.).

214 From *The Works of John Wesley, Vol. 3: Sermons III, 71–114,* edited by Albert C. Outler (Abingdon Press, 1987). Copyright © 1987 by Abingdon Press. Used by permission.

215 From *Dogmatics in Outline*, by Karl Barth, translated by G.T. Thomson (SCM Press, 1949). Used by permission.

216 From THE PURPOSE OF THE CHURCH AND ITS MINISTRY: REFLECTIONS ON THE AIMS OF THEOLOGICAL EDUCATION, by H. Richard Niebuhr. Copyright © 1956 by Harper & Brothers, Publishers, Inc. Copyright renewed 1984 by Florence M. Niebuhr. Reprinted by permission of HarperCollins Publishers, Inc.

217 From *Vatican II: An Interfaith Appraisal*, edited by John H. Miller. © 1966 by University of Notre Dame Press. Used by permission.

219 From REACHING OUT by Henri Nouwen. Copyright © 1975 by Henri J.M. Nouwen. Used by permission of Doubleday, a division of Random House, Inc.

220 From *Treasure in Earthen Vessels: The Church as a Human Community*, by James M. Gustafson (Harper & Brothers, 1961). Used by permission of James M. Gustafson.

221 From *Elements of Faith*, by Christos Yannaras (T. & T. Clark, 1991); pp. 121–122. Used by permission.

222 From *The Ante-Nicene Fathers, Vol. 5* (Wm. B. Eerdmans Publishing Co.); pp. 422–423.

223 From *Documents in Early Christian Thought*, edited by Maurice Wiles and Mark Santer (Cambridge University Press, 1975); pp. 170–171. Copyright © 1975 by Cambridge University Press.

225 From *The Faith by Which the Church Lives*, by Georgia Harkness (Abingdon Press, 1940); pp. 69–70. Copyright, 1940, by Georgia Harkness. Used by permission of Abingdon Press.

226 From *The Business of Heaven*, by C.S. Lewis. Copyright © 1984 by C.S. Lewis Pte. Ltd. Reprinted by permission of HarperCollins Publishers Ltd.

227 Taken from *An Introduction to Christian Doctrine* by John Lawson. Copyright © 1980 by John Lawson. Used by permission of Zondervan Publishing House.

228 From *A Black Theology of Liberation*, by James H. Cone. Copyright © 1986, 1990 by James H. Cone. Published by Orbis Books, Maryknoll, NY 10545. Used by permission.

229 From *The Church*, by Hans Küng. Reprinted by permission of Sheed & Ward, an apostolate of the Priests of the Sacred Heart, 7373 South Lovers Lane Road, Franklin, Wisconsin 53132.

230 Marjorie Hewitt Suchocki, *God—Christ—Church: A Practical Guide to Process Theology* (The Crossroad Publishing Company, 1986). Copyright © 1982 by Marjorie Hewitt Suchocki. Used by permission of The Crossroad Publishing Company.

231 Reprinted from *Christian History* Magazine, Issue 37, p. 22, by permission of David F. Wright.

232 From *Patrology*, Vol. II, by Johannes Quasten (A Christian Classics Reprint, 1984).

236 From *The Collected Works of St. Teresa of Avila, Volume One*, translated by Kieran Kavanaugh and Otilio Rodriguez © 1976 by Washington Province of Discalced Carmelites ICS Publications 2131 Lincoln Road, N.E. Washington D.C. 20002 U.S.A.

237 Quoted in *The Christian Theology Reader*, edited by Alister E. McGrath (Blackwell Publishers, Ltd., 1995); p. 312. Used by permission.

239 From *The Works of John Wesley, Vol 1: Sermons I, 1–33*, edited by Albert C. Outler (Abingdon Press, 1984). Copyright © 1984 by Abingdon Press. Used by permission.

240 Reprinted with the permission of Scribner, a Division of Simon & Schuster from THEOLOGY OF THE SACRAMENTS by Donald M. Baillie. Copyright 1957 by John Baillie; copyright renewed © 1958 by Ian Fowler Baillie.

241 From PASTORAL THEOLOGY: ESSENTIALS OF MINISTRY by Thomas C. Oden. Copyright © 1983 by Thomas C. Oden. Reprinted by permission of HarperCollins Publishers, Inc.

242 From *The Ante-Nicene Fathers, Vol. I* (Wm. B. Eerdmans Publishing Co.); p. 484.

243 From *Early Christian Fathers*, translated and edited by Cyril C. Richardson (Collier Books, Macmillan Publishing Co., 1970). Used by permission of Westminster John Knox Press.

244 Reprinted with permission from *Hildegard of Bingen's Book of Divine Works*, edited by Matthew Fox, Copyright 1987, Bear & Co., Santa Fe, NM.

245 Reprinted from THE BOOK OF CONCORD, edited by T.G. Tappert, copyright © 1959 Fortress Press. Used by permission of Augsburg Fortress.

246 From *Institutes of the Christian Religion*, by John Calvin, translated by Henry Beveridge (Wm. B. Eerdmans Publishing Co., 1989).

248 From WORSHIP by EVELYN UNDERHILL. Copyright, 1936, by Harper & Brothers. Reprinted by permission of HarperCollins Publishers, Inc.

249 From *The Oxford Book of Prayer*, edited by George Appleton (Oxford University Press, 1985); p. 3.

251 From *A New Handbook of Christian Theology*, edited by Donald W. Musser and Joseph L. Price. Copyright © 1992 by Abingdon Press. Used by permission.

252 From *The Church Confident*, by Leander E. Keck. Copyright © 1993 by Abingdon Press. Used by permission.

253 *Early Christian Fathers*, translated and edited by Cyril C. Richardson (Library of Christian Classics). Used by permission of Westminster John Knox Press.

254 From THE LITTLE FLOWERS OF ST. FRANCIS by St. Francis of Assisi. Copyright © 1958 by Beverly Brown. Used by permission of Doubleday, a division of Random House, Inc.

258 From *A Serious Call to a Devout and Holy Life*, by William Law (Paulist Press, 1978). Used by permission of Paulist Press.

259, 260 From *John and Charles Wesley: Selected Prayers, Hymns, Journal Notes, Sermons, Letters and Treatises*, edited by Frank Whaling. Copyright © 1981 by The Missionary Society of St. Paul the Apostle in the State of New York. Used by permission of Paulist Press.

261 From *Lucretia Mott: Her Complete Speeches and Sermons*, edited by Dana Greene (The Edwin Mellen Press, 1980). Used by permission.

262 From *Living the Christian Life: A Guide to Reformed Spirituality*, by Robert H. Ramey, Jr. and Ben Campbell Johnson (Westminster John Knox Press, 1992). Used by permission.

263 From *The Illustrated Book of Christian Literature*, copyright © 1998 Hunt & Thorpe. Text © 1998 Robert Van de Weyer. Abingdon Press edition published 1998; p. 157. Reprinted by permission of Hunt & Thorpe.

Acknowledgments

264 Reproduced from THE REFORMED READER: VOLUME 1 edited by William S. Johnson and John Leith. © 1993 William S. Johnson and John Leith. Used by permission of Westminster John Knox Press.

266, 267 From *The Works of John Wesley, Vol. 2: Sermons II, 34–70,* edited by Albert C. Outler (Abingdon Press, 1985). Copyright © 1985 by Abingdon Press. Used by permission.

268 From *Phoebe Palmer: Selected Writings,* edited by Thomas C. Oden (Paulist Press, 1988). Copyright © 1988 by Thomas C. Oden. Used by permission of Paulist Press.

270 Reproduced from NATURE AND DESTINY OF MAN by Reinhold Niebuhr. Used by permission of Westminster John Knox Press.

271 *Church Dogmatics, Vol. IV, Part 2,* by Karl Barth, edited by G.W. Bromiley and T.F. Torrance (T. & T. Clark, 1956); pp. 499–500. Used by permission.

272 From *Mere Christianity,* by C.S. Lewis. Reprinted by permission of HarperCollins Ltd.

274 From *Nicene and Post-Nicene Fathers of the Christian Church, First Series, Vol. II.* (Wm. B. Eerdmans Publishing Co.); pp. 509–510.

276 From *The Works of John Wesley, Vol. 2: Sermons II, 34–70,* edited by Albert C. Outler (Abingdon Press, 1985). Copyright © 1985 by Abingdon Press. Used by permission.

277 Reproduced from NATURE AND DESTINY OF MAN by Reinhold Niebuhr. Used by permission of Westminster John Knox Press.

278 From *Credo,* by Karl Barth. Copyright © 1962 Charles Scribner's Sons. Reproduced by permission of Hodder and Stoughton Limited.

279 From THEOLOGY OF HOPE by JÜRGEN MOLTMANN. English translation copyright © 1967 by SCM Press, Ltd. Copyright renewed 1995 by SCM Press, Ltd. Reprinted by permission of HarperCollins Publishers, Inc.

280 From *I Have a Dream: Writings and Speeches that Changed the World,* by Martin Luther King, Jr. Reprinted by arrangement with The Heirs to the Estate of Martin Luther King, Jr., c/o Writers House, Inc. as agent for the proprietor. Copyright 1963 by Martin Luther King, Jr., copyright renewed 1991 The Estate of Martin Luther King, Jr.

281 From *Religion, Revolution, and the Future,* by Jürgen Moltmann (Charles Scribner's Sons, 1969). Used by permission of Jürgen Moltmann.

282 From AND STILL I RISE by Maya Angelou. Copyright © 1978 by Maya Angelou. Reprinted by permission of Random House, Inc.

283 From *Systematic Theology: Perspectives from Liberation Theology,* edited by Jon Sobrino (Orbis Books, 1993). Copyright © 1993, 1996 by Orbis Books. Used by permission.

284 Reproduced from A COMPEND OF LUTHER'S THEOLOGY edited by H.T. Kerr. Used by permission of Westminster John Knox Press.

285 From *George Herbert: The Country Parson, The Temple,* edited by John N. Wall, Jr. (Paulist Press, 1981). Used by permission.

286, 287 "Sinners in the Hands of an Angry God," by Jonathan Edwards, from *The Works of President Edwards, Vol. 7,* edited by S.B. Wright (Yale University Press, 1929–30). Used by permission.

288 From *The Works of John Wesley, Vol. 2: Sermons II, 34–70,* edited by Albert C. Outler (Abingdon Press, 1985). Copyright © 1985 by Abingdon Press. Used by permission.

289 Reproduced from NATURE AND DESTINY OF MAN by Reinhold Niebuhr. Used by permission of Westminster John Knox Press.

290 From *The Business of Heaven,* by C.S. Lewis. Copyright © 1984 by C.S. Lewis Pte. Ltd. Reprinted by permission of HarperCollins Publishers Ltd.

291 Marjorie Hewitt Suchocki, *God—Christ—Church: A Practical Guide to Process Theology* (The Crossroad Publishing Company, 1986). Copyright © 1982 by Marjorie Hewitt Suchocki. Used by permission of The Crossroad Publishing Company.

292 From *A New Handbook of Christian Theology,* edited by Donald W. Musser and Joseph L. Price. Copyright © 1992 by Abingdon Press. Used by permission.

293 From *Christian Confessions: A Historical Introduction,* by Ted A. Campbell (Westminster John Knox Press, 1996); p. 162. Used by permission of Westminster John Knox Press.

294 Quoted in *The Christian Theology Reader,* edited by Alister E. McGrath (Blackwell Publishers, Ltd., 1995); p. 357. Used by permission.

296 From *Nicene and Post-Nicene Fathers of the Christian Church, Second Series, Vol. III.* (Wm. B. Eerdmans Publishing Co.); pp. 561–562.

297 From *Nicene and Post-Nicene Fathers of the Christian Church, Second Series, Vol. IX.* (Wm. B. Eerdmans Publishing Co.); p. 99.

298 From *The Pilgrim's Progress,* by John Bunyan, quoted in *John Bunyan: Grace Abounding to the Chief of Sinners and The Pilgrim's Progress,* edited by Roger Sharrock (Oxford University Press, 1966); pp. 266–267. Used by permission of Oxford University Press.

299 From "On the Resurrection of the Dead," by John Wesley, quoted in *A Compend of Wesley's Theology,* edited by Robert W. Burtner and Robert E. Chiles (Abingdon Press, 1954); p. 281. Copyright 1954 by Pierce & Washabaugh. Used by permission of Abingdon Press.

300 From *Dogmatics in Outline,* by Karl Barth, translated by G.T. Thomson (SCM Press, 1949). Used by permission.

301 From *The Business of Heaven,* by C.S. Lewis. Copyright © 1984 by C.S. Lewis Pte. Ltd. Reprinted by permission of HarperCollins Publishers Ltd.

303 From *The Hope of the Christian,* by Otto Hentz (A Michael Glazier Book, 1997); pp. 62, 64. Used by permission.

304 Reproduced from THE REFORMED READER: VOL. 1 edited by William S. Johnson and John Leith. Used by permission of Westminster John Knox Press.

306 From *The Works of John Wesley, Vol 4: Sermons IV, 115–151,* edited by Albert C. Outler (Abingdon Press, 1987). Copyright © 1987 by Abingdon Press. Used by permission.

308 From *And the Life Everlasting,* by John Baillie (Oxford University Press, 1934; sixth printing, 1959); pp. 204–205, 251–252, 286–287. Used by permission of Oxford University Press.

309 From DELIVERANCE TO THE CAPTIVES by Karl Barth. Copyright © 1961 by SCM Press Ltd. Copyright renewed. Reprinted by permission of HarperCollins Publishers, Inc.

310, 311 From *The Business of Heaven,* by C.S. Lewis. Copyright © 1984 by C.S. Lewis Pte. Ltd. Reprinted by permission of HarperCollins Publishers Ltd.

312 *From My Sister, My Brother,* by Karen Baker-Fletcher and Garth KASIMU Baker-Fletcher (Orbis Books, 1997). Copyright © 1997 Karen Baker-Fletcher and Garth KASIMU Baker-Fletcher. Used by permission of Orbis Books.

313 Reproduced from EARLY CHRISTIAN FATHERS (Library of Christian Classics) edited by Cyril Richardson. Used by permission of Westminster John Knox Press.

314 From *Gregory of Nyssa: The Life of Moses,* translated by Abraham J. Malherbe and Everett Ferguson (Paulist Press, 1978). Used by permission of Paulist Press.

315 From *The Illustrated Book of Christian Literature,* copyright © 1998 Hunt & Thorpe. Text © 1998 Robert Van de Weyer. Abingdon Press edition published 1998; p. 148. Reprinted by permission of Hunt & Thorpe.

316 From *Institutes of the Christian Religion,* by John Calvin, translated by Henry Beveridge (Wm. B. Eerdmans Publishing Co., 1989).

317 From *Jeremy Taylor: Selected Works,* edited by Thomas K. Carroll (Paulist Press, 1990). Used by permission of Paulist Press.

318 From *The Works of John Wesley, Vol 4: Sermons IV, 115–151,* edited by Albert C. Outler (Abingdon Press, 1987). Copyright © 1987 by Abingdon Press. Used by permission.

320 Kierkegaard, Søren; *A Kierkegaard Anthology,* edited by Robert Bretall. Copyright © 1974 by Princeton University Press. Reprinted by permission of Princeton University Press.

321 From *The Business of Heaven,* by C.S. Lewis Copyright © 1984 by C.S. Lewis Pte. Ltd. Reprinted by permission of HarperCollins Publishers Ltd.

323 From *The Cruelty of Heresy: An Affirmation of Christian Orthodoxy.* Copyright © 1994 C. FitzSimons Allison. Reproduced by permission of Morehouse Publishing, Harrisburg, PA.